THE RISE AND FALL OF
JESSE JAMES

JESSE JAMES
(From a photograph owned by Howard Huselton, Kansas City)

FRANK JAMES
In late middle life

COLE YOUNGER
Aged about 65

The Rise and Fall of

JESSE JAMES

by

ROBERTUS LOVE

Introduction by Michael Fellman

"He was hunted, and he was human"

University of Nebraska Press
Lincoln and London

First Bison Book printing: 1990
Most recent printing indicated by the last digit below:
10   9   8   7   6   5   4   3   2

Library of Congress Cataloging-in-Publication Data
Love, Robertus.
The rise and fall of Jesse James / by Robertus Love; introduction
by Michael Fellman.
p. cm.
Originally published: New York: G. P. Putnam, 1926.
ISBN 0-8032-7932-9
1. James, Jesse, 1847–1882. 2. Outlaws—West (U.S.)—Biog-
raphy. 3. Frontier and pioneer life—West (U.S.) 4. West (U.S.)—
History—1848–1950. I. Title.
F594.J25L68   1990
364.1'552'092—dc20
[B]
89-24965   CIP

Reprinted by arrangement with David F. Richmond

To

MR. H. L. MENCKEN

THE JESSE JAMES OF AMERICAN LETTERS

INTRODUCTION BY MICHAEL FELLMAN

On September 26, 1872, the Kansas City fairgrounds bustled with ten thousand funseekers. In the midst of the throng three armed men rode up to the ticket booth. One of the men dismounted, grabbed the tin cashbox from the ticket counter, and emptied its contents of $978 into his pockets. When Ben Wallace, the ticket taker, ran out of the booth and tried to wrestle back the money, one of the mounted accomplices shot at him, but, missing him, hit instead the leg of a small girl in the crowd. The three men then galloped off into the nearby woods.[1]

Reporting this event in the next day's *Kansas City Times,* Major John N. Edwards denounced the crime but lavished praise on its perpetrators. Men "who can so cooly and calmly plan and so quietly and daringly execute a scheme . . . in the light of day, in the face of authorities and in the very teeth of the most immense multitude of people that was ever in our city," he wrote, "deserve at least admiration for their bravery and nerve." Two days later, Edwards wrote an editorial on "The Chivalry of Crime," placing the Kansas City fair robbers in the traditions of heroic Sir Walter Scott characters and legendary European bandits. Just as had heroes of old, these bandits robbed not stealthily but "in the glare of day and in the teeth of the multitude. . . . The nineteenth century with its Sybaritic civili-

zation is not the social soil for men who might have
sat with Arthur at the Round Table, ridden at tourney
with Sir Launcelot . . . shivered a lance with Ivanhoe
. . . or met Turpin and Duval and robbed them of their
ill-gotten booty on Hounslow Heath." Eighteen days
later, in a letter to the *Kansas City Times* signed Jesse
James—but also signed Jack Shepard, Dick Turpin and
Claude Duval, legendary European bandits all—the
robbers bragged of their heist and offered to pay the
hospital bill of the little girl. They proclaimed themselves morally superior to the corrrupt Grant administration in Washington—"who can steal millions and
it is all right"—and they concluded with a flourish to
the multitudes: "We kill only in self-defense. . . . We
rob the rich and give to the poor." Robin Hood and his
Merry Band had just paid a visit to Missouri. Five days
following this missive, Jesse James wrote the *Kansas
City Times* denying any connection with the crime and
charging that he and his companions wished to clear
their names by turning themselves in to the authorities
but were prevented from doing so by their knowledge
of the fact that they could never receive a fair trial.[2]

Nine years later another Missouri newspaper retold
the story of the fairground exploit. In this version the
rider who dismounted went up to the cashier and asked,
"What if I was to say I was Jesse James, and told you
to hand out that tin box of money—what would you
say?" The cashier replied, "I'd say I'd see you in hell
first." "Well, that's just who I am—Jesse James—and
you had better hand it out pretty damned quick, or"—
and the bandit then concluded his argument by pointing his Colt revolver at the cashier's head.[3]

Robertus Love, a St. Louis newspaperman who for
many years covered the bandit beat, handles this in-

cident in a fairly plain manner in *The Rise and Fall of Jesse James* (pp. 119–20). He omits the bullet wound to the little girl, the chivalric and noble outlaw legends with which John Edwards glorified the bandits, the self-proclaimed, self-publicizing linking of Jesse James to famous European bandits and James's self-exculpation in his later letter. He relates the bare bones of the holdup, the same approach he takes to many of the other actions of the James band.

At other places in his lively narrative, however, Love repeats some of the more fabulous aspects of the story of Jesse James. In Chapter 10, "An Astounding Instance of Jesse's Honesty," Love relates a story that was told to him in 1925 by the small-town newspaperman Charles S. Murray, whose brother, "Plunk," was an "eye-witness" to the events in question. The story begins in Missouri in the 1870s. Sheriff Oscar Thomason of Clay County rode out toward the James farm with a small posse to arrest the James boys. Wishing to escape, but not wanting to kill the brave Thomason, who was a Confederate veteran like the James brothers and most of their outlaw colleagues, Jesse instead shot Thomason's splendid horse from under him. This stopped the sheriff without injuring him. Years later, in Texas, Jesse saw Thomason's son on the street and, saying he felt mighty sorry that he had killed his father's fine horse (and implying that he could easily have killed the rider instead if he had chosen to), pulled out his fat wallet and gave Thomason, Jr., $125 to pay for the long-dead steed.

In 1944 the historian William A. Settle, Jr., tracked down Thomason's son William, who told Settle that his father had told him that he had already dismounted when Jesse shot his prize horse, and that many years later Jesse and his group had come upon Thomason and others at a camp in the country, not on a city street. After a wary greeting the two parties shared a meal. Jesse asked Oscar if he needed money, and over Oscar's protests pressed $50 on him. The horse, however, was never mentioned. In this instance William Thomason's narrative as told by William Settle is pared down and unromantic, while the version Love repeats is the glorified story of a swashbuckling and noble outlaw.[4]

The ultimate granddaddy Jesse James story is the one Love recounts in Chapter 26, " 'The Perfect Crime'— Jesse's Masterpiece." This is the tale of the poor country widow who, while feeding Jesse, Frank, and the boys a meal, bursts into tears and tells them that the local banker is coming by that very afternoon to foreclose on her farm. Jesse modestly lends her the sizable amount of money outstanding on the mortgage, then rides down the road, hides a while, and holds up the repaid and up to this point smug banker riding back to town in his buggy. Love tells his readers that he got this story off Samuel E. Allender, a St. Louis detective, and that Allender heard it directly from the mouth of Frank James.

"Jesse's Masterpiece" was the most widely told folktale about the bandit king. Versions of it have been collected by folklorists all over the rural South and West.[5] William Settle tells us that as late as the 1930s rural folks would all repeat variations of this story to him—telling him that it happened just over the next holler, or that, "a friend of my grandpa was out riding one day when he saw. . . ."[6]

Examination of the origins and spread of such stories gives us the key to the thorny historical problem of coming to terms with a folk hero who was also a live person. In *The Rise and Fall of Jesse James,* Robertus Love was wrestling manfully not only with a bandit who had once really lived and robbed for sixteen years before being shot down by the traitor Robert Ford but with the most legendary of American outlaws, our very own Robin Hood. Love claims to be an "anti-bandit" analyst who has separated fact from legend, but, in keeping with most of his fellow Missourians of his era, he is also full of sympathy for Jesse and the boys. Wanting to report objectively, he succeeds sometimes, but he also presents the stuff of the legends.

Love is not to be blamed for this fusion of romance and reality, the very blend that has so long been the version Americans have wanted to share. Indeed the James boys themselves and their publicity agent, John Edwards, worked on that mixture of the human and the superhuman when they justified the gang's robberies. Jesse and Frank knowingly wrapped themselves in legend, probably sincerely, even while they looted, and when necessary shot down or cut the throat of the odd bank teller or railway express clerk. Their mother would tearfully protest her boys' innocence to reporters after each and every robbery. As well as being romantic about themselves, the James boys also were plenty shrewd: they often went into hiding in faraway Tennessee and Texas, and they made sure that no photographs of themselves came to light to help the detectives hunting them. Their chief disguise was their legend, however, and they knew its value. If they convinced their neighbors that they robbed from the rich and gave to the poor, they could gain the camouflage of the neighborhood, the better to carry on with their occupation. They were not merely seen as noble outlaws, there is every reason to believe that they saw themselves that way. Throughout their outlaw careers legend was at least as large a part of their reality as was the calculated use of force to appropriate other people's money.

Faced with the difficult task of sorting out and presenting these inherently legendary figures, Robertus Love tries at times to be the realist, as when he suggests that they robbed banks and trains because they wanted and needed the money, and because there were violent techniques to achieve those ends which they had learned as Civil War guerrillas. But Love also shares the widespread belief that his subjects were basically men of honor, always gallant to the ladies, honest in everyday dealings, and as much victims of an unfair manhunt as aggressors against the community.

Right on his title page, Love quotes John Edwards's maxim about Jesse—"He was hunted, and he was human." At the end of the Civil War, the Unionist Radicals who dominated Missouri did not permit Jesse and his fellow Confederate guerrillas to surrender, this story goes. (In fact, many noted guerrillas did surrender and lived on in peace with their neighbors.) The story goes that they had to keep alive, and so they could only carry on as outlaws. The authorities hounded them unmercifully. Finally, in the dead of night, the Pinkertons, those alien mercenaries, threw a bomb into the James house that maimed their long-suffering mother and killed their dim-witted little half-brother. Whatever the Jameses did, they were driven to do—the fault was in others. Besides, the Jameses held up banks and railroads, the central agents of the outside oppressors who exploited the little people of Missouri. Exploiting and destroying them, the James gang gave much vicarious pleasure as well as the fabled bundle of greenbacks to rural Missourians who saw themselves as helpless victims and the Jameses as their avengers.

Not only did the James gang redress the current wave of economic and social injustice caused by outside capitalists, they also squared accounts for the southern defeat in the Civil War. Most rural Missourians were of southern origins and many had supported the Confederacy during the Civil War. They were branded as collaborators and traitors by their Union neighbors. They had been the objects of Union attacks. As a result of the war, they had lost political control of Missouri to Radical Unionists who rode mighty arrogantly in the saddle. Many a young man, the Jameses and the Youngers among them, had ridden as guerrillas. They and their backers very much needed postwar moral justifications for their brutal wartime activities, and they wanted to get back at postwar Unionist power. The exploits of noble outlaws could retrospectively explain and justify what otherwise would appear to be inhuman wartime brutality, thus ennobling the Lost Cause.[7]

After the war, rural Missourians also wanted vengeance against the forces of industrial development that were invading their traditional lands. For them the James gang could serve as resistance fighters. Some modern historians even more explicitly than Love have considered the gang to be "social bandits"—men who got even with capitalist exploiters, serving themselves and avenging the people.[8] They were soft—giving generously to the little people. They were hard—stealing from the oppressors and killing the villains who duplicitously called themselves the forces of law and order. Doubtless many rural Missourians felt very good when they rallied to the honor of these outlaws. The

James boys were undoubtedly popular in their own day. For example, as Love points out, after the Pinkerton fire-bombing, popular defense of the Jameses nearly was translated into political amnesty from the Missouri legislature. However, it was not the gang in itself, but the already legendary heroic outlaws who were thus honored. The James boys as emblems, not the James boys in fact, were always the figures at issue.

There was a deep popular need (and there still is, of course) for outlaws. The very same people who respect the law in their own lives often identify with those who can break it, particularly when there is an element of social justice associated with the bandit. This urgent feeling for the righteous outlaw creates a market for the romance of the daring and noble outlaw. While Mother James would weep to reporters, denying her poor hunted boys ever had done wrong, John Edwards, in his newspaper columns and in his *Notable Guerrillas* (1877) would cast them in the roles of Robin Hood and his band.[9] Edwards, as Love points out, was an alcoholic fantasist who wanted heroes to identify with and defend. Though a journalist, he was not a reporter at all, but a writer of legends in the high heroic tradition. Even knowing this, Love could not escape the framework that Edwards had created around the James gang because it was so deeply appealing, even to him. And the reader of Love's book, in 1990 as in 1926 or in 1876, shares this desire to suspend credulity. Reviewing Love's book in the *Nation* in 1926, R. F. Dibble put the matter very nicely when he commented that Love "habitually tries to differentiate between fact and fiction, with the result that the reader generally accepts the fiction and doubts the fact."[10] We want the story, not the boring facts.

It should be emphasized as well that Love was ambivalent about both the legend and the bandits. He wanted to avoid either whitewashing the James boys or "devilizing" them, but he did some of each. His argument is based on divided feelings. Near the start of his book, Love states that the Jameses preferred the simple life of Mother, Home and Hearth, but "once got a-going in the wrong direction" they became good boys gone bad. When he is in this mode he condemns the robbers. For example, on page 211 he clearly sides with the citizens of Minnesota who shot down many of the gang robbing the Northfield First National Bank: "The professional dead shots had failed miserably, the amateur sharpshooters had carried off all the honors of the day." Yet two pages later Love fully identifies with the bandits as they attempt to ride out of Minnesota: "The Minnesotans did not know the wellnigh superhuman resourcefulness of their quarry . . . what height of superlative degree these frustrated bank robbers were able to . . . endure." When they were hunted underdogs, Love sympathized with the Jameses. When they were cold-blooded bank robbers holding the power of life and death over unarmed men, Love again identifies with the victims, at these times *against* the James boys.

Insofar as he believed that Jesse always remained at heart a devout and orthodox Baptist, Love is willing to defend his honor. If Jesse and Frank were always fine to the ladies, always helping them, always remaining faithful husbands, never philandering, Love could believe in their essential goodness. (Here it must be added that in other legends each boy fathered many a bastard.) In later life Frank James and Cole Younger were upstanding men, honest in business, contrite about their earlier outlaw careers. Such behavior and attitudes prove to Love that these men had never been hardened "criminal types" but only victims of circumstance.

In his ambivalence and in his underlying sympathies, in his effort to be a tough newspaperman and in his identification with his subjects, Love writes within the traditional legendary construction of the James legend. You were supposed to fear the outlaw you also esteemed, hate the crime and admire the daring criminal. This mixture of detachment and attachment lends value to Love's book rather than detracting from it. The compelling power of the legend is at least as important a subject as is its hokiness. In 1966 William Settle would do an admirable demolition job on the historical James boys. But even Settle urges us to read Love for its literary and legendary richness. This is the fullest account of many of the major incidents of this most famous of American outlaw careers. It is far better than the other wildly sensationalistic popular histories that preceded and followed it. As a rule of thumb, for accurate history, one can be warned about accepting the "eyewitness" accounts that Love frequently repeats, while accepting the recreation of events from contemporary newspaper accounts, which Love does with great skill and accuracy, insofar as the accounts themselves were accurate. The stories of the robberies, especially the long and careful account of the Northfield heist and its aftermath, are unsurpassed in the literature.

As a simplification and codification of the James legend, *The Rise and Fall of Jesse James* is the most important book ever written. This is the "authentic version" not of the history but of the story of Jesse James. It is fast-paced, stirring, emotionally satisfying, a story told by a master storyteller. Here are humans who could be heroic written about for readers who hunger for personified, mythic combat with those powerful forces out there that make them uncomfortable and angry.

Current heroes of this variety have become superhuman as a species. They can fly faster than speed of light, live forever, know absolute truth, destroy Old Nick and his human minions. In 1876 or 1926 our grandfathers and great-grandfathers thrilled to the exploits of people of flesh and blood who, aroused, could *approach* the superhuman, while ending up either really and truly dead from an assassin's bullet, like Jesse, or socially redeemed and perfectly ordinary, like Frank. They were more than we were when they were riding high, but in the end they were just like us, and thus we are approximately like them. The scale of the stories is human—the aspirations are superhuman.

Robertus Love captured this stuff of human-sized legend, and he did it with flare and energy. Taken for what it is, *The Rise and Fall of Jesse James* is a jim-dandy of a read. So pop some popcorn, put on your old slippers, sit back, and enjoy.

NOTES

1. *Kansas City Times,* September 27, 1872.
2. *Kansas City Times,* September 29, October 15, 20, 1872.
3. *Neosho* (Missouri) *Times,* August 18, 1881.
4. William A. Settle, Jr., interview with William H. Thomason, Liberty, Missouri, December 18, 1944, in Settle, *Jesse James Was His Name* (Columbia: University of Missouri Press, 1966), p. 207, n. 31.
5. As late as 1948, Margaret Gillis Figh collected a southern version of this story: "Nineteenth-Century Outlaws in Alabama Folklore," *Southern Folklore Quarterly,* 25 (June 1961), 130. Two

excellent folkloric treatments of James are Kent L. Steckmesser, "Robin Hood and the American Outlaw," *Journal of American Folklore,* 79 (April–June 1966), 349–55, and Orrin E. Klapp, "The Folk Hero," *Journal of American Folklore,* 62 (January–March 1949), 17–25. Also see Steckmesser, *The Western Hero in History and Legend* (Norman: University of Oklahoma Press, 1965), and W. E. Simone, "Robin Hood and Some Other Outlaws," *Journal of American Folklore,* 71 (January–March 1958), 27–33.

6. Settle, 171–72, 227 n. 39. The earliest printed version Settle found was in the *Boonville* (Missouri) *Weekly Advertiser* for March 19, 1897.

7. For a discussion linking these wartime and postwar meanings of the James story, see Michael Fellman, *Inside War: The Guerrilla Conflict in Missouri during the American Civil War* (New York: Oxford University Press, 1989), pp. 247–66.

8. Two first-rate treatments of this interpretation of the James gang are David Thelan, *Paths of Resistance: Tradition and Dignity in Industrializing Missouri* (New York: Oxford University Press, 1986), pp. 70–77, and Richard White, "Outlaw Groups of the Middle Border: American Social Bandits," *Western Historical Quarterly,* 12 (October 1981), 387–408. The modern discussion of social banditry was begun by E. J. Hobsbawm in his two books *Primitive Rebels: Studies in Archaic Forms of Social Movement in the Nineteenth and Twentieth Centuries* (New York: Pantheon, 1965), and *Bandits,* rev. ed. (New York: Pantheon, 1981). Also see the antiromantic attack on this form of analysis of bandits by Anton Blok, "The Peasant and the Brigand: Social Banditry Reconsidered," *Comparative Studies in History and Society,* 104 (September 1972), 494–503.

9. John N. Edwards, *Noted Guerrillas, or the Warfare on the Border* (St. Louis: Bryan, Brand, 1877), and Jennie Edwards, *John Edwards: A Biography, Memoirs, Reminiscences and Recollections* (Kansas City: Jennie Edwards, 1889).

10. R. F. Dibble, review in *The Nation,* 123 (July 14, 1926), 40–41.

IN PLACE OF A PREFACE

THE first chapter of this book is of a prefatory character. It must be read in full if you are to peruse the narrative understandingly. I have been asked how and where and when I gathered the raw material here made over into a history of the Missouri Border Bandits whose outlaw careers were in effect a continuation of the Civil War. The text of the work itself supplies this information to a degree which seems adequate.

In explanation of the use of the perpendicular pronoun in many instances, I may say that the recording of certain personal contacts with some of the individuals more or less prominent in this true tale has seemed to me of value in enhancing the verisimilitude. Without such contacts the book could not have been written with its present quality of authoritativeness.

The author may be permitted to suggest that this task has not been easy. As a rule the historian has a sufficient supply of dignified documentary matter to enable him to record items without holding them under suspicion. In this instance it has been necessary for the writer to examine and analyze a vast accumulation of unreliable material along with much that is reliable. Employing common sense plus integrity of purpose and minus all personal bias, he has rejected the rubbish and accepted the real. You will find, as you read, that all apocryphal incidents are qualified with conjectural terms.

Notwithstanding some minor errors which in all probability have crept into the chronicle, the author believes that his book is about ninety-nine per cent accurate; and he knows that it is no less than one hundred per cent honest.

ROBERTUS LOVE.

ST. LOUIS, January, 1926.

———

(In writing the chapters in this book which cover the Minnesota bank raid, pursuit and capture, the author has made use of many facts recorded in a volume published in 1895 by The Christian Way Company, Northfield, Minn., compiled by George Huntington from original and authentic sources. The work is entitled "Robber and Hero," the subtitle being "The Story of the Raid on the First National Bank of Northfield, Minnesota, by the James-Younger Band of Robbers, in 1876." It is thoroughly reliable.)

CONTENTS

THE RISE AND FALL OF
JESSE JAMES

THE RISE AND FALL OF JESSE JAMES

CHAPTER I

INTRODUCING A MILD-MANNERED MISSOURIAN

SHORTLY before the writer began the task of chronicling this unique chapter of American history he had a confidential talk with a mild-mannered Missourian who is registered in the old family Bible as James Robert Cummins, born January 31, 1847. To the casual reader that name means nothing. It is highly probable that here for the first time the full name of this man appears in print. Yet our Mr. Cummins enjoys—the verb is used in strict fidelity to fact—a certain remarkable notoriety. His distinction is due in part to the interesting circumstance that he rode with Jesse James, of whose historic group of outlawed Missourians this Confederate veteran of the Civil War is the sole survivor. It is due in greater part to the extreme credulity of the American people, who seem to enjoy being humbugged.

Accepting the P. T. Barnum dictum at full face value, literary artists of the blood-and-thunder brand have created a Cummins myth the demolition of which is an integral part of our present purpose, which in its larger aspect is that of transforming the tale of Jesse James and his companions in freebootery from its long-time status of myth and miracle to that of documented historical veracity.   Stated more simply, this historian intends to tell the true story of the celebrated Missouri outlaws, known alliteratively as the Border Bandits.

With the letter "g" interposed between the last two letters of his correct cognomen, Mr. Cummins of Missouri is known throughout the United States of America, in the Canadian provinces, in Mexico, in Australia, even in Europe.   For wellnigh half a century our now venerable friend has been exploited to a considerable section of the reading world in sundry paper-bound books and in hundreds of newspaper articles, written mostly by persons who knew less about the real Cummins than the average man knows about the great star Betelguese or the explosive potentialities of the atom.   So far as this earnest and anti-yellow investigator has discovered, not one of these ready writers ever has learned the real name of James Robert Cummins.   All have miscalled him Cummings—Jim Cummings.   One may forgive the Jim; but the mis-handling of his surname for so many years, with the man still alive and measurably active, is a crime comparable only with the unforgettable Crime of '73 which from the testimony of its own date was committed about the time when Mr. Cummins first passed from tragic fact into terrific fiction.

"Jim Cummings!" do you exclaim, incredulously?   "What!—Jim Cummings still alive?"

The same!   The selfsame Jim who rode and robbed with Jesse James and rode away.   The veritable Jim who, in the red years just preceding the post-war riding and robbing, rode hell-to-split with Bloody Bill Anderson on the Missouri-Kansas border in the Civil War. The indubitable Jim who, as a slim blue-eyed boy of sixteen, was accounted the most skillful horseman in all that rough-and-ready outfit of Confederate guerrillas, made up altogether of youths and lads to whom the saddle was the native seat and the stirrup the natural footgear. The identical "Jim Cummings" who, with the bridle reins between his teeth and the little "g" between the end-letters of his family name, has ridden for full five decades up and down and across the pages of paper-backed literature—a mythical fire-frothing fiend, an impossible he-devil, the manufactured hero of penny-a-liner literary outlaws whose product has been about three per cent fact and 97 per cent fiction.

Yet not all of the crude books wherein has been created and kept a-going the Jim Cummings myth have related solely or chiefly to this our living Mr. Cummins in the proud capacity of hero. Many of them, in fact most, have heroized the apparitional Cummings but incidentally. The bulging bulk of the heroization has appertained to the late Jesse Woodson James, the late Alexander Franklin James, or the late Thomas Coleman Younger, singly or the trio complete. Mr. James Robert Cummins, albeit he has his niche, is not of caliber to fill a quartet with the other three.

As Jesse James, Frank James and Cole Younger these thrilling three Missourians, perhaps not so mild-mannered in their impetuous youth as is the octogenarian Mr. Cummins of today, have galloped and gallivanted through imponderable reams of print, both paper-clad and cloth-bound, until now the imaginary hoofbeats of their mythical horses promise to echo forever down the tiled corridors of Time, clitter-clatter and lickety-split and hell-bent for heroes' heavens.

However, in the interest of justice to the departed and to the cause of history, let us inspect also the obverse of the shield.   Certain books and a vast bulk of newspaper print have devilized rather than heroized the two James brothers and Coleman Younger, the three outstanding figures in the most amazing crew of bandits that ever engaged in freebooting.   The devilization has passed far beyond the limits of truth.   Characters impossibly inhuman have been bestowed upon these outlawed men.   They have been represented as ogres of brutism, monsters of cruelty, dehumanized demons always athirst for blood: which, as a matter of proof-rich fact, not one of them ever was.

An elementary analysis of these men—who they were, what they did and how and why they did it, when and where they operated, their military and civic environments and the all-round genesis of their outlawry—will convince any open-minded investigator that the Jameses and the Youngers were quite intensely human beings in the ordinary sense.   In certain respects they were extraordinary individuals, yet they were neither subnormal nor supernormal.   They committed robberies, and infrequent murders incidental to robberies, from time to time through a long period of years.   It was their avocation to rob banks and railway trains, not ignoring an occasional stagecoach; but that was not their preferential vocation.   They preferred the simple life, with its present and prospective rewards comprising the sacred trinity of Mother, Home and Heaven; but having once got a-going in the wrong direction, they found it next to impossible to stop unless at a point immediately underneath a rope specifically noosed to fit their own necks with a fatal tightness.

They were a unique half-dozen, over and beyond their ordinary human qualities, the two Jameses and the four Youngers—"the James boys and the Younger brothers," as Missouri remembers them. Upon perhaps a score of raids they rode and robbed and rode away. Here they raided and robbed an unsuspecting bank. Yonder a proud express train was compelled to pause whilst being looted by them and their occasional confederates. After ten years of intermittent outlawry the Youngers fell by the wayside. The Jameses, lasting sixteen years, established a world's record in the matter of keeping out of the law's clutches. The fact startles, when presented thus nakedly and boldly. How was it possible? Why was it permitted? The charmed-life theory falls like a shot stag when the facts in the case are analyzed. And yet . . .

Out of Nowhere rode these raiders, into Nowhere they rode away. Like mounting thunder they appeared, like melting mist they disappeared. After a raid and a robbery, or now and then an unsuccessful attempt at robbery, the hoofbeats of their horses failed swiftly into silence. Always their Nowhere—in the case of Frank and Jesse James at any rate—opened for them its friendly gates. The sheriffs and marshals with their official posses, the impromptu posses of armed and enraged and outraged citizens, the Pinkertons and other able detectives—all failed to find the awesome and mysterious Nowhere of the James boys. Jesse and Frank outwitted all of them.

It happened half a century or so ago: today it could not happen, not even in Maddest Missouri.

Just why the sheriffs of hundreds of counties in a dozen states, the police forces of scores of cities and thousands of towns, the wide-spreading detective nets of Allan and William Pinkerton, and all the other man-hunting agencies failed to catch or to kill these two outlawed brothers, although during the sixteen years from 1866 to 1882 the avid sleuths were on the trail almost constantly, will develop as this narrative proceeds. The wise peruser will read between the lines, where frequently the marrow of the matter inheres.

Jesse James, to be sure, was killed at last; but it is important and interesting to bear in mind that it was no sleuth who got Jesse—it was a traitor in the camp, "the dirty little coward that shot Mr. Howard and laid poor Jesse in his grave," as the far-famed ballad has it. Nor did any officer of the law or any private detective figure in the final "surrender" of Frank James, who "came in" at last of his own accord; and as to Jim Cummins, absolutely the last soldier of the Civil War to return home—more than thirty-four years after Appomattox—it must be admitted that all the man-hunters failed utterly. There were reasons, and they will reveal themselves in the course of this astounding story of yesteryear.

This history of the James-Younger bandit brotherhood is not going to be a preachment. No wise-worded "moral" will be offered as tail-piece to any of these chapters. The story of the careers of these men, told as this writer intends to tell it, carries a moral which almost shrieks from every page. If perchance any moronic youth ambitious to emulate Jesse James or any other of the border bandits should read this record, his will be less than a twelve-year-old's mind if he lacks the sense to perceive that in the present state of society a Jesse James is an impossibility.

Necessarily the true tale involves the tragedies into which the deeds of these outlaws drew each of themselves and the innocent family of each. From the outset their ultimate downfall was inevitable. These free-booting fellows were not happy in their business. They led most uncomfortable lives. If as an organized band or as individuals they menaced society, as indubitably they did, also were they themselves menaced constantly by a thousand demons of danger. During all the years of their outlawry they lived most uneasily as to personal environment. For much of the time they existed precariously as to financial security for themselves and for their families. Grim prison doors yawned for them just ahead on every road they traveled. Always in the shadows at the roadside lurked grimmer Death. In the midst of life they courted death every day and every night.

These bandits of the border were neither he-devils nor heroes. They were merely men with strong zest for life, determined never to violate the first law of nature, the law of self-preservation, whatever other statutes they might fracture upon occasion. This normal attitude toward self-defense—the ancient and ordinarily honorable case of Life vs. Death—and not their personal choice, made them desperate men, desperate to a degree far beyond the cheap and ephemeral criminals of these times. Yet, on the other hand, they were by no means such dangerous men as are the crackbrained fellows who nowadays shoot so readily and upon such slight provocation. None of the murderous robbers of today is "driven" to crime. The Missouri bandits of yesterday insisted that they had been driven into outlawry, and they had many friends who agreed with them in that respect. In some parts of Missouri this feeling still persists.

Not long ago I revisited after many years the beautiful little cemetery at Lee's Summit, Missouri, where lie buried all in a row the one-time outlaws Coleman, James and Robert Younger and their excellent and unhappy mother. Not far from the Younger family burial-plot three gravediggers were plying their trade.

"What do you people living here in the old home town of the Younger brothers think about them?" I inquired of Gravedigger No. 1, who was old and worn.

No. 1 turned up another spadeful of damp earth, ejected some tobacco juice to dampen it further, and replied:

"Jest what we-all think about other good families around here, sir; them Youngers was all good people."

"And what do you say?"—this of Gravedigger No. 2, a middle-aged man. "What about their outlawry?"

"They was drove to it," averred No. 2, who said no more.

Gravedigger No. 3 was a youngster.

"What is your view of the Youngers—and the James boys too, for that matter?"

"Well, I reckon, from all I've heard, they wasn't so bad as they've been painted, Mister."

Gravedigger No. 2 expressed the settled conviction of hundreds of citizens of what we may term the James-Younger country, otherwise the Missouri counties of Clay and Jackson, bordering on Kansas. It is a conviction based partly upon tradition and partly upon close personal acquaintance with the Younger family in Jackson or the James family in Clay. Whether "they was drove to it," or rode to it when they might have ridden in any other direction, will develop as this narrative proceeds upon its gunpowdery and gory route, conclusions being left to the reader.

Why should any intelligent writer try to make either heroes or he-devils out of a group of men, now dead and done for, who were neither better nor worse at heart than are innumerable other human beings now at large under conditions such as keep them out of the penitentiary or off the scaffold? Why try to "excuse" them for the wrong they did? Why, on the other hand, muckrake in mythical tale-ology and fork forth the oozings and drippings of gore they never shed, when, forsooth, the true tale is gory enough to glut the most encarnadined maw?

"But why, good sir," ask you, "why tell the sorry old story over again at all? Why rake up all this horrible past and rattle its bloody bones over your typewriter? Why burst forth in blood and thunder——"

Stay, good friend—forbear! Right there have you

touched the quick of the tender spot. It is because your present chronicler cordially despises the thunder-blooders and all their output that he has set himself to the exceedingly difficult task of quieting the thunder and drying the blood. Herein he purposes to mop up and tone down. The residue, he ventures to hope, may turn out to be measurably satisfactory to those who love truth for its own sake, to whom the nude fact is more welcome than fiction of the balloon-tire brand surrounding a tiny inner tube of truth.

As a matter of fact, the sorry old tale never has been told. Parts of it have been told truly, parts tragically mistold. Until now, no writer ever has tried to tell the tale with measurable completeness, which task involves at least a running analysis of motives, with a halt here and there for more intensive scrutiny or a detour now and then into the byways of history.

But, perhaps you are asking, what about Jim Cummins, recently introduced and suddenly side-tracked? Impatient friend, Jim Cummins will keep until the more serious business of this bloody but not thundery opus is transacted. For the present we shall leave our picturesque friend Mr. Cummins, known personally to the historian since the summer of 1902, in his comfortable quarters at the Confederate Home of Missouri, near Higginsville, a Mid-West "Main Street" metropolis. We shall reserve Jim chiefly for our ultimate chapter.

Therefore, be patient. Jim Cummins, the real Jim— not the "Jim Cummings" of myth and miracle—will be presented to you as the wandering Ulysses of an Odyssey of tragedy and comedy the like of which no

penman since the ancient days of Homer of the bloomin'
lyre, save the unbugled operator of the modern typewriter now under hand, ever yet has discovered the raw
material for writing.

CHAPTER II

PARTLY to account for Jesse James and his outlaw career and associates, it is necessary to delve into history and excavate certain crimson characters whose names still flash fierily from the otherwise dusty archives of the Civil War on the Missouri-Kansas border. Like all the members of the post-war bandit crew save Jim Cummins, "their bullets and their bones are cold." But they survive in the nightmare memories of old men and women who in childhood or youth had high and horrid reason to shudder when their names were spoken.

Chief amongst these men of blood and horror whose records we are briefly to examine were William C. Quantrill, William F. Anderson and George Todd. To most of those who are aware that such men once existed, the first and second of the trio are known as "Charley Quantrell" and "Bloody Bill" Anderson. These guerrilla chieftains were the war-time tutors of the two Jameses, two of the four Youngers, Jim Cummins and several of the other young men of western Missouri who became outlaws on the border shortly after the war was ended for the rest of its millions of participants throughout the great republic.

These youths who were graduated from war banditry into civic outlawry served under these leaders of irregular Confederate forces in Kansas and Missouri, chiefly in Missouri. Guerrilla warfare schooled them in violence. Some of them for about three years, others for perhaps a year and a half, and one or two for a few months only, rode and fought, raided and robbed, slew and looted with Quantrill or Anderson or Todd. Quantrill quarreled with his lieutenants, or they with him, and long before the conflict closed Bill Anderson broke away to lead a guerrilla outfit of his own, and toward the end George Todd superseded Quantrill in chief command.

Let us take up first the man Quantrill, whose name, more than sixty years after his death, still is misspelled "Quantrell" in most of the newspapers which give him occasional mention and in all of the lurid fictions printed between covers and purporting each to be the true story of the terrible rough rider from Kansas. *A True Story of Charles W. Quantrell and His Guerrilla Band* is the title of a recent book dignified by cloth binding. Though the title-page sets forth that the "true story" is told by one "who followed Quantrell through his whole course," virtually all of the misstatements of fact and the rehashings of fiction current for six decades with regard to Quantrill's earlier career are presented as important factors in accounting for the blood-madness of the man.

There never was a Charles W. Quantrell. There was a William Clarke Quantrill, who smeared his name in blood upon the maps of several states. His only authentic biographer is Mr. William Elsey Connelley, secretary of the Kansas State Historical Society, by birth and breeding a Kentucky mountaineer. In the preface to his *Quantrill and the Border Wars* Mr. Connelley calls Quantrill "the bloodiest man known to the annals of America." On the closing pages of his valuable volume the Kansas historian writes of Quantrill:

"Of the Civil War in America he was the bloodiest man. Of the border he was the scourge and terror. Idolized for his ferocious blood-madness, he forgot his mother. Embarked in savagery, he forswore his native land. Professing allegiance to an alien cause, he brought upon a fair land fire and sword, desolation and woe. To manifest a zeal he did not feel, he had recourse to slander, betrayed his companions and aided in their murder. With red hands he gave fair cities to torch and pillage, and reveled in the groans and cries of the helpless and innocent victims of his ruthless and inhuman crimes."

That indictment stands upon the record as reconstructed by the painstaking labors of Mr. Connelley. His accumulation of evidence, documentary and verbal, utterly undermines the structure of misrepresentation which since the year 1865 has housed the memory of W. C. Quantrill as a "hero." The flimsy temple of the hero-worshippers is demolished, razed beam and rafter, fallen roof and lintel, leaving only a sorry residue of crumbling bones and dried-up gore to indicate what once was a reeking shambles created by America's bloodiest man.

Even the men who fought under Quantrill did not

know his real name. To them he was "Charley Quantrell." The misspelling of his surname was not at his own instance, but he professed to be one Charles Quantrill. In Kansas, before the Civil War, he operated as a thief and murderer under the alias of Charley Hart. At intervals in those years, beginning with his arrival in Kansas Territory in 1857, he wrote poetic letters to his mother and his sister, back in Ohio, in a chirography as symmetrical and delicate as that of a cultured woman. In these letters he pretended to be striving hard to earn money so that he might help the home-folks, who were struggling in poverty. His mother was a widow with several children, one son being a cripple; William C. was the eldest child. That he never sent home a dollar is proved conclusively by Mr. Connelley.

Before the war began, Quantrill invented a sensational tale of which he made much use during the rest of his life, which ended violently when he was two months under the age of twenty-eight years. All of the literary bandits who have written about Quantrill have made much use of this tale. Even some writers who are high-minded and substantial citizens have helped to pass along this monumental lie, taking it for granted that the story must be true because of its long and wide currency. Our venerable friend the Kansas historian quieted the Quantrill fabrication in his book dated 1910, yet still it squeaks here and there just as if it doesn't know it's dead, as instanced by the book about "Charles W. Quantrell" mentioned above.

Quantrill told the men in his guerrilla outfit, some-times called the Black Flag Brigade, that he was fighting for vengeance. He claimed to be a Southerner, a native of Hagerstown, Maryland. His elder brother, he represented, lived in Kansas some years before the beginning of the war. The brother wished to go to California and invited William—or "Charley"—to come out to Kansas and go with him. "Charley" went; the brothers outfitted and started westward by way of the Old Santa Fé Trail. Each had a wagon and a four-mule team, loaded with supplies. A free negro boy was taken along as cook and hostler.

One night when the caravan was camped beside the Cottonwood river a band of thirty-two Kansas Jayhawkers came along, killed Quantrill's brother, shot "Charley" himself in leg and breast, robbed him and the body of the slain man, stole all the mules, wagons and supplies, and carried off the negro. The Jayhawkers, Quantrill said, left him "for dead." For two days and nights he watched beside his brother's body, shooing off buzzards with feeble cries and feebler gestures. An old Shawnee Indian found him there, took the wounded youth to his shack and "nursed him back to life."

Quantrill, so his story ran, vowed eternal vengeance against the Kansas people. He joined the company of Jayhawkers that had murdered his brother. From time to time he managed to get one or another of the men separated from the rest. Bang!—a bullet entered the exact center of the unsuspecting fellow's forehead. In this manner Quantrill ran up, after several years of untiring effort, a tally of all but two of the marauding band, each victim being shot exactly in the center of the forehead. Thirty to one!

Many of the guerrillas conceived themselves to be fighting for vengeance. Relatives of many of them had been murdered or mistreated otherwise by Kansans in the border warfare over the Free-Soil problem, preceding the Civil War. They accepted Quantrill's tale gladly, as partial justification for their own course in fighting under such a bloodthirsty leader. Because of his supposed wrongs and his desperate course in redressing them, Quantrill became their immediate and intimate hero. The guerrillas who survived the war continued to believe the Quantrill invention, for it was altogether that. To this day most if not all of the small group of surviving Missourians who rode under the Quantrill banner believe that their chief told them the truth and that he was a much-wronged man.

Quantrill, being the eldest child, never had an elder brother. He was born not in Maryland but at Canal Dover, Ohio, where he grew up under abolitionist influences. When about 20 years old he emigrated to Kansas Territory, where he taught one term of school. In Ohio he had been a youthful schoolmaster. Aged Kansans who attended his school in the territory state that he was a good teacher, so we shall let that one white point do what it may by way of offsetting his predominantly red record. Mr. Connelley shows that at about the time when Quantrill pretended to have lost his beloved imaginary brother and to have begun killing the murderers by the center-shot process, the Ohio youth was in a Kansas settlement stealing things from a colony of boyhood friends who had come out from Canal Dover at his solicitation.

Those who would justify Quantrill in slightest degree

by reason of any wrongs he ever suffered have not a scant spadeful of ground upon which to stand. Here was a Northern man leading a body of Southerners; an abolitionist-reared Ohioan pretending to serve the cause of the South because he hated abolitionists; a fairly well-educated young man who, before the South seceded, became an associate and accomplice of the most ignorant and vulgar and vicious of the Kansas pioneer flotsam; and who, after the war began, kept up his pretense of being a Southerner and actually caused his followers to believe him such. Quantrill entered guerrillaism as an avenue of escape from the consequences of his own pre-war crimes. Renegade is one term which partly describes the man Quantrill.

Of the abnormality of this man there can be no question. He was not in any sense an ordinary human being. The conditions on the border, in the midst of which maelstrom of blood and terror he dwelt for four years before the war, could not have produced the Quantrill we know. They contributed, but back of this environment was something deeper, darker, more dreadful.

The scourge and terror of the border undoubtedly inherited certain unconquerable tendencies toward a career of crimson violence. His father was an embezzler, his mother has been described snappily as "a hell-cat." One of his brothers became a thief and a low scoundrel. An uncle was one of the most spectacular criminals of the generation preceding the Civil War, being a confidence man and a forger, serving sentences in several state prisons; he married and deserted six women, and attempted to murder the woman who had been his first wife; he defrauded people right and left, and for offenses petty or serious he saw the insides of jails in St. Louis, Cincinnati, New Orleans and other cities. Quantrill's paternal grandfather was accused of sharp practices in horse-trading and was a professional gambler; a brother of this progenitor was a pirate. If we must offer "excuse" for Quantrill's blood-thirstiness, let us look to his heredity. Every man is a sort of modified sum total of his ancestors.

Quantrill's biggest and bloodiest exploit was the sacking of Lawrence, Kansas. Ostensibly he assaulted this famous little Free-State city in retaliation for the attack of Gen. James H. Lane of Kansas upon the small town of Osceola, Missouri, where Confederate stores and many houses were burned, much plunder being hauled away to Kansas by the Federal invaders. But Quantrill told one of his chief lieutenants, Capt. William H. Gregg, who became after the war a reputable citizen and was a deputy sheriff of Jackson County, Missouri, and an acquaintance of the present writer, that "he longed to get even with Kansas." In a speech to his captains before the start from Missouri he said, according to Gregg:

"We can get more money and more revenge there than anywhere else in the state of Kansas."

Galloping into Lawrence early on the morning of Aug. 21, 1863, at the head of about 450 men, by far the largest force ever under his command, Quantrill ordered every male citizen shot to death and the houses of the people put to the torch. His order was carried out as far as was possible in a day's bulleting and burning. The guerrillas murdered 182 men that day. Part of this tally went to the pistols of Cole Younger and Frank James, and not an insignificant part of it to Bill Gregg's sixshooters. Jesse James was not at Lawrence; he never served directly under Quantrill. Jim Cummins was not at Lawrence. John and Robert Younger were boys at home, too young to be in the war.

Jesse James, Jim Younger and Jim Cummins served under Anderson and Todd. Bill Anderson possessed a cutthroat personality if ever any man has been so furnished. He was one of the earliest of the border guerrillas and one of the fiercest. Before the war he was a cattle thief in Kansas. His men did more killing at Lawrence than did the squad of any other of Quantrill's lieutenants. A year or so later Bloody Bill was operating more or less independently in Missouri, chiefly north of the Missouri river. In his guerrilla band were Jesse James, Frank James, Jim Younger, Jim Cummins and some others who became outlaws after the war closed.

In the September of 1864 occurred the incident known as "the Centralia Massacre." Bill Anderson, with 84 men, attacked a railroad train which had stopped at the town of Centralia, Missouri. He found aboard 26 Federal soldiers, captured them, lined them up along the track and shot them to death. That happened about noon. Late in the afternoon of the same day, not far from Centralia, Anderson and George Todd joined forces and wiped out the Federal command of Maj. H. J. Johnson, who had 260 raw recruits known as mounted infantry. They became dismounted infantry when they faced an almost equal number of veteran guerrillas; their commander actually had them dismount to fight the most skillful and desperate cavalry outfit then operating upon American soil! Some of the men detailed to hold the horses, back of the line, escaped. All the rest of the command, more than 200, including Major Johnson, were shot to death within a few minutes. Jesse James is said to have shot Johnson.

The well-mounted rough riders charged down upon the militia recruits drawn up in line of battle. The latter fired but one volley. The guerrillas rode in amongst the frightened Federals, pistoling them. Their work done, they rode out again, leaving but one of their own men behind. The two Jameses and the two Jims, Younger and Cummins, were quick and accurate marksmen in the Centralia affair. Jim Cummins still shudders when he recalls that holocaust of human extermination. It was war—of a sort.

Not long after the Centralia slaughter Bill Anderson was killed in battle. George Todd, an illiterate man from Canada who was a stonemason in Kansas City before the war, succeeded to the command of Quantrill's forces when the latter lost his hold, and kept up the gory adventuring until a Federal bullet dropped him in a skirmish at Independence, Missouri. Quantrill became active again late in 1864, gathered about him 33 of his old followers and invaded Kentucky. His band crossed the Mississippi river on New Year's Day, 1865, at a point north of Memphis aptly named Devil's Elbow. Of the future border bandits, Frank James and Jim Younger were in the expedition to Kentucky.

Members of this final and fatal Quantrillian expedition supplied two explanations of the movement. Some of them averred that Quantrill hoped to make his way into Virginia, where he expected to join Gen. Robert E. Lee's army and enjoy the general immunity at the forthcoming inevitable surrender. He knew that if he surrendered or was captured in Missouri he would be hanged. Other guerrillas who went to Kentucky said in later years that Quantrill's purpose was to drive his flying wedge through to Washington, assassinate President Lincoln and thus become, as he fancied, the supreme "hero" of the war.

Quantrill was asleep in a hayloft on a farm in Spencer County, Kentucky, when the Federal guerrilla outfit of Capt. Ed Terrill, a boy of nineteen with a record remarkably bad for one of his youthfulness, rode down upon him and his. The battle was swift and decisive. Quantrill received a wound which paralyzed his lower body. Twenty-seven days later he died in a hospital at Louisville. Before his death he mentioned his mother and his sister, up in Ohio, as those to whom he wished to leave a considerable sum of cash which he had accumulated. But later he thought of Kate Clarke, a girl he had induced to ride away with him from her home in Jackson County, Missouri, and with whom he had lain in the brush up in Howard County, that state, most of the summer of 1864, letting Todd and Anderson carry on the guerrilla warfare. Quantrill forgot mother and sister, and bequeathed his money to his mistress. She opened in St. Louis a house of ill repute which was notorious for years following the end of the war.

Quantrill was a handsome young man with a most winning smile. In the heat of battle the smile developed into a musical laughter. Whether pistoling soldiers in a fierce horseback onslaught or dispatching prisoners taken—"no quarter" was the first rule of the Black Flag Brigade—the guerrilla chieftain accompanied the sharp crackle of his weapons with the sardonic lyric of his laughter. This is a fact attested by many of his men, who feared him and adored him.

Of Bill Anderson our surviving friend Jim Cummins has this to say: "My first idea of this man was that he was the most desperate man I ever saw, and I've never had any reason to change my opinion of him."

And, as all of us must admit, Jim Cummins has seen quite a considerable number of desperate men in his day!

George Todd was a man of commanding presence, a "noble figure" on horseback, utterly without fear of man or of God. His wrath in battle has been described as a thing terrible to behold. He killed men with great gusto, and mercy was not in his make-up.

Quantrill, Anderson, Todd—tutors of Jesse James and the rest of the original James-Younger gang of border bandits! Quantrill was a good teacher—in a little log schoolhouse out on the Kansas plains before the war.

CHAPTER III

THE GENTLE BOYHOOD OF JESSE JAMES

JESSE JAMES was a good boy. That is the simplest way of stating a simple fact. Yet those who have swallowed, unmasticated beforehand and undigested afterward, the tales told anent Jesse's alleged inborn cruelty as both boy and man, may require some complexity of clinching testimony to re-establish the Missouri outlaw as a "bad man" developed through extraordinary circumstances from a good boy.

A favorite form of recreation indulged in by romanticists who write about notorious outlaws is that of inventing infantile or early boyhood wickednesses for their subjects. Most of these bushrangers operating on the outer edges of the vast arena of letters have not been impelled to employ their own powers of invention with regard to the James boys of Missouri: they have been content to follow in the main some early-day Eastern "biographer" whose easy conscience permitted him to assume that, since the Jameses turned out to be bad men, Frank and Jesse must have been bad boys.

That egregious Outlander, happily anonymous and forgotten, started something which his copyists have kept a-going. He set in motion the silly stories detailing alleged boyhood cruelties practiced by Frank and Jesse James. Never having touched Missouri soil, probably fearing that even if he dared try to cross the state aboard a railway train he might be caught, killed and scalped by the Jameses, he sat in the safety of his Eastern eyrie and gazed from afar upon the simple lives of two Missouri farm-lads, his own ferocious imagination transforming those average and ordinary boys into little ogres of brutality.

According to that petty penny-a-liner, Frank and Jesse were totally unlike all the other boys of their rural neighborhood in Clay County, Missouri. They enjoyed nothing more keenly than the cutting-off of cats' tails and ears, not to mention the caudal and auricular parts of dogs. Tiny bonfires built of dead leaves and living songbirds afforded them a higher thrill than the wearied besiegers in mythical times got when at last the towers of Ilium toppled in flames. When the hapless beasts or birds, including pet squirrels and domestic fowls, had contributed to their tormentors a satiety of ecstasy through audible protests or visible writhings, the boys enjoyed another "kick" by scooping shallow graves in the kitchen-garden and burying their victims alive. Then, leaping upon the graves, they tamped the soil by doing a devil-dance upon the mounds.

These are but a few of the imaginary cruelties practiced by the James boys when they were little fellows. Testimony of their old neighbors, including that of boys and girls who played with them, attended the same schools and churches and participated in social "parties" along with them, paints a picture altogether different. We find that in their boyhood both Frank and Jesse were notably fond of animal pets. In the case of Jesse this tenderness toward dumb beasts continued until the day of his death; and there is nothing to indicate that Frank James ever mistreated an animal.

When Jesse James, stricken by an assassin's bullet, lay dead upon the floor of his home, a small dog cut capers around the corpse. He was one of the chief mourners, and he showed plainly his grief. Ten days earlier the dog had been given to Jesse by the latter's half-sister, at the home of their mother, "to take to the children." The trip to his home required a horseback ride of two days. Jesse James carried the little dog in his arms all the way.

Frank and Jesse James, we learn from the neighbors, were just like other boys. They were neither wickeder nor more saintlike than the average American lad who grows up in a rural community. They were healthy, hearty youngsters. They played like other farm-boys everywhere; they romped and they wrestled; they went swimming in the creek hard by; they built snow forts and achieved average marksmanship as snow-ballers; they fought in earnest, as the other fellows did, when a playmate became aggressive or when they themselves picked fights and went after the other fellows. There was nothing whatsoever in their small-boy careers to differentiate them from millions of other lads growing up on American farms just before the outbreak of the Civil War: that is to say, nothing from the inside out.

From the outside in there was much to make their

early experiences and impressions different from those of the vast mass of boyhood in other sections of the United States. It is to be emphasized that on the Missouri-Kansas border the war began about seven years before the South Carolinians fired upon Fort Sumter. Roughly dating it, from 1854 to 1861 Western Missouri and Eastern Kansas were fighting each other with a ferocity and a fatality hardly possible of adequate description to the present generation.

The border was a realm beyond the law. It was a narrow realm, yet by no means small in its effect and influence upon the abolitionist movement in the North and the secessionist movement in the South. It was exactly as natural as human nature that Missouri and Kansas fought each other. Kansas was being peopled by Northerners, many of them from New England. Missouri, along the western border, already was settled by Southerners, people from Kentucky, Tennessee, Virginia and other slave states.

Free-Soil Kansas settlers invaded the border counties of Missouri and carried off slaves. Slaveholding Missourians, and many Missourians of the Border-Ruffian type who had no negroes but believed in the institution of slavery, invaded Kansas Territory and voted without warrant in the elections, hoping to make Kansas a slave state. Kansas Jayhawkers and Red-Legs, Missouri Border Ruffians and Bushwhackers—the descriptive titles are suggestive.

When Emerson's "sublime fanatic," John Brown of Osawatomie, set himself to the insuperable one-man task of eradicating slavery, beginning specifically in Kansas Territory, the border warfare already was well in progress. John Brown was by no means the only man along the border who believed himself to be above the law. There were thousands of others, in Missouri and Kansas, who from motives good or bad erected themselves upon platforms of opinion and activity so far above the law that they could not see the American Constitution nor the state or territorial statutes even with the aid of strong moral or mental spyglasses.

Hell broke loose on earth along the border. In time the fight lost its dignity as a direct issue between Free-Soilism and slavery. It became largely a vulgar, vicious, vain conflict, man to man, hand to hand, between the baser human passions. On both sides of the border-line were many who made the warfare a matter of immediate personal interest—as they conceived it. Kansans entered Missouri, seized slaves, and sold them back for ransom. Missourians went into Kansas and killed Kansans who had seized or were supposed to be intending to seize slaves. Kansans, on pretext of liberating negroes, invaded Missouri and stole horses, cattle, hogs, even chickens, carrying their loot to Kansas. Missourians retaliated in kind, though with a lesser measure of success. Both sides of the kettle became coal-black.

Kansans and Missourians ambushed and shot each other. Missourians and Kansans hanged each other to trees or to barn rafters. Robbery and murder were so frequent on both sides of the line that such crimes ceased to be sensational news and became wellnigh commonplace events.

Enter now, by your leave, the two little Jameses.

Alexander Franklin, known to outlaw history as Frank, was hardly eleven years old when hell cracked wide open along the border; he was born Jan. 10, 1843. Jesse Woodson, Frank's little brother, was about seven, having begun his unique career Sept. 5, 1847. Jesse was born at the old homestead three or four miles from the small village of Centerville, now Kearney, in a house still standing in 1926 though considerably altered, enlarged and made over. Frank's birthplace was a cabinlike domicile about three miles away.

The parents of the James boys were from Kentucky. Both belonged to substantial pioneer families whose forebears had traversed the old Wilderness road in the long-drawn trek which resulted in the winning of the earlier West. Logan County was the Kentucky center of the Jameses. The Coles settled at and near Lexington, in the bluegrass region.

Miss Zerelda Cole, born a century ago, had a mind of her own. Though educated in a Roman Catholic convent at Lexington, she married a Baptist minister. She would not permit religion to interfere with love. For that matter, love became her religion. In time the element of hate entered and wellnigh destroyed her little heaven on earth, though love never waned: it waxed, increasing in its intensity from year to year until the end. She hated only those who hated those she loved, or who through a sense of civic duty or in expectation of getting quick (though hardly easy) money, sought to harm her loved ones.

Robert James was a student in an academy at Georgetown, Kentucky, when he met Zerelda Cole at some religious gathering. "Love at first sight" is the brief recorded history of that meeting. Young James was in his senior year and was studying for the ministry, though not cultivating theology systematically. In those pioneer days many a youth was graduated directly into the pulpit from a small academic institution, or even from a puncheon-floored country schoolhouse, without having received a smattering of scholastic instruction in theology.

Robert and Zerelda did not wait until the young man's graduation. They were married a short time after they first met. He was twenty-three, she but seventeen. The young husband remained at his studies until the next spring. His mother, widowed and rewed, had removed to Missouri. Less than a year after Robert and Zerelda were united, the young couple visited Robert's mother in Clay County and liked Missouri so well that they made up their minds to remain. In the meantime Robert had been ordained to the ministry and had become the Rev. Robert James.

The twenty-four-year-old preacher acquired some fertile land near Centerville and built a house. His dwelling was small, his acres wide. Two or three years later he built a larger house. This is the celebrated Samuel farmhouse, named for Dr. Reuben Samuel, who became husband of the Widow James in 1857. He was a physician who also practiced farming, as the Rev. Robert James had done.

In the pioneer days there were many country clergymen who preached on Sundays and farmed during the week. Mr. James was energetic in both lines. He organized two neighborhood congregations, known as Providence and New Hope, which have withstood time's ravages and remain as monuments to his pious zeal. He became known widely throughout his section as an evangelist, holding "protracted meetings" or "revivals" here and there and mustering many converts into the fold. Jesse Edwards James, a Kansas City lawyer who is the only son of Jesse Woodson James, recalls the fame of his grandfather as a wholesale immerser of converts:

"I have had old men and women tell me of seeing him go into the water and baptize sixty converts at one time. At the time when my grandfather thus baptized so many without leaving the water, my father, Jesse James, was fourteen months old, and he was held up in his mother's arms and saw the ceremony. Years afterward, when my father had returned desperately wounded from the border wars, he was baptized not very far from the same place."

After living for about ten years in Missouri and cultivating his farm by working hard between Sundays, the young minister made up his mind to go to the California gold fields and try to acquire enough gold to educate his growing family. He got almost nothing from his labors in the Master's vineyard. There were three children. Susie had followed Jesse into the world after an interval of about two years. Jesse was not quite four when his father was ready to start the long trip overland. The child clung to his father. "Don't go, Pa; please don't go away and leave us!" Jesse is said to have pleaded, his tears falling. He made a great to-do over the impending separation.

The Rev. Mr. James looked at his wife, who looked at him. For a moment both were silent.

"Zerelda," he said, at last, "if I hadn't promised those other men I'd go with them, and hadn't gone to so much expense already, I'd surely stay at home. Poor little Jesse!—he needs me. But you have the negroes to help you, and I reckon I ought not to back out now."

Little Jesse still clung, still pleading.

"It's all right, Jesse," said his father. "I'll come back home with lots of money and send you and Frank through college, and maybe you'll grow up to be great and good men. You'll have a better start than your father had, anyhow."

He set Jesse down, said goodby to all, climbed to the seat of his covered wagon and set his direction resolutely toward the Far West. They never saw him again. The caravan reached California and the gold region nearly four months later. Less than three weeks after the journey's end came final journey's-end for the Rev. Robert James. He took sick and died. Many years afterward his two outlawed sons visited Maryville, California, where he was buried; they tried to find his grave but were unsuccessful.

Tragedy first entered the old homestead when the news came from California. The young widow took another husband a couple of years later, but divorced him because he was unkind to Frank and Jesse. Dr. Samuel, third and last spouse, fulfilled all requirements; he stood by "the boys" until Jesse was slain and Frank "came in," stood trial, was acquitted and settled down to good citizenship. Like the Rev. Mr. James, he was a Kentuckian of excellent family.

Both Frank and Jesse were schooled deeply in the old-fashioned religion. Every Sunday the family drove to church and took part in the worship. Sunday-school, preceding the sermon, found the two boys and Susie present, singing the oldtime songs and reciting golden texts along with the rest of the neighborhood children.

Jesse James remained thoroughly orthodox in his religious beliefs as long as he lived. This, perhaps, is a hard nut for you to crack; but, being a simple statement of fact, it goes down upon the record. A Baptist minister who preached at Kearney when Jesse James was a youthful member of the flock met the strayed reveler some years later, when he had become an outlaw.

"Jesse," said the old pastor, "why don't you stop these things you're doing?"

"If you'll tell me just how I can stop," Jesse replied, "I'll be glad enough to stop; but I don't intend to stop right under a rope."

"Well, anyhow, you ought not to forget your religion, Jesse. You were brought up religiously. Your father was a good man of God. I'm sorry you've forgotten your bringing-up, Jesse. Get back to your religion!"

The outlaw thrust his hand into his inside coat-pocket and drew forth a small book which he handed to the minister.

"It was a copy of the New Testament," said the venerable clergyman, in relating the incident shortly before this was written. "I looked through it and was astonished. Never in my life have I seen a Bible so marked up, showing such constant usage. I handed it back to Jesse James. He smiled, as usual, replaced the Testament in his pocket, and his eyes blinked fast."

Jesse James believed in a personal God and in a personal Devil—probably in a considerable number of the latter! He accepted the orthodox Heaven and the orthodox Hell, his faith being implicitly simple. He expected to go to Heaven when he died, for he believed that he had lived the best life he possibly could live under all the circumstances, and that, therefore, he was entitled to salvation.

The outlaw's mother testified at the inquest over his body that when Jesse left her home for the last time, less than two weeks before he was shot down, he said to her at parting:

"Well, mother, if I never see you here again we'll meet in Heaven."

And, incidentally, his faithful mother was comforted by the same belief, which she cherished until she died.

CHAPTER IV

FRANK AND JESSE JOIN THE GUERRILLAS

FRANK JAMES was a good-enough boy. Local history has it that Frank as a little fellow was just as good a boy as Jesse was up to the latter's fifteenth year, but that as the elder brother grew into the big-boy period he got to be "a little wild." Frank, being nearly five years older than Jesse, was that much farther along toward maturity throughout the border-war era. It is to be assumed that Frank took into his soul somewhat more of the blood and iron of those years, which may account in part for his wildness. A big boy in the midst or the vicinity of shooting and looting may be calculated to take it all more seriously than does a smaller boy.

Frank James, throughout adult life, was a serious-minded man. Jesse was virtually the reverse. Frank "took things seriously," Jesse with apparent light-heartedness. Frank was more or less morose, Jesse constitutionally cheerful. Frank was for thinking out a proposition, Jesse for going at it on the instant's edge. Frank counseled moderation, Jesse was inclined to radical action.

Just here may be the very place for suggesting that if these two brothers, as outlaws, had been alike as two green peas and Frank like Jesse rather than the other way about, their period of outlawry in all probability would have been punctuated by a full-point—or a pair thereof, in the form of bullets—long before it attained its world-beating record of sixteen years.

Life was by no means all play for the Jameses when they were boys. They were brought up to work, and work hard. On a Missouri farm three-quarters of a century ago such things as labor-saving devices were unknown. Farm work meant real work, sweat-o'-the-brow toil, back-wearying labor. From the time they were big enough to drive a horse and hold the handles of a plow, Frank and Jesse made "hands" on the old home farm. They planted, hoed, plowed, harvested. Wheat, corn, hay, garden truck, all were grown there. Horses to feed and curry, cows to care for and milk, hogs to call and corral, firewood to chop and split—the chores alone were enough, winter or summer, to keep the two growing lads in healthful exercise.

The hard work had its compensations. The open air and the physical effort gave the boys good health and hearty appetites. There was always plenty of wholesome food on the table. The mother of the Jameses, in addition to her oldtime religion, had the old-fashioned notion that good cooking is necessary to the conservation of good food; she was a capable cook, of the Kentucky pioneer persuasion.

Preceding paragraphs alluding to the border warfare have indicated the altered environment which gave the little Jameses impressions differing widely from those of boys in, let us say, New London County, Connecticut, or Albermarle County, Virginia. They dwelt but a few miles north of the Missouri river. Immediately south of that river and of Clay County lies Jackson County, the center of before-the-war riding, raiding, robbing and rapining in Missouri. Much of this devilism had seat also in Clay County. What the James lads didn't see or hear, they heard about. The grownups, seated on the front porch in summertime or before the blazy fireplace in wintertime, talked it all over in presence of the children. Expressions of opinion were wellnigh as violent as were some of the desperate deeds under discussion.

So it happened that the Jameses and their playmates, instead of continuing to play the oldtime game called town ball, precursor of the form of sport that has made Walter Johnson famous, engaged in games of grimmer and ghastlier genesis. They played, whenever they could induce some boy to stand for the chief character, "Old Jim Lane" or "Old John Brown." Neither John Brown nor General Lane was old, as we estimate age today; but the brief word was prefixed in those times to indicate that he whose name it preceded was ancient in sin and crime and all manner of iniquity.

Border Missouri men and women hated Brown and Lane, to whom they ascribed in their impetuous fury much of their miseries. Border Missouri boyhood most naturally shared this feeling. It was difficult to find any boy who would undergo the ignominy of playing the character of Jim Lane or John Brown. However, boys who sought the ecstasy and honor of shooting or hanging Brown or Lane—in play, mind you—were able to obtain raw material for those characters by agreeing to reverse the cast and themselves submit to the disgrace the next time they played the exciting and satisfying game.

Thus it came about that General Lane, "the Grim Liberator," was shot or drowned or hanged many times over, in Missouri, by boys who resented his Free-Soil activities, many years before he poked the muzzle of a revolver into his own mouth and killed himself, when an about-to-be-disgraced Senator of the United States; and that some years before John Brown was hanged in Virginia for his so-called treason to that state, the border boys had shot him full of holes or stretched his neck beneath many an overhanging limb. Incidental to these executions were much raiding and robbing, all done in play and yet not altogether guiltless of violent feelings.

Should you seek seriously for the germ of the genesis of all-round outlawry in Missouri, invented and carried on by men born on the border in the Roaring Forties and reared there in the Riproaring Fifties, ignore not the seven shuddery years preceding Sumter.

Frank James had turned eighteen when North and South finally clashed in arms. He was old enough and big enough to go into the army—a tall, slim, sinewy fellow of nervous activity. Already he possessed two essential military qualifications: he could ride hard and he could shoot straight. It is a local tradition that when Frank and Jesse were boys big enough to share the ambition of all country lads for firearms practice, a relative of the family who had been a scout on the plains of the Far West and had won repute as a dead-center shot paid a long visit to the Samuel farm. He drilled the boys in plain and fancy marksmanship. They had known only the one-barrel shotgun. This Wild Westerner introduced to them the rifle and the revolver. Under his tutelage the boys made rapid progress toward preparedness for their forthcoming military life, not to mention their anti-civil careers which followed.

Frank James enlisted under one of the lieutenants of Sterling Price, commander of the Missouri State Guards (of Southern persuasion). He fought in the fierce battle of Wilson Creek near Springfield in Southwest Missouri, Aug. 10, 1861, where the Federal commander, Gen. Nathaniel Lyon of Connecticut origin, perished in a heroic effort to hold back the advancing hordes of General Price and Gen. Ben McCulloch, the latter being of the regular Confederate forces. With the exception of the first battle of Bull Run, three weeks earlier, Wilson Creek was the first important clash of arms in the Civil War.

Frank James paid a visit to the homefolks some months after Wilson Creek and was frank and fiery in advocacy of the Southern cause. He is said to have flourished a Colt's navy pistol somewhat threateningly by way of emphasizing his political leanings. Local Federal militia resented this, and the young soldier was arrested and locked in the little jail at Liberty, the Clay County seat. An oath of loyalty to the Union, signed "Franklin James," apparently had no effect, for when Frank got out of jail he remained loyal to the Confederacy and proved it some time later by joining the growing squad of young dare-devils led by William C. Quantrill, the renegade guerrilla chieftain from Ohio by way of Kansas.

Afterward Jesse also was caught up into the guerrilla outfit, though not directly under Quantrill. The boy had remained at home during his brother's earlier wartime activities, being too young for soldiering. He was cultivating corn, trudging between the handles of an oldtime bull-tongue plow, one day in June, 1863, when the Hell's imps which for years had been raging all around him swooped down with specific fingers not altogether phantasmal, clutched him, carried him aloft, shook him violently for a time and then let him drop into the midst of the fiery furnace.

Jesse had not been burning with zeal for the cause which ultimately became lost. He did not intend to permit himself to be burned up in the Hell's-fire of border hatreds if he could help it. And he was able, as it turned out, to spit some fire himself.

That June day a large squad of Federal militia visited the Samuel farm. Dr. Samuel, stepfather of the James boys, met the visitors and inquired their mission.

"You have been entirely too loud in your disloyal expressions," the leader informed him, "and so has your wife. Furthermore, you folks are friendly to that damn cutthroat Quantrill, and you harbor his men. We've come to teach you a lesson."

One of the regulators produced a stout cord. The doctor's hands were bound behind his back. He was escorted to a tall tree with an overhanging limb. A rope was noosed about his neck. One end was tossed over the limb and caught by several home-staying soldiers as it descended. They pulled hard, drawing the victim up until his feet were well off ground. The pulling end of the rope then was tied around the trunk of the tree, and the regulators of private opinion publicly expressed left the doctor to choke slowly to death.

Mrs. Samuel saved his life. She had followed the execution party, keeping considerably to the rear. As soon as the militiamen departed, she ran forward and cut her husband down. She was an excellent nurse, he a skillful physician. Though about half dead from strangulation, Dr. Samuel recovered. His escape from death was due chiefly to the zeal of his tormentors for haste in completing decimation of the male members of the family found at home. They went looking for little Jesse. They found him in a distant cornfield, plowing as straight a row as any lad of fifteen could be expected to plow. He was a rather baby-faced boy, seeming younger even than his years. The lesson-teachers had another rope along, but when they saw what a little fellow Jesse was they hesitated.

"Don't let's hang him—this time," the leader counseled. "He's too young to go and fight like that tall wild devil Frank. But let's teach the cub a lesson, anyhow."

The lesson comprised a whipping along between the rows of corn. One of the teachers used the stout rope as a lash. Jesse released the plow handles and made toward home, the stern schoolmaster administering a fraction of the lesson at every other step. The militiamen made off before the pupil got to the farmhouse; they went to teach similar lessons to other Southern sympathizers.

When Jesse reached the house, running hard, his eyes were blinking more rapidly than ever. As a child he had suffered granulated eyelids. Throughout the rest of his life he had the involuntary habit of blinking. They were large eyes, of a light blue shade. Your present chronicler has no prejudicial attitude with regard to blue eyes; in fact, he is measurably fond of them. He states a simple fact when he sets down here that virtually all of the noted outlaws he has known in a long experience as a newspaper writer have had blue eyes. The eyes of most of them were of a steel-blue tint. Frank James had such eyes; so also has Jim Cummins. The most spectacular bank robber that ever lived, the late Henry Starr of Oklahoma, who does not belong to the present narrative, sighted along the barrels of his sixshooters with eyes serenely blue.

The blue eyes of Jesse James were dripping as well as blinking, when he reached the farmhouse. The boy was hurt both physically and spiritually. That rope-lashing had been an insult as well as an injury. The proud old Kentucky pioneer blood of the Jameses and the Coles was outraged. Jesse James was crying both from physical pain and from humiliation.

"What have they done to you?" demanded his mother, whose eyes were dry.

Jesse mumbled out what they had done to him. He wore a work-shirt of the blue-check pattern common to farmhands in those days. The back of his shirt was damp—with sweat, and with something else.

"Come here!" commanded his mother.

Jesse had been making for the water-trough in the back yard.

"You come right here to me!"

Jesse obeyed his mother. She turned him around, grabbed a handful of the wet garment and drew the shirt up over his shoulders, exposing the boy's bare back. It was livid with long welts, from some of which blood trickled. Then, for the first time since the military visitation, Zerelda Samuel began to weep.

"Don't cry, Ma," the boy pleaded; "don't you cry, now. I hate to see you cry—I just can't stand it, Ma. I'll go and join Quantrill and get even!"

Members of Quantrill's command were in the neighborhood. After the resuscitated Dr. Samuel had attended to his welts and Mrs. Samuel had provided him with a clean shirt, Jesse went and found some of these men and begged them to take him along as a member of the guerrilla force. They laughed at him— after they had sworn at his regulators. Quantrill couldn't use little blue-eyed babies, they said. Jesse returned home, disappointed and chagrined. Plowing corn had lost its interest for Jesse.

Some days later the regulators reappeared. This time they were determined to kill both Dr. Samuel and Jesse James. They had heard that Jesse had failed to take his lesson seriously: he had been in communication with Quantrill's men, no doubt giving them valuable information—he had "informed" on the Federal militia.

Both the doctor and his stepson happened to be away from home. But the doctor's wife was there, and her daughter, little Susie James. Susie was twelve years old—goin' on thirteen. Mrs. Samuel and Susie were arrested—military arrest. They were placed in jail at St. Joseph, Missouri, as persons disloyal to the Union. Their incarceration lasted for several weeks.

There were two little Samuels, quite too young to hurt the Union or to help the Confederacy, which the Federal authorities permitted Mrs. Samuel to take along to jail. These were Sallie Samuel, past three years old, and Johnnie, whose months were about fourteen.

Incidentally, the next-born of the Samuel family was named in honor of Mr. W. C. Quantrill, though his name was misspelled, as usual, in the christening: they called her Fannie Quantrell Samuel. The guerrilla chieftain was known to his followers, as we have seen, as "Charles W. Quantrell." It is to be assumed that Fannie's name, had she been born a boy, would have been Charles Q. Samuel. Let us pause to record the birth of the last-born of the Samuel children, Archie Payton Samuel, July 22, 1866. Archie, at the age of eight and a half years, is a tragic little figure in a later chapter of this narrative.

When Mrs. Samuel was liberated and returned home, Jesse's back no longer was black and blue. His eyes were as blue as ever and they blinked fast and furiously when he greeted his mother.

"Ma, it's a damned outrage, that's what it is!" blubbered Jesse.

"Hush, son! You haven't been brought up to swear."

"Huh!" ejaculated Jesse; and a moment later his chubby round face was a flower-garden of smiles. As boy and man, he could smile at slightest provocation; he could smile, and he did, in a certain manner, when putting a bullet through head or heart of soldier or citizen   There were times when Jesse James had what some have been pleased to term a disarming smile.

Jim Cummins lived on a farm, his birthplace, a few miles from the Samuel homestead. Jim was about eight months older than Jesse James. The boys had played together from time to time. Jim was a thin stripling and Jesse a slight lad when the pair, with two other boys of the neighborhood, left home together and joined a guerrilla force affiliating with the groups under George Todd and Bill Anderson. The squad the four boys joined was under immediate command of one Fletcher Taylor, who made a remarkable record as a fighter. As "Fletch" Taylor his name is written redly in the annals of the Quantrillians, and as Charles F. Taylor after the war he made a fortune in the lead and zinc mines at Joplin, Missouri.

Jesse and Jim presently got under immediate wing of Bloody Bill Anderson, who said of Jesse at 16, "For a beardless boy, he is the best fighter in the command."

George Shepherd, another of Quantrill's and Anderson's most expert shooters and looters and a future member of the James-Younger outlaw band, extended a fatherly wing above Jesse toward the end of the war. Instead of going to Kentucky with Quantrill on the latter's foolish and fatal expedition at the end of 1864, as Frank James did, Jesse went to Texas with George Shepherd and some other veteran guerrillas. The boy had suffered ghastly wounds in battle. He was to suffer another, no less ghastly, when he returned to Missouri to surrender.

CHAPTER V

BEFORE proceeding to the bloodier business of this narrative it is of importance that the late Capt. Thomas Coleman Younger be introduced. His military title was won when he fought as a regular Confederate in the Iron Brigade of Brig.-Gen. Jo Shelby of Missouri, toward the end of the war. For nearly three years prior to that service he was a guerrilla lieutenant under Quantrill and Anderson.

When I was a very small boy in Missouri, somehow a book that gave me a tremendous scare got into my hands. It was one of those once-familiar paperbacks; you may find some of them today, though not a copy of that one, in the cheaper sort of shops where second-hand books are sold. In that old paperback, dog-eared already from frequent handling by older readers, was a full-page picture of a terrible monster-man named Cole Younger shooting no less than fifteen men at one discharge of his formidable weapon. I could read print but slowly, though I could grasp the import of a picture quickly enough.

The text explained the terror-trickling illustration. It seems that this Cole Younger person, or ogre, had captured the fifteen men in battle and had pronounced immediate sentence of death by thunderous word of mouth, "You must DIE-UH!" Then he placed the fifteen in line but not side by side. The first man faced the executioner, the second stood immediately behind the first, the third behind the second, and so on to the last. Cole Younger, standing a few feet in front of the first man, lifted his long rifle and pointed it at the center of that luckless captive's forehead. There was nobody present to call time. Taking deliberate aim, Cole pulled the trigger. One by one the fifteen fell, each man shot precisely through the center of the forehead!

In the old woodcut illustration you could see them falling. 'Twas truly a prophecy of moving-picture realism. The first to feel the bullet was stone dead, prone on the ground. The second was writhing in dissolutional agonies. The third, fourth, fifth, and possibly the sixth, were in rhythmical process of falling, No. 3 being already down to hands and knees, No. 4 beginning to crumple. The rest of the victims, still fairly in alignment, awaited the swift impact and passage of the leaden pellet—or perhaps already it had passed through their several heads and was speeding to bury itself in a tree far beyond, or possibly to kill a cow in the next county.

Anyhow, that single bullet killed every captive, so asserted the text with comparative calmness. The small boy spelled out the account of the multi-execution, gazed sharply and shudderingly at the picture, wondered vaguely why at least one or two of the men did not duck their heads and evade the bullet, and for a considerable number of years he remembered the mighty marksman called Cole Younger as a veritable demon masquerading in man's form.

Not long ago, grown much older and possibly some-what wiser, I visited the pretty little town of Lee's Summit, in Jackson County, Missouri, and called at the home of Miss Nora Hall, a middle-aged lady of substantial family and charming hospitality. In the cosy living-room I occupied a chair which, I was mildly startled to learn, had been one of the favorite resting places of the late Thomas Coleman Younger, Miss Hall's "Uncle Cole." Close by was a still cosier lounging retreat, a sofa or settee, which I was given to understand had been Cole Younger's first choice when the one-shot executioner of the doomed fifteen chose to take his ease whilst reading Gibbon's *Decline and Fall of the Roman Empire*, or the Kansas City *Star*, or—yes, truly—the latest copy of his weekly church paper!

"Yes, indeed," said Miss Hall, "Uncle Cole just loved to lie there on the sofa and smoke his pipe, or a cigar, and read. He was a great reader, Uncle Cole was. He liked to read history, for one thing, and he knew a great deal about history. He liked theological works, too; you know he was always deeply interested in religion, probably would have been a minister if the war hadn't come along and changed everything for him and his family; and he always kept up with the news of the day, being a constant reader of daily newspapers. Uncle Cole knew politics backward and forward. He would have been in the United States Senate, I some-times think, if it hadn't been for the war. I remember hearing him say once, after he came home from Minne-sota, that he got into the war without trying to get in and it took him forty years to get out of it."

Offhand, I had heard about the reading propensities

of Cole Younger, and was glad to have them verified by his favorite niece in the house where she lived, where "Uncle Cole" also lived for a dozen years until he died in the bedroom directly above that living-room.

My memory harked back a very considerable number of years, to the old paperback and the awful illustration. In those intervening years much water had poured through the mill-races of the grown-up boy's information and impressions regarding the chief figure in the 15-to-1 massacre. Long ago had he ceased to shudder when he read or heard the name Cole Younger; and now he was able to smile at himself when he recalled that as a little boy on a small farm he had been afraid to go out to the woodpile for an armful of stovewood or down to the spring for a pailful of water, lest the miraculous monster Cole Younger should get him.

"Miss Hall," I ventured, rather sheepishly, "one question in particular I wish to ask you—but please don't laugh. Did your uncle ever mention having seen the book with the picture in it showing him shooting fifteen men with one bullet?"

Miss Hall did laugh, gaily. "Yes, he did; and Uncle Cole had a good laugh over that story and picture."

Which goes toward proving that T. C. Younger, after all, was human. Yet there was some slight basis for the 15-to-1 fiction. When Younger was fighting as a guerrilla under Quantrill, he was in command of a squad of twelve rough riders who had been sent out from the main force to reconnoiter. At a farmhouse in Johnson County, Missouri, the party stopped for refreshments, hitching the horses back of the dwelling.

On the front fence several bed-quilts, washed by the women of the house, hung drying in the sunshine. One of the guerrillas, on the lookout, saw a group of fifteen Federal soldiers riding up the road. Younger's men took position behind the quilts, at his order. As the enemy came directly opposite, the Quantrillians arose and fired one volley. It is related that only one of the fifteen got away, which is not notably marvelous. It was comparatively easy for the romancer of the paperback to twist that incident into his impossible thriller.

Cole Younger, born on a fine farm a few miles from Lee's Summit—it is the Jackson County Poor Farm now and the buildings resemble a university plant—is remembered by the very few surviving octogenarians of the town and time as "Bud" Younger. He was born Jan. 15, 1844, and was one year younger than Frank James, his comrade in guerrillaism, his accomplice in banditry, and his traveling companion and partner in the latest and most legitimate enterprise of the two men's lives—a Wild West show. Younger made money enough out of that venture and out of his lecture engagements in Texas and other Southwestern states to buy the house in which he lived and died and which he presented to his favorite niece, Miss Hall.

It is hardly to be assumed that any Jackson County family will be offended through the statement that there is no better blood in their county than that of the Youngers and their kin. Should you ever happen to visit Kansas City or any other point in Jackson, particularly Lee's Summit and its rural environs, it may be wise for you to reserve expression of opinion as to the Younger brothers, unless your view be favorable. Nobody would shoot you, but you might commit a sad breach of etiquette by remarking to a prominent lawyer, doctor, banker or farmer that in your opinion the Youngers (his own close kin) were a mighty low-down set. The family connections are remarkably numerous, and some of them are leading citizens.

Col. Henry W. Younger, a Union man in sentiment and sympathy, was the father of the four outlaws and half a dozen other children. He was a man of solid substance, owner of more than 3500 acres of splendid farming land in Jackson and Cass Counties and of a prosperous livery business at Harrisonville, in Cass, when he was murdered and robbed by Federal soldiers from Kansas commanded by a captain named Walley. Colonel Younger had been to Independence, capital of Jackson County, where he had sold a drove of cattle from one of his big farms. Driving toward Harrison-ville in a buggy, he was shot down about five miles south of Independence, July 20, 1862. The murderers turned his pockets inside out, stole $400, missed several thousand which Colonel Younger carried in a belt beneath his outer clothing, and left his body by the roadside.

The wife of Colonel Younger and the mother of the four outlaws was a daughter of the Hon. Richard M. Fristoe of Jackson County, who had served in the Missouri Legislature and on the bench. The Fristoes were of the first-family grade, as were the Youngers, in local pioneer life. Mrs. Younger, a refined and delicate woman, passed through the horrors of the pre-war fighting and the Civil War, saw the large property left by her murdered husband swept away in the strife, heard the accusations of banditry against at least two of her sons, and died in 1870 after many years of semi-invalidism due chiefly to the results of harsh treatment at the hands of Kansas Jayhawkers and Red-Legs and the Jackson County Federal militia.

Part of this harshness was because of her son Coleman's activities as a guerrilla. Much of it must be laid to the same devilish spirit that inspired her husband's murder. The Younger brothers were deeply devoted to their mother, risking their lives in wartime and later to visit her and to give her substantial aid and comfort.

The writer of this narrative has been amazed at many discoveries in the course of his inquiry into border banditry. Perhaps the palm of amazed surprise must go to the discovery that the Missouri outlaws had such a host of apologists, amongst whom were several men of outstanding character. For the present we shall name but two of these—General Shelby and Major Edwards. One of the staunchest friends and defenders of the Youngers and the Jameses, up to his death in 1889, was John Newman Edwards, in honor of whom Jesse James named his only son, Jesse Edwards James.

Edwards was a native of Virginia who removed to Missouri as a youth and was editing a weekly newspaper in the fine old town of Lexington, on the Missouri river, when the Civil War opened. Not far from Lexington is the small town of Waverly, where Joseph Osborne Shelby, a native of Lexington, Kentucky, was operating a rope factory when the war interrupted his business. Shelby, known to familiar history as Gen. Jo Shelby, came of an aristocratic family. His paternal grandfather was the first governor of Kentucky. The Shelbys were related to the Kentucky Prestons, Breckenridges, Bledsoes, Marshalls, Bentons, Hamptons, Blairs. B. Gratz Brown of St. Louis, Horace Greeley's running mate in the presidential campaign of 1872, was a cousin of Jo Shelby; so also was Gen. Frank P. Blair of St. Louis, "the man who saved Missouri to the Union" in 1861.

John Edwards met Jo Shelby at Waverly early in 1862, when the latter returned from the Confederate service east of the Mississippi to recruit a regiment in his home county. This unit was the nucleus of "Jo Shelby's Iron Brigade" of cavalry, which fought for three years in the regular Confederate service west of the Mississippi and made glorious history. The remnant of Shelby's brigade never surrendered. With General Shelby at its head, this force of about 1000 veterans in gray marched into Mexico at the close of the war, proffered its services in turn to General Juarez and to the French supporters of Emperor Maximilian, and cut its way through bands of Mexican guerrillas to the Castle of Chapultepec, where Jo Shelby and John Edwards, his adjutant, after acquiring baths, boiled shirts and bootshines, were received in gracious audience by Maximilian and his Empress, the beautiful Carlotta. Edwards became the historian of that unique expedition and likewise the chronicler of the activities of Shelby's Iron Brigade, writing two big books about astounding adventures in which he took a gallant part and never once mentioning himself in the text of either tome.

Jo Shelby, when he died in 1897, was United States marshal at Kansas City. The general knew personally all of the ex-guerrillas who became outlawed after the war—a dozen or more in number. Never were they unwelcome at his home near Page City, in Lafayette County. The Youngers, the Jameses, Jim Cummins and the rest of them found refuge there when hard pressed, and the courtly Kentucky-born Missouri brigadier would have sacrificed his life rather than turn one of them over to the civil authorities.

Major Edwards was no less devoted to the outlaws: he was, if possible, even more so than was General Shelby. Edwards was a man of strong emotions. He was indisputably an honest man, a man of unimpeachable honor. He believed firmly that the border bandits were well-intentioned men who had been persecuted into outlawry. Like the old gravedigger at Lee's Summit, he felt that "they was drove to it."

In the last twenty years of his life no man in Missouri journalism had such a following as Major Edwards enjoyed. He was, in a certain sense, the Horace Greeley of his state. He was primarily an editorial writer. His editorials in daily newspapers of St. Louis, Sedalia, St. Joseph and Kansas City, written chiefly in the oldtime floridly rhetorical style, were copied throughout the country. He was emotional, poetic, visionary. It was a book which Edwards wrote, *Noted Guerrillas*, published in 1877, that set the Youngers and the Jameses upon the highway leading toward lasting fame as heroes.

When Major Edwards, who dearly loved his whisky toddy, as for that matter did General Shelby, got himself secluded from mankind in the presence of a ream of copy-paper, a bundle of lead-pencils and a bottle of white man's liquor, he could and he did make the exploits of the post-war bandits as wartime guerrillas appear manyfold more marvelous than the facts really supported; and the facts were marvelous enough.

Be it far indeed from this humble penman to accuse the gallant major of inditing a paragraph out of which an unbridled imagination might evolve such a tale, for instance, as that of the Cole Younger massacre-miracle with which this chapter begins; yet any student of the war on the border must admit, if he reads Edwards on the noted guerrillas, that the brave and brilliant soldier-journalist who exchanged a flashing sword for a slashing pen was quite capable of believing that Younger could have performed that feat if the young Quantrillian had set his mind and his muscle resolutely thereto. Indeed, there seems to have been nothing a guerrilla could not do in the way of hairbreadth escapes, hair-raising slaughter of enemies, or other deeds of desperate daring—if you happen to have emptied Edwards into your mental archives.

A most lovable man was Major Edwards. A very brave and a highly honorable gentleman and scholar was he. A knightly and a valiant fighter was the major, with sword and pistol, with pencil and pen. A master of the editorial English of the Seventies and the Eighties was Editor Edwards. Yet—yet his imagination was more masterful still, and once he mounted that fiery steed it ran away with him, frothing red

CHAPTER VI

THE ONSET OF POSTBELLUM OUTLAWRY

POSTBELLUM banditry in Missouri began with a St. Valentine's Day surprise party. The gentle saint of love and romance, however, had nothing to do with it, in inspiration or in execution. The "function" was altogether the creation of a combination of demon-gods operating in the war-disordered brains of a dozen young daredevils who had ridden and robbed and slaughtered with Quantrill, with Anderson, with Todd. All of these men, according to popular belief and the law of probabilities, were ex-guerrillas, less than a year out of the crimson course of the Civil War on the border.

Liberty, county seat of Clay, native county of the Jameses, was the town selected for the first manifestation of peace-time violence. Weary of the war which had raged around the place, irregular and regular, for a decade, little old Liberty was glad to be again at peace. Many of the undesirable citizens of Clay and the adjacent counties had departed, to return not. Hundreds of them, along with perhaps as many citizens who were desirable, had fallen in the fray. Some had suffered strangulation at the noosed ends of ropes, dangling from convenient trees. Many others, kit and boodle, had drawn stakes and decamped; for these the changed conditions in Clay and Ray and Platte and Jackson Counties had become uncomfortable, not to say menacing. Men who had fought for the Union and men who had struggled against the Union had "come in" and settled down again. Enemies of years past had become friends—with reservations. Everybody was heartily glad that the war was over—with exceptions.

The exceptions were some of the young fellows who didn't seem to know the war was over. Hard riding and straight shooting had become their habitual exercise. On scores of raids had they ridden, stirruped and spurred and sixshootered, hooting, shooting, looting. They had taken by violence what they needed, plus what they wanted. Horses for fresh mounts, store merchandise, household goods, any sort of plunder which they fancied, had been theirs without the asking. Only the bullet had spoken.

That St. Valentine's day in 1866 dawned bright and cold. The sun shed slanting rays upon the roof of the county courthouse which, quite unsuspected by the sheriff and his deputies who were a bit late in getting on duty in their offices, was to become that very day and to continue for more than sixteen years the seat and center of this weary old world's most amazing man-hunt.

Business places fronting on the courthouse square were opening, the hour being about 8 o'clock. Girls of romantic inclinations, on their way to school, were stopping by the post office to inquire for mail, hoping that the youths they fancied had sent them Valentines, and fearing that they hadn't. A few grinning lads who had mailed "comics" to the girls were lounging about in the hope of watching their victims open the merry missives. It was "business as usual" in Liberty, though too early in the day for most people to be out.

On the hill beyond the public square sat William Jewell College, a Baptist institution then in its early years. Students who lived or boarded in the town were gathering collegeward. One of these was "Jolly" Wymore, son of a well-to-do citizen. His first name was George, but such was his amiable disposition that nearly everybody called him Jolly. He was a bright lad of nineteen, who had perhaps more friends than any other student at William Jewell. Jolly was the life of many a party where the young people gathered to play such games as kiss-your-partner. Liberty being Baptist, Methodist, Presbyterian, dancing was taboo. Jolly Wymore, ambitious to earn his diploma and win his way forward, accepted his share of the kisses without letting the pleasant pastime interfere seriously with his studies.

Little Jimmy Sandusky, several years younger than Jolly, was another college student, of the preparatory department, on his way to school, books and slate under arm, his neck muffled with one of those oldtime "nubies" that kept small boys from getting the larynx chilled. The nubia conserved and accelerated the vocal cords, so that Jimmy and his playmates could yell almost like grown men.

Almost, yet not quite so loudly and so fiercely! Jolly Wymore and Jimmy Sandusky were to hear, that crisp February morning, the wild Rebel yell of the earlier Sixties, made wilder far than when it "rang through Shiloh's woods and Chickamauga's solitudes." It was the border guerrilla's modification of the more modest and less frightful Rebel yell of the true "fierce South cheering on her sons." It was, to describe the indescribable, the howl of the hyena, the yelp of the jackal, the yip-yip-yaw-aw-aw of a regular human devil riding hell-bent for blood and boodle. It was the baleful bleat of the men who had followed Bloodluster Quantrill and Bloody Bill Anderson into battle and ridden out with smoking pistols. It was the most terrifying sound that any human being ever heard.

At the northwest corner of the Liberty square on that long-gone day stood, as it stands now, the substantial brick building in which the Clay County Savings Association did its banking business. The bank was as solid as the building, though shortly after that day it liquidated its business and ceased to be. The shock the bank received that morning more than sixty years ago wrecked it as a financial institution. It was the shock of an onset of a round dozen of he-devil youths lately released from the restraints, so to say it, of war. They were graduates of guerrillaism, bearing diplomas that made them bachelors of freebootery. Some of the dozen were, in time, to acquire the master degree.

Fortunately we have not only the bank building itself as a standing relic of the first bank raid, robbery and murder committed by these graduates, but also a living eye-witness to that historic crime. Little Jimmy Sandusky saw it and heard it. He is the venerable Judge James M. Sandusky, a prominent attorney and banker in his native town. Judge Sandusky has supplied the writer with this brief page out of his past:

"I saw the robbery of the bank at Liberty in February, 1866. I was a small boy on my way to college, and was about half a block away when I saw several men sitting on their horses in the middle of the street in front of the bank. One of them fired and killed a student, George Wymore, about nineteen years old, standing on the corner of the street across from the bank.

"In a short time other men came out of the bank, mounted their horses, and rode east on Franklin Street about three blocks, and then turned north and left town on the road leading from Liberty to what is now Excelsior Springs, and crossed the Missouri river that night at some point in Ray County.

"As they were leaving town a few citizens were in the street, firing at them, and they were returning the fire. They were pursued by the sheriff and a posse, but no one was captured and no one injured. There was that night a blinding snowstorm, and it was intensely cold. Mr. R. L. Raymond, who lives in Liberty, was one of the posse.

"I think there were about ten men in the robbery. No one was recognized. I do not remember that they were disguised in any way. I do not think there was more than suspicion as to who the parties were. There was a man from Gentry County examined before a magistrate and discharged.

"My information is that about $60,000 was taken, and lost. About $45,000 of this was in United States bonds, and the balance was gold and currency."

Other citizens of Liberty state that the number of men in the raiding party was twelve. It was not far past eight o'clock when the desperadoes entered the town. The savings bank opened for business at an hour much earlier than similar institutions are wont to open now. Sixty years ago life was simpler, and sterner, than it seems to be today. Men worked longer and harder. On that morning Greenup Bird, cashier, and his son William, bookkeeper, were the only men in the banking place until two strangers entered most abruptly. From that moment the business-as-usual rule was suspended.

From different directions, in small groups, the men rode into the town, concentrating in the square. There were a few words of ostensible greeting, some gestures of pointing, and again the party split. Three men rode away together, but after going a short way they separated, each taking individual position a few hundred feet from the bank. From these posts they were able to observe the actions of citizens and detect any movement of a hostile kind.

The nine others rode to the corner of the bank building, where the door was located. Two men dismounted, threw their bridle reins over hitching posts, and entered the bank. The others divided, three riding to the right and four to the left, thus covering the two sides of the building which were exposed to the streets. These seven did not halt, save momentarily; they continued to ride up and down, watching nervously the adjacent stores and dwellings.

Inside the bank a scene the like of which became uncomfortably common in the succeeding years was being enacted. For the first time in America, perhaps for the first time anywhere, a bank was being robbed in broad daylight and in a time of peace. Each of the men who entered the bank drew a sixshooter of Colt's navy pattern and aimed it at the head of a Bird. There were, as we know, two Birds and two bandits present.

"Open the vault, and do it quick, or I'll blow your head off!"

Thus to the senior Bird the robber who held a bead on him. Cashier Bird, though he had no precedent for action in exactly such a predicament, chose to retain his head unblown: he opened the vault, situated at the far inner corner of the large banking-room. It is a substantial vault, as I can testify. Early in 1925, by invitation of Mrs. Minnie Duncan, an enterprising woman who for sixteen years has carried on a millinery business in the old bank and who lives in the commodious upper story of the building, I stood erect and hatless within the veritable vault that was robbed by the young Missourians who invented the industry of daylight bank robbery.

The vault is as big as a bathroom. Its walls are of stone, brick and mortar; ceiling and floor of similar material; door metallic and massive. On the shelves where in other days reposed bonds and coin and currency I found stored the latest models of ladies' bonnets. To what genteel and gentle uses, messieurs, is this once-violated crypt of commerce put! Accidentally one of my hands brushed a spring model of delicate shade—the obliging milliner had switched on the electric light—and I felt that somehow I too was become a Vandal. I was glad to escape from that denatured cash-crypt, yet not so glad as was Greenup Bird six decades earlier.

Accepted utterly without verification, for all these years there has been a prevalent notion that Jesse James (then a youth of eighteen) was one of the men who robbed the Liberty bank. Though Jesse was not on horseback anywhere upon that specific day, being flat on his back at home in bed, there clings to the authentic history of the raid one incidental episode suggesting his presence and participation.

Jesse James was of a jolly sort, say what you may. One adds nothing to the myth supporting his alleged general heroism when one states the plain and proved fact that Jesse did most dearly love his little joke. Apparently no situation in which he ever found himself involved was too deeply tragic to turn him aside from his lifelong propensity for cracking a joke.

Like (and likewise most unlike) Abraham Lincoln, Jesse James bolstered up his courage by telling funny stories and indicating in other ways that he could see the funny side of things. One of the chasmal differences between these two Americans, each unapproachably famous in his own line, lay in the matter of temperament. Each, in his individual way, was highly temperamental, though by no means so in the artistic sense; but melancholy was the chief characteristic of the Lincolnian temperament, whilst an indwelling cheerfulness was paramount in the emotional makeup of Jesse James.

It is indisputable, being based upon an ample archive of testamentary proof, that this Missourian who during eighteen of the thirty-four years of his life must be classed as more or less of an outlaw, in wartime and afterward, was throughout his career a person who possessed in a degree wellnigh superlative what we understand as "the saving sense of humor." Whether this sense saved Jesse at any time, or all the time until the bullet entering the back of his head put him past all earthly saving, we are entitled to leave to the learned individuals who practice the new-time science of psychology. It is a most engaging point, but we must pass it by as inert, like all mere points. This is a tale, and a true one, of progressive action.

When the robber who entered the bank-vault and helped himself to sundry bundles of bonds and several boxes of coin and currency had handed his spoil to his accomplice who still kept the younger Bird at bay under pistol-point, he paused briefly to take a last lingering look at the elder Bird, his own especial charge. The fact that he knew the cashier's name proved him no stranger to Liberty, though it did not prove that he was Jesse James.

"All birds should be caged," remarked the robber, grinning. "Get inside the vault, Mr. Bird, and step lively!"

Mr. Bird did not enjoy the pun. He obeyed the mandate, nevertheless. Slamming the heavy door shut, the two robbers quickly rejoined their friends outside the bank.

"Right there on the doorsill," said Mrs. Duncan when I myself emerged from the cage and was about to make exit from the millinery stronghold, "is the place where the robbers laid their wheat sack filled with bonds and money, to be picked up by other members of the band as the two who got the loot were unhitching and mounting their horses."

But both the Birds were free by that time, the vault door failing to operate its own spring lock when the robbers closed it upon Greenup Bird. The cashier and his son rushed to the windows and yelled out that the bank was being robbed. Already the actions of the mounted men had aroused suspicion. Several citizens had appeared in the open, wondering what was happening.

The outcry by the Birds changed forthwith the scene outside. There was immediate and excited running to and fro on the part of citizens, there was sudden galloping up and down street by the horsemen. Also there was shooting, promiscuous, intentionally wild, by the raiders, to frighten off anybody who might interfere with the remounting of the two active participants in the looting. Also that most terrifying of all sounds heard on the border, the Rebel guerrilla yell, was ripping through the February air.

Jolly Wymore, at this moment, was standing just across the street from the eastern side of the bank. He had paused in his walk toward the college to witness the actions of the mounted men. Apparently he did not understand the situation. It was not until the bank officials gave the alarm that young Wymore became aware.

The youth started to run around the corner, probably intending to carry the alarm to men in places of business. He had gone but a short distance when one of the bandits shot him down. It is a tradition that other desperadoes pumped bullets into his body and that he received five wounds. In any event, the most popular young fellow in Liberty lay dead upon the sidewalk when his neighbors dared approach the spot.

A few of Liberty's citizens had found firearms and were shooting, give and take; but the dozen outlaws, with their sack containing $72,000 in bonds and cash, shortly disappeared from the scene, galloping clitter-clatter out of town, hurtling back a bullet now and then and emitting their dreadful beast-bawl until the ultimate house was passed.

It was a clean get-away. Unless a member of the raiding squad be living somewhere now, a man of eighty or past, no person alive knows the identity of any of those young desperadoes. Certain Libertyites made accusations against certain former guerrillas whom they professed to have recognized in the gang. One Bill Chiles was of the number accused. Bill heard the news promptly and left the state in a hurry. J. F. Edmunson and Jim White were arrested at St. Joseph, Missouri, on suspicion; they were released when preliminary examination before a justice of the peace failed to connect them with the robbery. Oliver Shepherd, the "Oll" of many escapades in Quantrill's time and until his killing as an associate of the Jameses and the Youngers, was "positively identified" as one of the raiders, according to doubtful authority. Red Monkers and Bud Pence, the latter a relative of the James brothers, were others whom suspicion fixed upon. They, like Bill Chiles, made themselves scarce in Missouri.

For years it was believed by many Clay countians that Cole Younger was one of the robbers. On a recent visit to Liberty I was informed that Younger, some years after the bank raid, paid a visit to his uncle, the Hon. Thomas Coleman, who served at times in the Legislature and was a leading citizen of Liberty.

"Cole, were you, or were you not, in the gang that robbed the savings bank here?" inquired the uncle, looking his namesake straight in the eyes.

"Uncle Thomas," replied the nephew eye to eye with the Hon. Mr. Coleman, "I was not."

Considerate reader, you may take that denial for what you may count it worth. There were very many times when Thomas Coleman Younger told the truth like ordinary mortals; but no man in peril of his life need be expected to give incriminating testimony against himself when not under oath.

Of course the Jameses were accused, though not officially, of participation in the Liberty job. According to friends who constructed an alibi for him, Frank James was in Kentucky at the time. Jesse was at his birthplace about a dozen miles from Liberty, still suffering from a bullet-wound in his right lung, received from a Wisconsin soldier when the young guerrilla was going into Lexington, Missouri, to surrender and take parole at the end of the war. His friends averred that at the time of the Liberty robbery Jesse still had to lean over a vessel at stated intervals every day and drain the pus from his wound.

Many Clay County citizens still believe that the leader of the Liberty bank raiders was Arch Clements, one of Bill Anderson's most accurate marksmen. Clements was killed at the age of twenty-two, in December, 1866, in a running fight at Lexington, when he went to that town to surrender himself to the United States military authorities as a Confederate, hoping to receive a belated parole. He had been one of the most dashing daredevils in the guerrilla outfit, and it may be suggested here that his chances for life, liberty and the pursuit of happiness—even had he survived to be paroled—were negligible. Clements had gone to Kentucky with the Quantrill expedition early in 1865, and had spent some time in that state with Frank James, his particular chum, after the death of Quantrill.

"Arch Clements," Frank James once told me, "was the bravest man I ever knew. He was absolutely without fear."

CHAPTER VII

MORE than eight months passed before another bank was robbed by mysterious Missourians. The snows had melted from the grave of Jolly Wymore, spring and summer had brought their gifts of grass and flowers, autumn's early frosts had begun to drift hectic leaves upon the mound. Gone but assuredly not forgotten were the Liberty bank raiders. They had ridden straight back into the Nowhere whence they came. Apparently, so far as Liberty was concerned, the incident was closed.

But late in October of that year 1866 five horsemen entered the battle-scarred town of Lexington and drew rein near the banking house of Alexander Mitchell & Co. It was noon. Business had yielded to the invitation of the dinner-bell. The bank was deserted. Cashier J. L. Thomas, having nothing else to do, stood in the doorway looking idly across the street, chewing a quill toothpick.

Disinterestedly, the cashier watched the five men dismount and hitch their horses in an adjacent alley. He observed that all the horses were fine-lookers. Two of the men walked slowly toward the bank. The cashier went back behind his counter: evidently a bit of banking business was in the offing.

The two strangers advanced to the cashier's window. One drew forth a fifty-dollar bond which may or may not have been one of the valuable papers missing from Liberty. In those days U. S. Bonds of $50 and $100 were used, at convenience, like ordinary currency.

"Can you change this for me, if you please, sir?" requested the holder.

"I reckon I can," the cashier replied, pleasantly.

He opened the cash drawer and was fingering some currency when he glanced up and saw four big revolvers pointed directly at his head. Two more men had appeared in the doorway with Colt's navies not concealed.

Cashier Thomas recalled the Liberty affair and accepted the situation with such calmness as he could muster.

"Now give us all the money you have in the bank," suavely demanded the man who had asked for the change. "Do it quietly and quickly and you won't be hurt; but if you don't, you'll get your head blown off."

Thomas complied, quietly and quickly.

"All right; thanks," said the polite robber, tossing the loot into a wheat sack held open by the man standing at his side. "Now don't you give an alarm, for if you do you'll be too dead to know it."

The two men backed to the door, keeping the cashier covered with their weapons. The two at the door backed away, pocketing their pistols. The four of them walked at normal gait into the alley, where the fifth had remained, looking after the horses. They all unhitched, mounted, turned into the street and rode out of town without any ado.

They may have been ex-guerrillas—most probably they were—though none of them uttered the terrifying yell. It was a quick and quiet affair throughout. Cashier Thomas waited until the clatter of the hoofs had died almost to silence before he walked out and informed the neighboring merchants that those five horsemen had robbed the bank of all the cash on hand, $2,000.

It was an hour or so before a dozen Lexington men found mounts and set out in the direction taken by the robbers. The posse spent a couple of days in riding about the country, making various inquiries, striking a possible trail here and there. Nothing came of the pursuit, save weariness and vexation.

Public meetings were held in Lexington, the idea being that something should be done about the matter. Country banks should be safe-guarded, if possible, against such incursions. There was that Liberty affair, where the bank lost $72,000 and a fine young man was murdered. Those two James boys of Clay County, wild young fellows by reputation, had been suspected at Liberty: well, probably they and their gang had robbed the Lexington bank. Beyond that, nobody had a theory. After a few weeks the mild excitement subsided, though the personnel of small-town banks throughout that general section of Missouri felt uneasy.

Lexington is on the southern bank of the Missouri river, a day's easy horseback ride east of Liberty and southeast of the James boys' home. Savannah, seat of Andrew County, where the daylight bank robbers made their third appearance, is a couple of days' journey by dirt road to the northwest of the Samuel farm. Four months intervened between the Lexington and the Savannah affairs.

The private bank of Judge McLain was the financial stronghold of Savannah. On the 2d of March, 1867, five horsemen rode leisurely into the little town. The hour was 12 o'clock, almost the same to the minute as the time of the Lexington robbery. As at Lexington, most of the townspeople were indoors at dinner.

Judge McLain and his son were in the bank, nobody else being present until four of the five strangers entered, the fifth being left to guard the horses hitched at a rack near by. Apparently Banker McLain had in mind the Lexington affair. Reasoning from analogies, he figured that it must be the same gang on a similar errand. The banker was a man of nerve. Without waiting for his visitors to make initial demonstration, he slammed shut his safe door, snatched his pistol from its shelf under the cash counter, and began firing at the quartet as rapidly as he could cock his weapon and pull the trigger. A brave man, a bad marksman!

The four men drew their weapons at the moment that Judge McLain drew his. All returned his fire. The wonder is that he was not shot to shreds in that close battle, but he received only one bullet. A ball from a Colt's navy revolver penetrated his breast. He fell heavily to the floor. Meantime McLain's son had rushed out into the street, bullets whizzing about his ears, and cried the alarm.

Unharmed, the thwarted robbers ran out to their horses and sped away, along with the fifth rider. They got not a penny of the McLain bank money. Savannah citizens were somewhat quicker than had been the Lexingtonians; mounts were found almost immediately, and the fugitives were pursued by a few men. By mid-afternoon nearly all the horses in town and a number from outlying farms had enraged citizens aboard and were galloping out some road. Groups were absent on the trail for several days, but nobody was caught.

"The James gang again!" cried many more than one. "Looks just like one of their jobs, from all a fellow hears."

Men named Samuel Pope and William McDaniels, the latter being known to his cronies as Bud, were arrested some time later on suspicion. They set up alibis and went free. Bud McDaniels, a Kansas City-an, if not a member of the James-Younger gang then became one later; and he will reappear in this narrative, and disappear tragically. William Chiles, James White and J. F. Edmunson, former guerrillas, also were suspected of complicity in the Savannah failure, but none was apprehended. Judge McLain recovered from his wound and was a local hero for years.

Violent events now were popping fast. Less than three months after Savannah came Richmond. That pleasant little city is the seat of Ray County, immediately east of Clay. It is less than a dozen miles northwest of Lexington. Ray County was to become, in time, an important part of the Jesse James country, with a certain farmhouse near Richmond as intimate center of operations tragic and comic, chiefly tragic. From that lowly homestead, visited time and again by Frank and Jesse James, Jim Cummins and other members of the outlaw fraternity, was to go forth the raw youth whose bullet cut short before early middle age the career of the king-bee bandit; and in the same house, not long before the end of Jesse James, one member of his band was to meet violent death at the hands of another member.

In the matter of fatalities resulting from the Richmond bank robbery of May 23, 1867, this was the reddest of all the raids allegedly ridden upon by the James-Younger combine. Deaths of at least eight persons may be traced thereto.

If the Lexington and Savannah fives were one and the same quintet, as appearances suggested, then it is in order to surmise that the Liberty and Richmond dozens were the same men, with a couple added in the latter affair. Some citizens averred that they counted fourteen men in the gang of robbers and murderers who invaded Richmond. This outfit, mounted on fast horses and emitting the unmistakable Rebel guerrilla yell, dashed into town firing right and left. Citizens ducked and darted hither and yon. Six of the mounted miscreants halted at the Hughes & Mason Bank, the doors of which had been closed and locked when the yelping devils were heard from afar.

With the other members of the gang sitting their horses hard by and keeping up the shooting and the hooting, the six broke into the bank and found about $4000, which they crammed into the customary sack. Out again, they rejoined their accomplices, who by now were having much less fun than they enjoyed at first.

Mayor Shaw of Richmond was the chief official hero of the tragic day. He found somewhere a hefty six-shooter and dashed across the street to a point where other citizens who showed fight seemed to be gathering. Apparently it was the mayor's purpose to take leadership of this impromptu posse. Before he reached the spot he was observed by three of the yelling riders, who charged down upon him. The mayor fired briskly at the trio, but they were too many for him; he went down, the autopsy showing four bullets in his body.

In the county jail, adjoining the courthouse and not far from the bank, were several prisoners who, it was alleged afterward by friends of the suspected ex-guerrillas, were held there because they had continued to express secessionist sentiments. The raiders made a bold attempt to break open the jail and liberate these men. B. G. Griffin, the jailer, and his son, a courageous lad of fifteen, sought to withstand the assault. The boy got a big revolver and took post behind a tree, from which inadequate shelter he was firing upon the murderous gang when some of them shot him dead. Jailer Griffin saw his son fall; he rushed forward and stood over the boy's body, shooting at the murderers until seven bullets struck him down. Several of his wounds were in vital parts. Father fell dead across dead son.

With their sack of loot the fourteen bandits finally galloped out of Richmond, evidently having suffered no injury from citizens' bullets. This outrage aroused the whole county and several counties adjacent, not omitting Clay and Jackson. The Jesse James country stood up on edge. Men of means subscribed to a fund for running down the robbers and murderers. Warrants were issued for eight men who were alleged to have been recognized as members of the gang.

These were James White, John White, Payne Jones, Richard Burns, Isaac Flannery, Andrew McGuire, Thomas Little and Allen H. Parmer. Most of them had served under either Quantrill, Bill Anderson or George Todd.

Allen Parmer, who three years later was to become a brother-in-law of the Jameses by marrying Miss Susan L. James, had been one of Quantrill's most deadly marksmen; he made a gory record at the Lawrence Massacre. As to the Richmond affair, Parmer had a perfect alibi, it being proved that he was working at an honest job in Kansas City when the raid took place. Later he removed to Northern Texas and became a prosperous citizen. At this writing (1926) Parmer is one of the small group of survivors of Quantrill's so-called brigade.

Three days after the Richmond tragedy, and on the day of the funerals of the three local victims, a posse of about twenty men from Kansas City learned that Payne Jones was at a certain house near Independence and went out after him that night. It was a rainy night, of pitchy darkness. A little girl named Noland was taken along as guide. Members of the posse surrounded the house quietly, but Jones discovered their presence. He flung open a door and bolted out, a double-barrel shotgun in his hands and two Colt's six-shooters in his belt.

The desperado discharged both barrels of his gun before the startled possemen could appreciate the situation. B. H. Wilson, a young member of the posse, was killed and the Noland girl wounded so seriously that she died in a short time. Jones threw down his shotgun, drew his pistols and made for the woods. He was pursued for some miles. Many shots were fired in the darkness by both Jones and his pursuers, but none found a living target. Payne Jones was murdered some years later by a former guerrilla comrade who bore him a grudge.

The night following the Payne Jones tragedy a posse of Richmond men ran down Richard Burns. Convinced of his guilt, they took him to a lonely spot far off in the woods. Burns begged for time to pray, which was denied him. He was hanged to a tree. When found a long time afterward, his bones had been picked by crows and buzzards, so runs the tradition.

Near Warrensburg, in Johnson County, just east of Jackson, a persistent posse pursued Andrew McGuire and caught him, about a month after the Richmond horror. The small posse resolved itself into a mob and hanged the captive to a tree, without trial.

After being chased like a scared rat from place to place, Thomas Little reached Jefferson City, the state capital, and found a steamboat about to depart for St. Louis. He bought a ticket and went aboard. Somebody at the capital who had recognized Little sent a wire to the St. Louis chief of police. The chief received the fugitive as the latter was leaving the boat at the wharf, and placed him in the St. Louis jail. There Little remained until it was considered safe to take him to Warrensburg, his home, where he was wanted on charges of robbing stores. It was not safe, however, for Tom Little. A home-town mob hanged him to a tree in the outskirts.

Suspected of participation in the Richmond crime, but not arrested, William Hulse and John (Jack) Hines of Jackson County disappeared from the state. Cole Younger, whose friends declared he was in Texas at the time of the raid, was named by some persons as a suspect. Both of the Jameses were suspected, both presented evidence toward alibis. The presentation, incidentally, was made by others, Frank and Jesse being discreetly under cover. Your outlaw historian has found no conclusive evidence for or against either Cole Younger or the James boys. The fact that neither of the three was included in the warrants mentioned should be recorded in their favor.

CHAPTER VIII

BANDIT BULLETS SING SOLOS IN KENTUCKY

THE Missouri counties of Clay and Jackson having become decidedly inhospitable territory for the Jameses and the Youngers—save in certain homes where never a door was closed against them in all the years of their outlawry—those young men kept themselves invisible to the naked eye of the public in their own country for many months following the Richmond tragedy. Under suspicion, though not under indictment, they were discreet enough to veil themselves effectually from the view of officers of the law and of private detectives. The Pinkertons, who in years to come were to have tragic relations with both the Youngers and the Jameses, already were beginning to scent the trails of the outlaw suspects. Far ahead upon those trails, the lifeblood of three or more Pinkerton operatives was to soak into the soil of Missouri and cry out for vengeance; and Vengeance, responding, was to operate in two directions.

For nearly a year all was quiet along the Missouri, but on the 20th of March, 1868, Missouri bandit bullets sang solos in Kentucky. That day the first of the bank robberies beyond the borders of Missouri by ex-guerrillas from that state was committed, in the town of Russellville.

James Younger and Frank James, who had invaded Kentucky with Quantrill early in 1865 and participated in a series of gory engagements, already had names more or less bad in that state because of those activities. Jesse James and Coleman Younger were but vague names to Kentuckians until the Russellville raid.

This quiet little Logan County town of about 3000 people had no suspicion that any of the rough-riding Missourians were in the vicinity until six men rode into the place, wounded two citizens, and rode out with about $14,000 from the safe of the local bank, a private institution operated by Nimrod Long and George W. Norton. About ten days before the raid a well-dressed stranger who said his name was Colburn called upon Nimrod Long in the Russellville bank and sought to sell a 7-30 note of the denomination of $500. He said he was a cattle dealer from Louisville. Interest coupons still were attached to the note; but it was offered at par, with the accrued interest thrown in. Long, knowing that such notes commanded a premium in Louisville, suspected that something was wrong and refused to buy it.

A week later "Colburn" paid the bank another visit, accompanied by a tough-looking individual. Mr. Long wondered mildly why a gentleman of Mr. Colburn's prepossessing aspect was traveling in such company. Colburn requested change for a hundred-dollar bill. Long suspected the bill of being spurious and declined to accept it. Three days later, on the afternoon of the 20th, at about 2 o'clock, Nimrod Long, a bank clerk named Barclay and a farmer named Simmons were sitting behind the bank counter when Colburn and five other men rode up, dismounted and hitched their horses to an adjacent rack. Colburn and another man entered the bank, the other four remaining just outside the door. A little later one of these went to the rear of the bank.

"Mr. Long," said Colburn, "can you oblige me by changing this fifty-dollar bill?"

Long took the bill in his hand, felt of its texture, remarked "This looks to me like counterfeit, Mr. Colburn," and was about to inspect it more closely when Colburn suddenly drew a big Colt, shoved the muzzle against Long's head and called upon him to "surrender." Wartime terminology still did service!

Long wheeled around and leaped for a door leading into a rear room. Colburn did not fire. He seemed to be astonished, not to say considerably chagrined, at the banker's unexpected effort to get away from the immediate menace of a cocked sixshooter. In Missouri such things were not done.

One of the other robbers had no compunctions against shooting. He had posted himself at the bank's back door. When Long reached the room leading to that exit this man, uttering not a word, poked a pistol within less than a foot of his head and blazed away. The banker got a glancing wound; the bullet plowed through his scalp for a couple of inches. He grappled with the bandit, seizing the weapon and trying to wrench it loose. The fellow gripped it tight and kept possession. Clubbing the pistol, he began beating Long over the head. After a few blows, the bleeding banker fell to the floor. In a few seconds he regained his feet and again tried to wrest the big revolver from his assailant, just as the latter was in the act of cocking it to fire again.

By this time Long found himself at the rear exit. He sprang outside and slammed the door shut; then he ran around to the front, yelling for assistance. Two of the robbers sat there on their horses, each carrying a rifle and each armed also with a revolver. They were firing up and down the street. When Long appeared in plain view they fired several shots at him. Nevertheless, the banker got around a corner without being hit again.

Whilst Long was making his spectacular exit, the man passing as Mr. Colburn was busy inside the bank. Barclay, the clerk, and Simmons, the farmer, were advised to stand still and keep quiet.

"Otherwise," said Colburn, "you'll both be killed."

Colburn's companion was placed on guard over Simmons and Barclay. The desperado who had shot Long and grappled with him entered the banking room and assisted Colburn in finding and sacking the loot. The familiar Missouri wheat sack became, for the first time in an alien state, the loot-bag of a band of robbers. In a cash drawer was about $9000 in currency, all of which was sacked. The door of the vault stood wide open. Several bags of gold and silver coin had been placed there by some farmers, on special deposit for safekeeping. This hard money amounted to about $5000. Into the sack went all. The bandits examined some boxes of bonds shelved in the vault but took none of them.

"Come out! Come on out, boys!" cried one of the mounted men.

A citizen named Owens had acquired a sixshooter and opened fire. The robbers turned their guns upon him; he got a serious wound and missed all of his targets. The men inside emerged with their plunder and unhitched and mounted, under cover of their companions' fire. At a signal from Colburn they dashed out of town at full speed, taking the turnpike road toward the town of Gallatin. Several citizens who quickly had armed themselves fired fruitless volleys.

Less than a quarter of an hour after the bandits vanished, about forty citizens of Russellville, carrying such firearms as they could find in a hurry and riding horses and mules commandeered from farm wagons, buggies and hitching-posts, began pursuit. Odds quite naturally were against them. The bandits were aboard splendid horseflesh. Those Missourians always straddled the best beasts available: to ride handsome and capable horses was a point of pride and honor for them all. Pursuers found that pursued had turned off the pike into the woods, about five miles from town. This discouraged further immediate effort to overtake the fugitives. Riding through brush and timber was a feat familiar to the Quantrillian raiders; sedate Kentucky citizens balked at the prospect.

Next day "Yankee" Bligh, of Louisville, a noted detective of that era, took to the trail. For about seventy-five miles southward he traced the robbers. At the edge of Nelson County, Bligh lost the scent; but up the road some distance one or more members of the gang had been recognized by residents and Bligh had fairly good clews to follow. He followed them, with William Gallagher, another detective, and with several Nelson County men, to the home of George Shepherd in that county.

This Shepherd was none other than the daredevil Quantrillian who, late in 1864, had taken the daredevil Andersonian, Jesse James, under his escort and, along with other guerrillas, had departed from Missouri and descended upon Texas. Shepherd was much older than Jesse and much wiser—permitting use of that word here—in ways of violence.

Dick Maddox, who is said to have killed more men in the Lawrence Massacre in 1863 than any other member of Quantrill's command, was himself shot dead in the spring of 1865, in Kentucky, as an item of gore in his chief's last fight. Maddox had left a young widow, who had remained in Kentucky after she went down to search for her husband's body or place of burial. George Shepherd, who had become enamored of the fair Mrs. Maddox in earlier years, had hied himself Kentuckyward. He either married the Widow Maddox or took her for his mistress. At any rate, the pair were living together on a farm in Nelson County.

The posse surrounded Shepherd's house and demanded his surrender. Shepherd tried to escape through the thin line, put up a hot-shot fight, but in the end was captured. He stood trial and was sent to the Kentucky penitentiary for three years. He refused to disclose the identity of his accomplices in the Russellville crime.

From the files of the Nashville (Tenn.) *Banner* these statements are extracted:

"The arrest of George Shepherd had been made first because he was by himself, the others of the gang having been traced to another part of the county. On gathering a posse to capture them, it was found that news of George Shepherd's arrest had gone ahead, and his cousin, Oll Shepherd, had immediately started for Missouri with one or two comrades. Inquiry easily developed information that Jesse James and Cole Younger went with him. It was then satisfactorily shown that Cole must have been the man who called himself Colburn at the bank. It was found also that Jesse James had been 'visiting' in Logan County a few weeks before.

"At that time Jim Younger and Frank James were a hundred times more notorious in Kentucky than Cole and Jesse, because the latter two had not done the state with Quantrill. It was a natural thing, then, on finding that Jesse and Cole had gone with Oll Shepherd, for the detectives to claim that the other boys were in it too, especially as no trace of a James or Younger could be found anywhere in Nelson County, where they had been stopping off and on for a year. So the cry of 'the Jameses and Youngers' was raised.

"More careful investigation developed the fact that on the day of the robbery Jesse James was at his hotel in Nelson County. He was slowly recovering from an old wound which would not heal, and this made it imprudent for him to ride on horseback on any violent trip. The romantic version of the raid is that it was undertaken to procure funds to send him on a sea voyage. Frank James had gone to California some months before.

"Bligh followed the retreating raiders till he was satisfied of their destination, and then sent word to the Jackson County, Missouri, authorities to look out for them. Oll Shepherd made a quick trip of it, and on arriving he was waited upon by a sheriff's posse. As they summoned him to surrender he broke for the brush and got about twenty bullets, which finished him.

"The rest of the party were heard from a day or two later, and as better information then had been obtained, Bligh and Gallagher went over with requisitions for Cole Younger, Jesse James, John Jarrette and Jim White, who were claimed to be the active participants with the Shepherds. However, the news of Oll Shepherd's death had given them warning to keep out of the way. The Younger residence was raided, but only the youngsters John and Bob were found at home. The balance of the band were never arrested.

"Bligh still holds that Jesse James was accessory to the job, though he admits that Jesse was seventy-five miles away when it occurred."

George Shepherd, who returned to Missouri and settled down in Kansas City after his release from the Kentucky prison, was an accomplished romancer, as you will discover more clinchingly when you read the forthcoming account of his stupendous feat of killing Jesse James some years before Robert Ford got the credit, plus a little of the cash, for actually doing that job. Shepherd told newspaper men, after he got back from Kentucky to his old home county, that he was not arrested at his Nelson County farmhouse the day after the Russellville robbery; he eluded the posse, he declared, and was chased nearly seven hundred miles.

"I was determined never to be taken alive," said George, "but when I was in a little drugstore in a Tennessee village I was leaped upon suddenly by three men who pinioned my arms before I could make any resistance at all. It was a complete surprise, and so I had to take my medicine."

The "romantic version" with regard to Jesse James, mentioned by the Nashville *Banner*, may or may not be true. Proof or disproof of such an item after nearly six decades hardly is possible. However, Jesse did go on a long sea voyage shortly after the Russellville raid; he traveled first to New York, by steamboat and train; after viewing the sights of the metropolis for the first time, he took passage on a steamship for Panama, crossed the isthmus with the other passengers, and upon reaching the Pacific side went aboard another ship and voyaged up to San Francisco. The young invalid made himself most agreeable to fellow-voyagers; they noted the cheerfulness of his disposition and commented thereupon. Though hardly more than a living skeleton, the blue-eyed youth smiled pluckily and cracked jokes with the well persons.

From the Golden Gate, after a brief sojourn in San Francisco, Jesse proceeded to Paso Robles, rejoining there his brother Frank, who had traveled by land to California some time earlier. The Jameses spent a year or more as guests of their uncle, Dr. Woodson James, who operated a hotel and sanitorium at Paso Robles Hot Sulphur Springs.

Undoubtedly Jesse James went to California for his health—probably in the slang sense, surely in the actual meaning of the term. He had been advised by a celebrated physician and surgeon of Kansas City, who had attended him for the terrible wound in his right lung, suffered when he was going in to surrender at the close of the war, to take a long sea voyage. The ocean air greatly improved his health, and the hot baths and other treatment at Paso Robles completed the cure.

Frank James also benefited in general health from the baths and the sanitorium treatment prescribed by his uncle, though he never became, as did Jesse, a heartily robust man. Frank, in fighting trim, weighed only about 140 pounds; he was tall and rather angular. Jesse, who had been a slim lad, filled out as he matured; his weight was around 170 pounds when he was residing for several years in and near Nashville, Tennessee, as a business man and farmer under another name. Nevertheless, Jesse suffered at times from the effects of his wounds until his death. When he was attacked by illness, such as malaria, a malady common to outdoors men in his day, the old war-wounds gave him trouble. Having been shot twice through the right lung, it was said that the lung was virtually destroyed.

Another reason for the James boys' trip to California was the hope, upon the part of their friends and themselves, that a sojourn of some considerable duration far from the scenes of their youthful activities might improve their chances for settling down at home and living like other folks.

"Stay away a while, boys, and it will all blow over," was the advice they acted upon.

There is no reason to doubt that they had had enough and to spare of the violent life and that the simple life appealed strongly to both of them, perhaps more strongly to Frank than to Jesse.

But it didn't "blow over." When they returned to Clay County and made that discovery they began to feel that they were in for it as a proposition probably permanent, and they began to study out such virtues as might be found in violence. It was then, and not till then, that the Jameses became desperate outlaws in full fact. Despairing of a peaceable future, desperation became their portion. They had got started wrong and they couldn't stop without bending their necks for the noose.

When in California the boys went to a tintype "artist" and, standing together, had a little likeness of themselves made, which they sent to their mother. Mrs. Samuel had the picture set in a locket which she wore on her bosom, beneath her dress, all the rest of her life.

If the Pinkerton detectives had killed Mrs. Samuel when they tossed a bomb into her house in 1875, instead of merely blowing off her right forearm, they might have found on her bosom a concrete aid toward identifying her sons, the outlaws. One of the principal reasons why the Jameses never were arrested lay in the fact that the sleuths had no pictures of them to show how they looked. Another reason, incidentally, was that the boys, knowing that they would be hanged if apprehended, were determined never to be taken alive.

CHAPTER IX

THE CLINCHING CLEW OF THE HORSE THAT DESERTED

NOT often did Jesse James leave a clew to his identity when he galloped away from a crime of violence, back into the mysterious Nowhere whence he came. On one most memorable occasion he did so; but even this notable dereliction must be qualified in the chronicling by the admission that he did not gallop away in his customarily grand manner, for the clew he left was the horse he had ridden out of his awesome Nowhere to rob a bank.

Though Jesse had an alibi ready-made, and his friends had another man to thrust into his place at this robbery, the unspoken testimony of his own high-stepping steed remains sufficient proof to the people of Daviess County,' Missouri, that he helped to rob the Daviess County Savings Bank at Gallatin and that it must have been Jesse who shot down the cashier, Capt. John W. Sheets.

This double crime took place Dec. 7, 1869, more than twenty months after the Russellville raid. It signified the definite re-entry of the James-Younger combination into the old home state after a long absence. In the intervening period the Missouri outlaws had been quiet enough to satisfy the most exacting advocate of law and order. The Jameses, as we have seen, had spent most of the time in California. Cole Younger is believed to have passed some months in the vicinity of Bastrup, Louisiana, where he had been stationed as an officer in the regular Confederate service in the latter portion of the war, after leaving the guerrilla outfit.

Jesse James, returning from California, had taken up his abode at the old homestead and begun plowing corn for his mother, thus resuming the pastoral occupation in which he had been interrupted some years earlier when the Federal militia lashed him along the corn-rows with a rope knout. That he was honest and earnest in his effort to "come back" hardly is to be doubted by any mind that is not prejudicially mean. So many bad things must be said of this man of tragic career that it is but fair to him and his that we mention the good things in passing.

There was a "protracted meeting," or series of revival services, at the Baptist church in Centerville, or Kearney as the home town was beginning to be called. Country people joined townsfolk in attending these meetings, where an exhorter of the oldtime type preached sermons of the old-fashioned orthodox severity, prayed with deep fervency for the repentance of sinners, and entreated those still outside the fold to come forward to the "mourners' bench" and wrestle with God for forgiveness of their sins.

One night a young man—he was in fact but a youth of twenty—who had been a back-row attendant almost from the beginning of the protracted meeting and had appeared to take serious interest in prayer and song and sermon, advanced to the mourners' bench. He was prayed over by the evangelist and by local brethren and sisters. He prayed to God for his own conversion to righteousness, and Kearney tradition has it that he prayed most fervently. Before the meeting was over he stood up rejoicing, and the minister announced that Jesse W. James was one of the evening's converts.

Jesse was taken into the church as a member in good standing, after being immersed in the creek where as an infant he had watched his father baptize scores of converts after a protracted meeting at which the Rev. Robert James had been the preaching and praying revivalist. For some months he attended church, prayed in public, and gave every evidence of being as desperately in earnest religious-wise as he had been in his earlier avocation as a rough-riding and quick-shooting guerrilla.

It is to be assumed that the emotional fervency of Jesse's religious tendencies, as in the case of many other revival converts from the days of Peter Cartwright to those of Billy Sunday, cooled down considerably as the months passed. Corn-plowing again proved to be a perilous occupation for the returned native. His name had been "removed" from the rolls of the Baptist congregation, and so marked for record, before he mounted his horse and rode into Gallatin with two men who still are believed in Daviess County and elsewhere to have been his brother Frank and the Jameses' oldtime comrade Cole Younger.

The Gallatin affair was accomplished by a force much smaller than went usually on a raid against a bank. The average number seems to have been about six. At Gallatin only three men were in the party. There seems to be less ground for believing that Younger was present than for the conviction that both of the Jameses were on hand. Nobody was recognized or identified, nobody captured, nobody confessed. One must rely solely upon circumstantial evidence to fix responsibility for that unpunished crime.

The circumstance of the horse is difficult to explain away.

The robbery and murder may be described briefly. Without any demonstration suggesting former guerrillaism the three men rode into Gallatin. They were quiet and orderly as they approached the bank. Two of them dismounted and entered. The third remained with the horses, his business being also to serve as lookout. Captain Sheets, who had been a Federal officer in wartime, and a young man named McDowell, who was making a deposit, were the only persons present until the bandits entered.

One robber laid a hundred-dollar bill on the cashier's counter and requested that it be changed into smaller bills. Captain Sheets picked up the bill and was counting out the change when the other outlaw thrust a Colt's navy toward him and demanded that he surrender the keys to the inner doors of the safe; the outer door stood open. The man who had requested the changing of the bill now presented a big weapon and held Captain Sheets a captive whilst his accomplice went back of the counter and took about seven hundred dollars from safe and till.

The two robbers whispered together for a moment, both studying intently the face of the cashier. An instant later the one who had kept Sheets covered with his revolver pulled the trigger. The cashier fell dead.

Two or three citizens already had tried to enter the bank on business. Threatening death, the man on guard outside had driven them off. They had given the alarm. Several men had snatched up such firearms as were close at hand and were gathering near the bank. The lookout robber called to his accomplices to hurry out. Already they were at the door. They rushed for their horses, the other man having mounted. The man carrying the bank money got into his saddle and he and the lookout were off, but the fellow who had shot Sheets had poor luck.

Bullets were whistling. Shouts were heard above the shots. The spirited animal which the third outlaw was trying to mount plunged and snorted. His rider had one foot in stirrup when the horse dashed away, dragging the man some yards. Struggling to release himself, the fellow succeeded, and his horse trotted away to a livery stable, probably preferring the company of his own kind.

One of the mounted robbers rode back, the fallen one was helped up behind him, and the double-laden horse carried his burden out of town, pistols cracking both from and toward the escaping outlaws. Within a few minutes several live-wire Gallatin men got horses and began pursuit. They felt reasonably confident of capturing the two men on the one horse. But a mile or so southwest of the town the fugitives met a farmer named Daniel Smoot, riding into Gallatin on a capable horse.

"Get down—and get away!" cried the robbers.

Smoot complied, seeing two large weapons pointing at him. He disappeared in a field. The man who had been riding behind mounted Smoot's horse. The three desperadoes thus easily outdistanced the pursuing parties. When near the small town of Kidder, some miles from Gallatin, they impressed into service a Methodist preacher.

"You know the roads," he was told. "Pilot us around this town so that we won't have to go through it."

The preacher did so; under the circumstances he became as honest, though by no means as earnest, at land-piloting as he was at sky-piloting. Just before the bandits advised him that he was free to proceed upon his way in peace, the one who was riding the Smoot steed remarked:

"I'm Bill Anderson's brother. I've just killed S. P. Cox—if I'm not mistaken in the man I shot. Cox killed my brother, and now I've killed Cox for vengeance. Been after him for five years. Goodby, parson."

Lieut. S. P. Cox of the Federal army was the man whose bullet was supposed to have been the one that finished the career of Bloody Bill Anderson, who fell in a running fight with soldiers in Ray County, Missouri, in the autumn of 1864. Jesse James, at that time, was a member of the guerrilla force commanded by Anderson.

The sheriff of Daviess County took possession of the horse that had refused to carry his rider out of town. It was an excellent piece of horseflesh, a large and living clew to the identity of the man who shot Captain

Sheets.   Simple enough was the problem, provided that the man who rode the horse into Gallatin was the owner; the animal, of course, might have been stolen.

The public's nine days' wonder as to whose horse it was came to an end Dec. 16, when the Kansas City *Times* carried a news story conveying the information that the mount had been identified, beyond question, as the property of "a young man named James, whose mother and stepfather live about four miles from Centerville, Clay County, near the Cameron branch of the Hannibal & St. Joe Railroad." The phrase "a young man named James" indicates that up to that time Jesse James had not become a notable celebrity in his own country. However, he was not altogether unknown to the Kansas City press, for the semi-editorial article went on to say, "Both he and his brother are desperate men, having had much experience in horse and revolver work." Incidentally, "horse and revolver work" is a bit of phraseology carrying much significance as applied to the activities of the James-Younger crew in the years that were to follow.

Bill Anderson had a brother, James Anderson, who also was a guerrilla.   Little had been heard of Brother Jim since the war closed.   He was understood to be somewhere around.   The alibi offered by Jesse James and his friends included a tale to the effect that Jim Anderson had called at the Samuel farmhouse shortly before the Gallatin affair and had proposed to Jesse that the latter join him in a job where both could get "a lot of money."   Briefly, the proposition was to rob a bank.   Jesse, as the tale goes, indignantly declined.

He was not engaged in that sort of business, and he advised Jim to keep out of it.

"Well, anyhow, Dingus, I need a horse," Jim is alleged to have said, "and I like the looks of yours. What'll you take for him, Dingus?"

The wartime nickname of Jesse James was used by Jim Anderson—whatever he may have said to Jesse. When the blue-eyed boy first arrived in Bill Anderson's vicinity he had some difficulty in adjusting a piece of his camp-in-saddle equipment.

"This is the dad-dingest thing I ever saw!" ejaculated the disgusted recruit.

Thereafter Jesse was "Dingus" to his comrades. Most of them would have employed an expletive much more profane than "dad-dingest," to express similar disgust; but little Jesse, fresh from home and mother, had not learned to swear like a guerrilla trooper. The fact is, he never did learn the art of profanity unbridled. After he became an outlaw he used a direct cussword occasionally, but there is ground for belief that the "removed" Baptist convert entertained to the end of his life the feeling that it was a sin to take the name of God in vain. A peculiar person, this Jesse James! There have been eminent pirates, by the way, so devout that they insisted upon holding company prayers on the edge of scuttling a ship. Well, anyhow, the fact that the hard-swearing guerrillas nicknamed Jesse from his innocuous expletive, by way of deriding his rural innocence, must go down upon the record of items to his credit.

We return now to Jim Anderson and the alleged parley with Jesse anent the horse. Jesse needed money more than he needed horseflesh, according to the story. He named the price, it was paid and Jim Anderson rode away on his purchase.

It is said that Captain Sheets resembled Lieutenant Cox. The most kindly theory of this murder is that Jesse James, suddenly struck with that resemblance, just as suddenly shot Sheets in the belief that he was shooting the man who slew, in battle, his old guerrilla chieftain. Jesse, as we have learned, was a quick actor.

Gallatin people believed, and their descendants believe, that the two men who entered the bank were Cole Younger and Jesse James, and that Frank James was the one who stood lookout. Whether guilty or innocent in this instance, Younger was unfortunate because of his commanding size. He was a big man, weighing around two hundred pounds, well-proportioned, a person calculated to attract attention and arouse admiration for his physical endowment. It was "the big man" who went behind the counter and got the money. It was the lookout, a tall, slim man, who rode back and picked up the man whose foot got tangled in the stirrup. It was this man, rider of the horse that ran away from him, who killed Captain Sheets, one of Gallatin's most useful and popular citizens.

That was not the last time Frank and Jesse rode tandem on a single mount. On another memorable occasion of double riding, the hat of one of them was shot off and left behind; but it supplied no clew of value, as you are to discover. Hats and horses are different.

CHAPTER X

OFFICIAL Liberty felt, after the Gallatin bank robbery and murder, that those wild young James boys should be curbed forthwith. Curbing involved catching. At that time catching them was not regarded as such a perilous enterprise as it proved to be later. They were not looked upon as supermen in any sense: merely as restless young fellows who, like many other ex-guerrillas, had acquired the habit of lawlessness during the war and, unlike most of their former comrades, did not seem disposed to come in and be quiet and orderly. The unprovoked slaying of Captain Sheets caused widespread indignation; and if those Jameses were of the Gallatin party—well, they were getting altogether too much of a menace to be left at large.

When two men from Gallatin arrived at Liberty with proof of the identity of the Jesse James horse that had broken loose and remained at the scene of the crime, local sentiment demanded prompt action against the owner of the mount. The owner's brother was included in this demand, for official Clay County felt reasonably sure that Frank had been with Jesse at Gallatin.

Capt. John S. Thomason, formerly sheriff of the

county, lived in Liberty. He had served in the regular Confederate army and was a citizen highly respected. Both as sheriff and as army officer he had given abundant proof of personal courage and of solid common sense. He felt that for the honor of Clay County he should lead an expedition to the home of the Jameses and bring the boys back with him to Liberty, where they would have opportunity to render an account of their deeds.

Captain Thomason owned a saddlehorse of which he was proud, and with reason; it was a splendid steed that had carried him through many a battle. He saddled this animal, polished his army pistols, and with his son Oscar and two or three other well-mounted and properly pistoled men set forth on the road to the Samuel farm.

"We'll bring the boys in," said the captain as his party left the courthouse square.

"All right, Captain; we'll do the rest," gaily promised a spokesman for the Circuit Court official staff.

The Jameses saw them coming. Frank and Jesse already had learned the value of vigilance. They advanced down the road to meet the enemy. They knew the Thomasons and were aware that the captain had been a gallant Confederate. There was brief parley, in voices loud enough to carry across a considerable distance.

"We want you boys to come to Liberty with us," announced Captain Thomason.

"We don't want to go to Liberty, and we don't intend to go," announced one of the Jameses.

"But you've got to come along," insisted the captain.

"Not until we get good and ready."

The next proceeding had to do with firearms practice, though the James boys apparently had no desire to kill any of the possemen. They seemed merely to wish to shoo them away.

Both sides fired. Nobody hit anybody. But when it became evident to Jesse James that the Liberty men meant stern business, he shot to kill—a horse. Taking good aim, he put a bullet through the head of Captain Thomason's veteran war-horse. The animal dropped dead, his rider sliding off without being injured. By this time the skirmish had taken both pursuers and pursued out of sight of the old homestead. The Jameses drew off, as did the deputies. Frank and Jesse disappeared from the neighborhood. Captain Thomason, after witnessing their discreet flight, walked up to the Samuel farmhouse and borrowed a horse from the stable.

"Your son Jesse has killed mine," he told Mrs. Samuel.

"Well, Captain," said the militant mother, "I reckon you're in great luck, at that, for Jesse must have killed your horse to keep from having to kill you."

"Maybe so—I don't know. But I'll see that he pays for my horse, some way," declared the indignant captain. "Those boys of yours, Mrs. Samuel, are getting entirely too wild."

"Why don't you people let my boys alone, Captain Thomason? If you did, they wouldn't be so wild."

Tradition states that there was much more give-and-take talk between the two, with Mrs. Samuel lecturing Captain Thomason, the captain lecturing her. The mother of the Jameses could hold her own in any duel of tongues, and at last the posse leader and his men rode away.

When Thomason returned to Liberty riding the borrowed horse there was much indignation. The captain was humiliated. However, his skin was whole, as were the hides of Oscar Thomason and the others, which was an item not to be despised in the reckoning.

In the years that followed, such a casualty as the killing of a horse seemed utterly insignificant in the catalogue of crimson deeds charged up against the James boys. Some of Captain Thomason's cronies joked him, from time to time, about the loss of his war-horse; but as the years sped, and as bullets sped manward instead of beastward, the incident was almost forgotten by disinterested citizens.

Jesse James remembered it.

When I visited Liberty in 1925 I met Mr. Charles S. Murray, for half a century connected with the publication of the Liberty *Tribune*, a weekly newspaper. The veteran printer and editor pointed to a rusty metallic object in the window of the *Tribune* office.

"That," he said, "is a rather interesting relic. It's the lock from the door of the jail where Frank James was confined for a time, early in the war, when he got a little too wild in his expressions of political opinion. They've torn down the little old jail, and that's about all that's left of it. Joe Smith, the Mormon prophet, also was a prisoner in that jail, long before Frank James was."

"Quite interesting," I admitted; "but what do you

know about the Jameses—from personal knowledge, I mean?"

"Oh, I knew them when they were young men and I was a boy. They used to be around here a good deal. They were quiet enough, as I recollect them—just like the average young fellows. But, of course, they changed, later."

"So I understand; changed considerably."

"You've said it," laughed Mr. Murray. Then he told me this strange little tale:

"My brother, 'Plunk' Murray, much older than myself, fought in the war as a guerrilla. He knew the Jameses and the Youngers, rode side by side with some of them in battle. Some years after the war closed he was down in Texas. With him was Oscar Thomason. Captain Thomason had died a few years before. Jesse James was a hunted outlaw then, as he had been for a long time. Probably hundreds of sheriffs and deputies, scores of detectives and thousands of private citizens were looking for him; he was worth money to anybody who could catch him—the rewards were big.

"One day Oscar Thomason and my brother were standing together on a street in a Texas town talking, when a young man passed them and turned around and came back. He smiled, reached out a hand and called both men by name: 'Hello, Plunk; hello, Oscar.' He was Jesse James.

"'Oscar,' he said to young Thomason, 'I've been wanting to see you for years.'

"Jesse still smiled, but Oscar was wondering, maybe a

bit uncomfortably, just why Jesse had been so eager to see him.

"'Well, Jess,' said Oscar, clearing his throat, which seemed just slightly husky, 'here I am; anything I can do for you?'

"'Nothing at all, Oscar,' replied Jesse; 'but I reckon maybe I can do something for you. I figure you haven't forgotten that time you and your father and those other fellows from Liberty tried to take me and Frank, up at the old home in Clay?'

"'I should say not, Jess,' Oscar admitted, trying hard to return Jesse's amiable smile.

"Plunk stood silent, wondering what the dickens Jesse James had up his sleeve, so to speak. He knew how quick on the trigger Jesse was, for he had seen the young guerrilla pop off Federal soldiers several in a bunch, firing sixshooters with both hands. He knew, quite of course, that Jesse had a couple of Colt's navies or probably a Colt and a Smith & Wesson concealed on his person, ready to hand. That fact was as certain as daylight.

"'Well,' said Jesse, pulling out—no, not one of his big guns—pulling out a big fat pocketbook, 'I've always been sorry I found it necessary to shoot that fine horse of your father's. Captain Thomason was a brave Confederate soldier. I didn't want to shoot him, so I shot his horse instead. I had to do it, Oscar. I always intended to pay the captain for that horse, but never got a chance. You fellows both know why. Since he died I've been hoping to run across you somewhere, so I could pay up. How much, about, was the horse worth?'

"Plunk told me," continued Mr. Murray, "that Oscar's eyes almost popped out, from sheer astonishment. Incidentally, Oscar felt considerably relieved, too. For quite a spell he couldn't answer Jesse, but finally he found his tongue.

"'Well, Jess, I reckon—well, my father wouldn't have taken any money for that favorite animal of his, but I remember hearing him say that he had been offered $125.'

"Jesse peeled off some bills from a roll out of his pocketbook and handed the cash to Oscar.

"'Here's settlement for that old account, Oscar,' he said, with a laugh. 'I'm glad to get it off my mind.'

"Young Thomason obligingly took the money. After Jesse had talked with Plunk and Oscar for a few minutes longer, about old times up here in Clay, asking about certain friends and enemies, and all the while keeping his eyes blinking in every direction, he smiled himself away. So there's a true story about Jesse James that's never been published."

"It will be, Mr. Murray—thanks to you," promised the bandit biographer. "It's just about the most astounding story I've ever heard, and I don't wonder that Oscar Thomason's eyes almost popped out of his head."

"Jesse James," remarked the Liberty editor, "was a queer combination."

"Undoubtedly he was!"

The story of another early attempt to catch Jesse James at his old home has been mishandled miserably by long-distance biographers. It is of date more than a year prior to the Thomason episode resulting in the loss of the horse; in fact, it happened only a short time after the Liberty bank robbery. Jesse, as we learned in the account of that affair, was confined to his bed much of the time, around that date, still suffering from the wound in his right lung which a soldier in a Wisconsin regiment had inflicted when the young guerrilla was going into Lexington, Missouri, to surrender, at the close of the war. After the boy had lain in the woods for a day or so he had been picked up and taken to a farmhouse, where he received surgical attention and nursing. Maj. B. J. Rodgers of the regular army, stationed at Lexington in charge of the bureau that received surrenders and passed out paroles, learned that Jesse's mother and her smaller children had gone to Nulla, a small town in Nebraska, to escape persecution from the Federal militia. Dr. Samuel, her husband, had accompanied his family and was practicing medicine in and around Nulla. Major Rodgers provided transportation and sent Jesse out to the Nebraska town, on a stretcher, so that the boy might have the comfort of dying under his mother's care. But Jesse refused to die there.

"Take me back home, Ma," he pleaded. "I don't want to die up here in the North."

His mother took him back. The whole family returned home. For many months Jesse lay in bed, slowly recovering. Shortly after the Liberty bank raid the local militia determined to go out to the farm, arrest Jesse James and see that he was punished for his activities in the war, or to kill him if he resisted arrest; they preferred, most likely, the latter course.

Six members of the home guards visited the Samuel

homestead about midnight, late in an unusually cold February. Jesse was asleep. Dr. Samuel responded to a loud rap on the door, inquiring who was there and what was wanted. This awoke Jesse, who peered through a window and saw half a dozen horses and one man. The other men were posted at different points near the house; two or three were on the front porch.

Jesse got up, drew on his clothes, buckled his cartridge belt around him, and with one of his big Colt's navy pistols in each hand stood ready for emergencies. He was weak but not very shaky.

"We want Jesse James," said the leader of the party. "Open the door!"

Dr. Samuel made pretense that the lock was out of order, thus giving Jesse a brief time in which to achieve preparedness. The man outside the door pounded on the panel.

"Open this door! We want Jesse James——"

"Here I am," said Jesse; "come and get me."

He fired a shot through the door. The bold militiamen turned and fled, Jesse firing another shot or two as they galloped down the road.

So far as it can be told at this late date, that seems to be a measurably accurate account of this incident. But the pen brigands have it otherwise. Let us introduce to you the late John William Buel of St. Louis, who wrote or compiled in his time more than sixty books. Some of his writings were worth while, others hardly so. Unknown to literary fame, he was a most prolific author and a versatile one, it being recalled that for a subscription-book publishing firm in his home city Mr. Buel wrote, one immediately following the other, a life

of Jesus and a life of Jesse James. Buel handled the
midnight raid on the old homestead by stating that
Jesse fired a shot through the door panel, which probably was a fact. Then he proceeds thus:

"A stifled groan told him that his aim had been
perfect. On hearing the shot, the other five rushed to
the front of the house. Jesse threw the door partly
open, and the light from the snow made the men outside
easy targets for his unerring aim, while he was so hidden
by the door and the darkness within that the attacking
party could not fire with the least accuracy.

"In half the time it has taken the reader to even scan
this report, three of the six men were lying dead in the
snow and two others were desperately wounded,
while the other fled in mortal terror. Suffering,
as he was, from a very high fever, Jesse lost no time
in mounting his horse, and with a hurried goodby he
again rode into the wilderness, leaving his mother and
her family with the dead and wounded.

"It was a ghastly scene" (verily it must have been, if
anything!) "there upon the white-shrouded ground, one
man dead on the doorstep, two others stiff and frozen in
their own blood which crimsoned the yard, while the
groans from the wounded made the place more
hideous."

Tradition has it that Jesse, sick and weak as he was,
did mount his horse and flee; which is not to be mar-
veled at, seeing that he had solid ground for expecting
the six scared-off regulators to return with perhaps a full
company of home guards, seeking revenge for the

fright they got when Jesse's bullet crashed through the door.

Jesse took refuge with relatives in Kentucky. Frank James is said to have been in that state at the time, not having returned to Missouri with the other survivors of Quantrill's men who invaded the Dark and Bloody Ground and made it still more bloody, early in 1865. Frank is said to have ridden into the Kentucky town of Brandensberg, some months before the Liberty bank robbery, and to have been sitting in the office of a small hotel when several members of a law and order committee entered and told him to consider himself under arrest as a horsethief. Much outlawry had followed the war in that region.

The story goes that Frank responded by opening fire on the vigilantes, wounding two or three of them, and that one of them shot him through the thigh. His wound is said to have kept him confined to bed for some months in the home of a friend many miles from Brandensberg, to which refuge he rode after shooting his way through the party that tried to arrest him.

The Jameses had many family connections in Logan and Nelson Counties, and those two sections of Kentucky became far-outlying provinces of the Jesse James country for many years to come.

CHAPTER XI

TIME and tide now swing the story of the border bandits into the Serious Seventies. The decade from 1871 to 1881 was the reddest and the most roaring of any in the nineteenth century, considered from the blood-and-thunder viewpoint. Throughout the United States in general it was not a notable decade, but for the small group of men who comprised the James-Younger fraternity of freebooters it was a ten-year period of tremendous import.

For Missouri it was the saddest era since the first state legislature sent Thomas Hart Benton to the United States senate and showed New England and the lower East that the raw new commonwealth on the western bank of the Mississippi had at least one man worthy of clashing with the intellectual steel of Webster and Calhoun. This community sadness was due to the activities, actual and imaginary, of the Jameses and the Youngers. There was much of the actual and more of the imaginary.

It must be admitted frankly that these Missourians gave their native state a running start toward a very bad reputation. The state suffered sorely for the sins of these her sons—sins which, multiplied and magnified by public press and private prejudice, grew before the decade's end into such stupendous accumulation of infamy and ignominy that "poor old Missouri" perforce must hang her head in shame.

The Missouri *Democrat,* now the St. Louis *Globe-Democrat* and always until recent years a strongly partisan Republican newspaper in spite of its name, coined the expression "poor old Missouri!" The coinage was an exclamation of contempt for the state because she seemed unable to put down banditry within her borders, not to speak of permitting her native-born and home-bred bandits to run at large in several other commonwealths and work their pernicious wills against law and order.

The Jameses lasted through the decade, the Youngers dropped out about midway. But it was Minnesota, not Missouri, that saw to the dropping out of the Youngers, excepting as to one of the four brothers, John, a minor figure in the outlawry; and even John Younger was attended to not by a state law-officer but by a Pinkerton detective. Incidentally, John took the detective along with him into the Unknown Beyond, and Jim Younger sent another Pinkerton to swift doom at the same time.

Missouri had become known as "the Robber State," that being the descriptive title which her sister commonwealths applied to her with no apologies. It was averred by reputable citizens that the values of Missouri real estate had been depreciated quite seriously because of the outlaws' energetic pursuit of the business of robbing banks and railway trains. It is not to be questioned that many prospective settlers were shunted into other Mid-West states because they looked upon poor old Missouri as in truth the robber state. Such was the terror created by thunder-bloody literature concerning the James and Younger outfit that many timid tourists, undeniably, detoured before they reached the Missouri line, proceeding through adjacent states.

However, the Serious Seventies saw the Missouri bandits operating in several states other than their own, without making over those alien communities into areas of dread and depreciation. Happily, the year 1870 was a blank in the program of the bandits. Their first reappearance after the tragedy at Gallatin was dated June 3, 1871, and at that time they went into the North a short distance. In that interval they had been rusticating in Kentucky, Texas, the Indian Territory, possibly elsewhere: now and then, no doubt, in their own counties, Jackson and Clay, where they kept so quiet that their presence was known only to their friends, or possibly also to some enemies to whom discretion counseled silence.

The capital of Wayne County, Iowa, which bears the classic-sounding name of Corydon, is but a few miles above the Missouri border. Situated in the midst of a rich agricultural region, in the heart of the hog and corn belt, it seems to have been assumed by the outlaws that the bank at Corydon should supply pickings worth their while. Accordingly, on that rare June day in 1871 they rode out of Missouri into Iowa—and out of Iowa into Missouri. Say what you may, those fellows loved poor old Missouri! They were always coming back home.

Just who robbed the Ocobock Bros'. Bank at Corydon no man knoweth unto this day. Certain signs indicated that it was the familiar Missouri gang, though no definite proof ever yet has been adduced. If we can rely upon what has been phrased as the concensus of opinion, the band of raiders was made up of Cole Younger, James Younger, Frank James, Jesse James, Clell Miller, James White and James Koughman. Anyhow, they were seven.

Because of an incident immediately following the robbery, the present chronicler is inclined toward the theory that Jesse James was at Corydon. Jesse, you are not to forget, never let opportunity for a joke pass by him unaccepted.

The bandits selected that particular day, no doubt, because an outdoor political meeting was to be in progress. There was public speaking in the courthouse square. Everybody in town would be at the speaking, and the bank robbery would be easy. So it turned out.

When the seven men rode into the town nobody paid them any attention. Just another group of young farmers, or farm hands dressed in their Sunday clothes, coming in to hear the speeches. In those days a political meeting in the Middle West possessed a pulling power far beyond the present strength of a similar gathering. Spellbinders awed the open-mouthed multitudes, and an army could have surrounded a town when some forensic celebrity was uttering wisdom or worse.

Three of the horsemen entered the bank, finding the cashier all alone. Each man poked a pistol at head or heart of the cashier. The latter gave up the keys to the safe. The robbers took nearly forty thousand dollars, which they carried away in a sack sacred to the great Wheat Belt. Their surmise as to the richness of the pickings had proved accurate. It was one of the handsomest hauls they ever made.

Before leaving the bank the bandits bound the cashier, hands and feet, gagging him also. This act, the like of which the Missouri outlaws never performed before nor afterward, seems to have been due to their desire to attend the political meeting. Those young men could talk politics with fluency, and they were Democrats in the midst of a Black Republican stronghold which, for the nonce, was listening to a Missouri Democrat of the rockribbed variety.

The orator of the day was the Hon. H. Clay Dean, a celebrated, brilliant and eccentric politician and lawyer of Northern Missouri. The bandits rode from the bank to the public square, one of them holding the loot-sack between his saddlehorn and his belly. It looked, of course, just like an innocent purchase of some Corydon merchandising commodity and not at all like forty thousand dollars in disguise.

The eloquent namesake of Henry Clay was in the midst of his fiery oration on the evils of Black Republicanism. One of the bank robbers, sitting his horse at the outskirts of the crowd—popularly supposed to be Jesse James, and it was just like Jesse to do it—interrupted the speaker:

"Mr. Dean, I rise to a point of order, sir."

"What is it, friend and fellow-citizen?" inquired the orator. "If anything of paramount importance, I yield to the gentleman on horseback."

All Iowan eyes turned toward the mounted man, whose companions sat their steeds close by.

"Well, sir," said Jesse James, "I reckon it's important enough. The fact is, Mr. Dean, some fellows have been over to the bank and tied up the cashier, and if you-all ain't too busy you might ride over and untie him. I've got to be going."

Then the robbers rode away. Suspecting his interrupter merely of trying to annoy him, and not knowing that Jesse was a good Democrat, the Hon. Mr. Dean re-knit the raveled threads of his speech. It was some minutes before the outlaw's hint was acted upon. By that time the indubitably bold raiders were well out of town. A posse followed, half an hour later, after an argument as to which road the seven strangers had taken. The trail led into Clay and Jackson Counties—and Nowhere.

About two months after the Corydon robbery Clell Miller of Clay County, a former guerrilla and a recent recruit to the James-Younger band—in which company he remained to a violent death farther north—was arrested near his home by detectives from Kansas City. He was taken to Iowa after extradition proceedings, underwent a four-days' trial at Corydon late in the next year, and was acquitted. The evidence was insufficient to identify him as one of the robbers.

Jameses and Youngers presented alibis, naming many persons in their home counties who, they averred, could testify to their presence in Missouri at the time the Iowa bank was robbed.

There was no jesting in connection with the next robbery supposed to have been committed by the border bandits, though Jesse James was one of the suspects. Five men robbed the Deposit Bank at Columbia, Adair County, Kentucky, on April 29, 1872. They entered the town on horseback by different roads, the group coming together in the public square at about half-past two o'clock in the afternoon. Three men went into the bank, the other two staying outside and firing revolvers for intimidation purposes.

Cashier R. A. C. Martin and two other men were in the bank. Martin refused to deliver up the keys to the safe and was shot to death. The other two citizens ran out. Unable to open the safe, the robbers got only the money in the cash drawer, about two hundred dollars. The whole party rode away without further incident.

Pursuers followed the trail into Tennessee and lost it in the fastnesses of the Cumberland mountains. Detectives from Louisville, Nashville and other cities worked for months, off and on, in the hope of capturing one of the murderous marauders and collecting the rewards offered, but nobody ever was caught. Cole and Jim Younger and the two Jameses were under suspicion. The fifth man remained anonymous.

A few oldtimers in Kansas City recall vividly an incident of Sept. 23, 1872, when the tin cash-box at the Fair Grounds, containing nearly ten thousand dollars, was seized and carried away. It was "Big Thursday" at the fair, and about thirty thousand persons had paid gate fees. A famous trotter of the time, "Ethan Allen," was the chief attraction. About 4 P.M. the treasurer of the fair association counted the day's proceeds, locked the cash-box and handed it to a young man who was instructed to deposit the money in a bank, arrangements having been made to receive the deposit after banking hours.

The great throng was quitting the grounds. Just as the man carrying the box stepped outside the main gate, three horsemen dashed up. People leaped aside to keep from being run down. One man dismounted, grabbed the treasure-tin, handed it to one of the men still on horseback, then remounted. The trio rode away, firing many shots into the air.

Confessions made years afterward by other members of the gang made it seem highly probable that Jesse James was the man who grabbed the tin box, Frank James and one of the Youngers other than Cole being his accomplices. A letter published in the Kansas City *Times*, some weeks after this sensational holdup, signed "Jesse James," named Cole Younger as the man who stole the box. There is little or no probability that Jesse James wrote the letter. There were times when the outstanding outlaws were not on amiable terms with each other, but never times when one of them told tales on another.

The next bank raid attributed to the gang opened new territory. By this time the band had two more recruits, Robert Younger, twenty years old, and Bill Chadwell, whose real name was William Stiles. Until we are ready to dispose of his bulleted remains in Minnesota, in the memorable centennial year of 1876, we shall call him Chadwell. Frank James and Jim Younger seem to have gone "prospecting" in the West, as far as Cheyenne, Wyoming. In their absence from Missouri, Jesse James, Clell Miller, Bill Chadwell, Cole Younger and his boyish brother Bob are supposed to have gathered somewhere in Jackson County and planned a trip to Southeast Missouri.

The town selected as objective point is Ste. Genevieve, where the first white settlement on Missouri soil was made. It lies close by the bank of the Mississippi. Then, as now, the predominant element in the populace comprised Roman Catholics of French extraction. Ste. Genevieve is one of those towns tritely described as "quaint." It was quainter in 1873 than now. The bank of the Ste. Genevieve Savings Association ordinarily carried much cash on hand. It has been averred that $100,000 was not an unusual total ready to the hands of any bandit outfit that might covet the currency. But, being far from the Jesse James country, quaint little old Ste. Genevieve felt secure against bank looters.

The outlaws are believed to have ridden horseback all the way to Ste. Genevieve, by a roundabout route covering perhaps four hundred miles. First they rode southward, making a stop with friends at a rural place in the hill country south of Springfield, Missouri, "Queen City of the Ozarks." Then they turned eastward, riding through the heart of the rugged Ozark ridges to Bismarck, a town on the Iron Mountain Railroad about seventy-five miles south of St. Louis. There they spent a day, resting up, man and horse. Resuming their long journey, they rode through St. Francois and Ste. Genevieve Counties to the town of the latter name, arriving on the morning of May 21, 1873. Before they got to Ste. Genevieve the group split, two men riding in from the north and three from the south.

O. D. Harris, cashier, and Firman A. Rozier, Jr., whose father was president of the Savings Association, were on duty. No customers were present. Three bandits went into the bank. All of them pointed pistols at Harris. Young Rozier was ignored; he ran out into the street, yelling that the bank was in the hands of robbers and murderers. He was rather rash, at that, for the two murderers and robbers outside fired three bullets at him, one of which passed through the cloth of his coat.

"Open the safe door!" was the succinct command heard by Cashier Harris.

"I'm in your power, gentlemen," said the obliging cashier.

It so happened that the bank was far along in process of liquidation, a fact which the robbers' advance agent had failed to learn. Most of the cash on deposit had been sent to the Merchants Bank in St. Louis. Instead of the expected $100,000, more or less, the raiders got only about $4000, much of which was in silver coin. The wheat sack was so heavy that it dragged the ground as they emerged from the bank with Harris walking in advance, pistol-persuaded. They permitted him to go about his business when all were mounted and ready to depart.

Not far out of town the bandit bearing the sack of silver dropped it when his horse stumbled. The whole party halted whilst this man got off his horse to pick up the treasure. When he tried to remount, the unwieldy loot-bag struck against the animal's flank; the coins made clinky sounds; the beast broke loose and bounded back toward Ste. Genevieve. A pretty pickle for hardworking coin-collectors!

It sounds almost like a scene from a modern movie thriller, but Ste. Genevieve tradition still holds it true that at this immediate moment a German-American farmer came riding a horse toward town.

"Here, you!—ride hard after that loose horse and catch him—bring him back here—quick!"

"Und vot do I get?"

"You get the horse, damn your Dutch hide! If you don't, you get a bullet right out of this here nice little Colt!"

The German looked at the muzzle of the sixshooter and rode hard after the loose horse. Some distance up the road he caught the animal. When he led it back and delivered it to the unmounted man, who had turned over the sacked silver to a companion, he sat his steed stolidly, in the middle of the road, and naively inquired, not to say demanded:

"Yah, I catch der horse, now. Vot do I get for dot?"

The leader of the expedition—it must have been Jesse James, none other—bent almost double with laughter.

"You get away mit your lifes, you tamned Tutchmans! Vot else you egspeck, hey, alretty yet?"

Everybody laughed, excepting the "Dutchman." The robbers rode away into their Nowhere, pursuit being brisk but ineffectual.

CHAPTER XII

JESSE JAMES has been credited or discredited with having invented the art, science or industry of train-robbing. That probably is because he was Jesse James. To him personally has been attributed, in public print and private theory, the first faint glimmering of the notion that, since a bank could be robbed, why not a railway train?

Largely because of his alliterative name, so easy to ejaculate from the tongue, Jesse James became, long before his final exit, a sort of sign or symbol of super-humanness in rough and ready outlawry. Had his name been John Williams, Joseph Richardson or anything similarly ordinary, the likelihood is that his reputation as a riproaring freebooter would not have been in his lifetime, and would not have remained until this day with promise of preservation to a far future, the most spectacularly impressive in all outlaw annals. When his proud parents named him Jesse, the late Mr. James was labeled to an unanticipated immortality.

Although it is a fact that Jesse possessed qualities unique, standing out in bold relief from the general dead level of the border-bandit personnel, there is little doubt that Lady Luck hovered above his christening with approving smiles—that the James and Jesse combination, the short and snappy cognomen and the likewise short and snappy Christian name of the Baptist preacher's blue-eyed boy, served him well indeed in his peculiar avocation: it was a stroke of genius on the part of Madame Nomenclature. In many respects Frank James was a far abler outlaw than Jesse was, and the same statement applies to Cole Younger; but both of them were outdistanced in the race to premier repute when the youngest of the three was christened Jesse James.

Well, perhaps Jesse James did invent train-robbing. If not he, then some member of his gang must have been the inventor, for the first railway train holdup that ever happened has been charged up to the James-Younger group; and since July 21, 1873, no reason has popped up from any source to dislodge belief in the justness of that charge-up. The chief wonder is that these enterprising Missourians, who are supposed to have invented daylight bank-robbing in 1866, waited seven years to start the sister industry of train-robbing.

It happened in Iowa, not in Missouri. The latter state, however, is entitled to such glory as inheres in being the place of the idea's genesis and development. The theory generally accepted is that Frank James and Jim Younger, when they went westward about the time the Ste. Genevieve bank raiders started southeastward, were under instructions from the committee of the whole to ascertain just when there was to be a big gold shipment from the West to the East.

There was to be such a shipment, by way of the Chicago, Rock Island & Pacific Railway, about the third week in July of that year. James and Younger are supposed to have returned to Jackson County about the time the other five got back from Ste. Genevieve. There is evidence to support the belief that the seven started from Jackson, on fresh horses, July 12, headed for Iowa.

Cole Younger and Frank James, according to reports which may be true or false, went to Omaha, Nebraska, to make inquiries as to the precise date on which the gold shipment was to come eastward. They left the rest of the band at Council Bluffs, Iowa, which point was attained after six days of hard riding from the home county. Council Bluffs became headquarters for the expedition. Frank and Cole are supposed to have learned that the yellow wealth would be whizzing through the little town of Adair, in the county of the same name, two counties east of Council Bluffs, on the evening of July 21—unless somebody stopped the train and got the gold beforehand.

The seven robbers mounted their horses and rode to a point a few miles west of Adair, where a sharp curve presented excellent opportunity for wrecking a train. Hitching their horses in the woods, they unspiked a rail from the track. They left the loosened rail in place but tied a long rope around it. The end of the rope was held by a couple of the bandits, lying concealed in shrubbery and grass some yards from the track.

At 8:30 P.M., on time, Engineer John Rafferty, one of the Rock Island's most faithful men, drove his train around the curve. "Hand on the throttle, eye on the track." John Rafferty was obeying regulations. His quick eye saw a rail, unaccountably yet none the less actually, move suddenly to the outside of the track as if somebody had given it a quick jerk.

Rafferty reversed, but the distance was fatally short. The huge locomotive plunged off the track and turned over on its side, crushing the engineer to death. The fireman was bruised but not injured seriously. Some of the passengers—there were two Pullman sleepers and five day coaches—were bumped and bruised.

The train conductor assumed that the engine had left the rails at the curve because of some ordinary wrecking accident; but this assumption was dissipated when seven hooting, shooting desperadoes arose from the brush, some on one side and some on the other, and rushed to board the train. Even then, the conductor could not comprehend the situation.

Train-robbing was a new thing altogether.

Two outlaws boarded the express car, held up the messenger and compelled him to open the safe. They got all the money it contained, hardly more than $3000. Twelve hours later an express train carrying $75,000 in gold passed safely eastward over the replaced rail. The advance agents of the outlaw band had made a miscalculation in time.

The passengers were somewhat longer than was the conductor in reaching realization of the startling fact that the train had been wrecked by robbers. Some of them, suffering from the shock of sudden derailment and stoppage, were too much bewildered to understand what they were expected to do when the robbers entered the coaches and ordered hands up. It was such a novelty!

The gang got several hundred dollars and a quantity of jewelry from passengers. They mounted their steeds and set their faces southward. Back for poor old Missouri, where, in spite of everything, it felt like home!

News of this outrage was published throughout the land, and even in Europe. If news is the unusual, then truly this was news. It was not merely unusual, it was unique. The outlaws had started something new, and as the very first sample of their novelty they had committed a murderous crime which might have resulted in many deaths instead of but one. Public indignation was such that for several months the bandits kept under cover more nearly opaque than ordinarily was the case.

The day following the Adair affair five men on horseback stopped for dinner at a farmhouse in Ringgold County, Iowa, just above the Missouri line. The farmer, who had not learned of the crime, had a pleasant conversation with the men. They talked politics, agriculture—and religion. One of the visitors was described thus by the host whom they had entertained with their sprightly talk:

"Seemed to be a kind of leader; five feet seven or eight inches tall, light hair, blue eyes, heavy sandy whiskers, broad shoulders, short nose, a little turned up; high, broad forehead; looked to be a well-educated man not used to work; age, thirty-six to forty."

But for the age, that was a fairly accurate description of Jesse James. Jesse was not quite twenty-six at the time. He was not well-educated, save in outlawry, but to a simple farmer a young man of Jesse's experience in travel and in general contact with the world might have seemed so. The farmer's descriptions of the other four seemed applicable to Frank James, Clell Miller and two of the Youngers. However, that supplies no proof. Personal descriptions frequently are misleading.

The next adventure in which, by implication of suspicion and certain other elements, the Missouri border bandits indulged themselves, was as old-fashioned as the robbery of a railway train was new-fangled. Stagecoaches had been robbed from immemorial times. The celebrated British knights of the road had given specimens of that industry to play-wright, poet, novelist, historian. Out in our own Wild West many a stagecoach had been held up and its driver and passengers made to stand and deliver.

There was, therefore, nothing new under the sun in the episode of Jan. 15, 1874, on the highway between Malvern and Hot Springs, Arkansas, save that it was a new sort of adventure for the highwaymen who held up the Hot Springs stage. Five men from Missouri, who had passed the night at Hot Springs, left that famous health resort that morning, traveling eastward. Having their own saddlehorses, they did not wait for the outgoing stage, but they did wait for the incoming coach. It was one of those big old Concord coaches, picturesque enough to deserve the honorable and romantic place it occupies in dignified fiction.

Fourteen passengers, men and women, were aboard, bound for the Springs and their hot and healing waters. The Hot Springs Reservation is a United States Government institution. The area including the hot springs was taken over by the government in early days to be preserved permanently for the benefit of the American people. The city surrounding the springs, with the scenery in and adjacent to the city, is one of the most beautiful places in America. In the days before Hot Springs had railway communication, it was assumed that only the rich could get there, traveling expenses being so high.

The bandits hid in the brush about five miles east of Hot Springs. An hour before noon the stage came lumbering along. The holdup men arose. Frank James, according to tradition, called shrilly upon the driver to halt. The passengers were ordered to alight from the coach. Lined up at the edge of the road, they submitted to search and seizure. Money and jewelry were turned over to the outlaws. Clell Miller and Jim Younger are supposed to have been the men who took the loot from each passenger and put it into the customary sack.

Former Governor T. A. Burbank of Dakota Territory was one of the passengers. One of the robbers remarked that Burbank looked like a detective. Another passenger had a Southern accent.

"Were you in the Confederate army?" inquired one of the highwaymen, a big, handsome man of genteel aspect.

"I was," replied the passenger.

"Name your regiment, company and colonel."

The passenger named them.

"So was I in the Confederate army," said the big robber. "I served under Gen. Jo Shelby of Missouri."

Thereupon he handed back to the astonished

Southerner the watch and chain and the wallet the traveler had given up.

"We never rob Southerners," said the large man, assumed to have been Capt. Thomas Coleman Younger, late of Gen. Sterling Price's army and earlier of Col. William C. Quantrill's guerrillas; "especially Confederate soldiers we hold exempt. I and the gentlemen of my present party, who have had the honor to relieve you gentlemen of your extra equipment because we need it perhaps more than you do yourselves, are old Confederates; and we are forced to follow this irregular business because we have been persecuted in our own homes, our families outraged, some of our loved ones foully murdered, because of our wartime sympathies and activities. No, gentlemen—and ladies," removing his hat and bowing low, "we never molest ex-Confederates; but," with a swift sidewise glance at Governor Burbank, "detectives, Pinkertons in particular, are not on our exemption list. We are sorry to have detained you, and now"—to the driver—"you may climb to your seat and drive ahead for the beautiful little city of Hot Springs and its waters of healing."

If it was Cole Younger who made that little speech, the 200-pounder from Jackson County did some big, tall talking not altogether truthful. Throughout their careers the Jameses and the Youngers were in the habit of insisting that their depredations were strictly against Northerners, and their apologists were still more insistent upon that point. The fact is that all of the banks they robbed, excepting the one at Corydon, Iowa, and the one they tried to rob at Northfield, Minnesota, were in Southern states, if we class Missouri as Southern, which is not strictly a fact. Missouri is sufficiently Southern, however, to clinch our contention here.

The further fact is that all of the trains they robbed, save one in Iowa and another in Kansas only a few miles west of the Missouri line, were in Missouri. In robbing a bank or a train they never inquired as to the political or sectional proclivities of their victims. Southern and Northern alike delivered up to them at pistol's point. The Hot Springs stage affair was exceptional.

Thus falls to ground another considerable slab from the flimsy structure which the friends of the Missouri outlaws constructed for them, the fabricated notion that they were engaged in outlawry because they wanted "vengeance." Our late friends from Missouri, once they got hell-bent for banditry, robbed banks, trains and stages primarily because they wanted—and very probably needed—the money.

CHAPTER XIII

THROUGHOUT the Serious Seventies many Pinkerton detectives hunted the Missouri border bandits. The famous agency founded before the Civil War by Allan Pinkerton devoted much time and talent toward capturing or killing the Jameses, the Youngers and their accomplices in outlawry, Frank and Jesse James being the chief objectives. From the headquarters in Chicago and from branch offices the most astute operatives in the service were sent out after the appearing, disappearing and reappearing free-booters. It was the most memorable man-hunt in American annals.

If the stage-robber who made the impromptu speech to impressed listeners in Arkansas was indeed Cole Younger, the orator had still stronger reasons for disliking detectives in general, and Pinkertons in particular, a few months later. Though the outlaws had been active for about eight years, intermittently, the fraternal ranks of the two leading families in the gang remained unbroken. The astounding fact stands forth that not a James, not a Younger, had been killed or caught, or even wounded. Their bullets and those of their associates had found fatal lodgement on a number of occasions but the four Youngers and the two Jameses had remained immune.

At last the tide turned. Before the first quarter of 1874 ended, one of the Youngers was thrust into a grave by the side of a road which his own lifeblood had crimsoned, the vital fluid of two Pinkerton detectives also having deepened the sanguinary stain.

This triple fatality was preceded by the first train robbery committed by the Missourians in their native state, which happened on the last day of January, at Gadshill, a way-station in Wayne County, Southeast Missouri, something more than a hundred miles below St. Louis. The place was a lonely outpost in the foothills of the Ozarks, on the Iron Mountain Railroad, now a part of the Missouri Pacific system.

Gadshill, evidently named by somebody who sought thus to honor the beloved Charles Dickens, whose home bore the same name, was a mere flag-station. A small shack beside the track was called "the depot" by brevet of courtesy. A rude dwelling or two comprised the rest of the settlement. The adjacent country, then but thinly peopled, was rocky and hilly.

The men who had robbed the Hot Springs stage, with the probable addition of Jesse James, who is said to have been in Louisiana at the time of the stage holdup, are believed to have accomplished the Gadshill job. The outlaws spent the two intervening weeks at a remote retreat in Missouri, near the Arkansas line. The Little Rock express train from St. Louis was due at Gadshill at 5:40 P.M., but not due to stop there. The season being midwinter, darkness had fallen.

Five strangers, all wearing blue overcoats, had been seen in the vicinity of Gadshill a day or two before the date of the robbery. Shortly before the train was due to whiz past the little station five men, only one of whom wore an overcoat—and that was a blue one—walked up to the depot, captured the station agent and five Ozark hillbillies who were there to see the train pass, and took possession of the premises.

The man in the blue overcoat, traditionally identified as Clell Miller of Clay, planted a signal flag in the middle of the track, and took off his overcoat and laid it on the track, thus making himself inconspicuous. Others turned the switch, to compel the engineer to stop the train if he failed to heed the flag. The express came along on time. The engineer obeyed the signal, supposing that prospective passengers were at hand.

When the conductor stepped to the ground alongside the station, lantern in hand, he looked first into the muzzle of a pistol pointed at his head, then into the face of the man who was pointing the pistol. It was a somewhat thin, angular face, with a wide forehead—a sort of triangular countenance, as the conductor described it. Frank James wore such a countenance, and tradition may be correct in assuming that the man who held up the conductor was Frank James. The outlaw marched his captive into the depot, where the original prisoners were corraled. Engineer and fireman were ordered to walk some little way into the woods, where one of the robbers held them under pistol persuasion.

Two men entered the Pullman sleepers and one the day coaches, compelling passengers to surrender valuables estimated to total about $2000. The express car was reserved to the last. More than $1000 was taken from the safe. Mail bags were cut open; a registered letter containing $2000 in cash was reported missing, after the affair.

At this robbery all of the bandits wore masks made of calico with eye-holes cut. They talked almost constantly, bantering passengers and trainmen. The loot being obtained, the members of the train crew were escorted to their several posts and told to pull ahead for Little Rock. The engineer yanked open his throttle and the wheels began turning.

"Hey, you, hold up a minute!" cried Clell Miller, waving his six-shooter.

The engineer suffered a second scare. He stopped the train, probably expecting to be shot or scalped.

"Don't worry," called Miller, reassuringly. "I just wanted to get my overcoat off the track before you run over it."

The other outlaws, who had left their overcoats out in the brush, laughed heartily at Clell Miller's predicament.

"Holding up a train is hot work, even on a cold night, Bill," remarked one, "and you surely ought to know that by this time."

Clell already was a veteran. An incident which suggests the presence of Jesse James took place just as the train first was ordered to go ahead. One of the outlaws handed to a member of the train crew a sheet of paper on which was written, all shipshape for newspaper publication, this brief account of the robbery, signed "Ira A. Merrill":

"The most daring on record—the southbound train on the Iron Mountain Railroad was stopped here this evening by five heavily-armed men and robbed of —— dollars. The robbers arrived at the station a few minutes before the arrival of the train and arrested the station agent and put him under guard, then threw the train on the switch. The robbers were all large men, none of them under six feet tall. They were all masked, and started in a southerly direction after they had robbed the train. They were all mounted on fine blooded horses. There is a hell of an excitement in this part of the country."

The train itself was bound in a southerly direction, which is to be taken into consideration if you are to appreciate the Jesse James joke. As to the excitement, the language employed by the volunteer reporter was expressively accurate. At Piedmont, seven miles below, the train conductor notified the telegraph operator, and in a twinkling the wires in each direction were conveying the news.

Posses of citizens from Piedmont and from Ironton, in the beautiful little Arcadia Valley to the north, set out in the hope of trailing the bandits. Both the railroad company and the express company offered large rewards. The state had a standing reward. Several public and private detectives from St. Louis combed the Ozark underbrush for some days. Capt. J. W. Allen of Chicago, known also as Lull, and James Wright of St. Louis, two of the most able of the Pinkerton operatives, were assigned to the task.

The Pinkertons knew that the Youngers had relatives

in St. Clair County, Missouri, about two hundred miles northwest of Gadshill. A rural watering-place called Monegaw Springs had been for some years an occasional resort and refuge for the Youngers. Acting on the theory that one or more of these brothers had taken part in the Iron Mountain train holdup, Allen and Wright proceeded to St. Clair County. They stopped first at Osceola, the county seat, the very town, by the way, the burning of which by Gen. Jim Lane of Kansas early in the Civil War was alleged by some of the guerrillas to be the chief occasion of Quantrill's day of sacking and slaughter in the Kansan city of Lawrence.

At Osceola the Pinkerton men enlisted Edwin B. Daniels, a former sheriff of the county. Daniels knew the rural districts thoroughly. He guided the Pinkerton detectives to the Monegaw Springs neighborhood. The three sleuths posed as cattle buyers. Near the Springs lived a farmer bearing the odd name of Theodoric Snuffer; he was related to the Younger family. Some distance beyond was the home of a widow named Simms.

"I know the Youngers by sight," said Wright to his companions, "and I reckon they know me; I served in the Confederate army, where I met some of the boys. I'll not stop at Snuffer's, therefore, but will ride on ahead."

Allen and Daniels stopped in front of Snuffer's and inquired the way to the Widow Simms's house. Snuffer directed them, and they rode on. In the Snuffer farmhouse at the time were James and John Younger, who kept themselves hidden from the ostensible cattlemen. They heard all of the conversation and watched from a window as the Pinkertons rode away.

At a fork in the road they observed that Allen and Daniels took the wrong direction. So they were not going to the widow's, after all! The Youngers mounted their horses and followed. About a mile beyond Snuffer's they caught up with the detectives. The hour was about 2:30 P.M. on the 16th of March, 1874. Daniels and Allen rode side by side. Wright was in sight not far ahead.

John Younger carried a double-barrel shotgun, Jim had two revolvers. John cocked both barrels of his gun and ordered Allen and Daniels to halt. Wright, up the road, drew rein, turned in his saddle and leveled a pistol at one of the Youngers. Apparently he changed his mind, for instead of firing he put spurs to his horse and dashed away. The Youngers ordered him to halt, but he kept going. One of them fired, shooting Wright's hat from his head.

Daniels and Allen, meanwhile, had obeyed the command to stop. The Youngers rode up.

"Drop your weapons in the road!" came the command.

Allen dropped two revolvers, Daniels one. Allen had another in his hip pocket, which he retained. Jim Younger dismounted and picked up the three weapons.

"Damn fine pistols," he commented. "You must make us presents of these."

"Where are you fellows from?" inquired John Younger.

"Osceola," Allen replied.

"What are you doing in this part of the country?"

"Rambling around."

"You were up here one day before," said Jim Younger.

"We were not."

"I've seen both of you, at the Springs. Some detectives have been around here; they're hunting for us all the time, and we're going to stop it."

"I'm no detective," Daniels said. "I can show you who I am and where I belong."

"Oh, I know you," one of the Youngers replied. Then, turning to Captain Allen, he asked, "What in the hell are you riding around here for, with all them pistols on you?"

"Good God! isn't every man wearing pistols when traveling, and haven't I got as much right to wear them as anybody else?"

"Hold on, now, young man—we don't want any of that!" John Younger cried. He was covering Allen with his cocked shotgun.

Daniels then had a few more words with the outlaws. Allen, in the belief that the Youngers intended to kill Daniels and himself, suddenly swept a Smith & Wesson out of his pocket and fired at John Younger. This was the first shot fired, save that at Detective Wright.

Allen's shot was followed immediately by one from each of the Youngers. The detective's left arm, which held the reins, dropped to his side. His horse took fright and jumped into the bushes beside the road. One of the Youngers rode past Allen and fired twice at him. The horse brushed against a sapling and knocked Allen out of his saddle. He staggered across the road and fell, having received a fatal wound.

Almost simultaneously John Younger fell out of his saddle, dead. At the end of the battle Daniels also lay dead in the road, a big bullet having struck him in the middle of the neck, crushing the bones.

Captain Allen, whose mortal wound also was in the neck, apparently from a buckshot, lingered for several weeks. He died in presence of members of his family who had rushed from Chicago to his bedside. He received a Masonic burial in Chicago. Daniels sleeps in the Osceola graveyard, John Younger under a tree in the orchard of Theodoric Snuffer.

Jim Younger got away.

From the testimony of surgeons who examined the wounds, it appeared that John Younger gave Captain Allen his death-wound after the Pinkerton man had given the outlaw his own, and that Daniels was killed by Jim Younger.

John Younger, killed at twenty-four, had comparatively little to do with the outlaw activities. He is not known definitely to have taken part in any of the robberies. He had, however, a bad record in Texas. For some time he lived in and near Dallas, where his older brothers Coleman and James found refuge from time to time.

One night early in 1873 John Younger took part in a drinking bout in a Dallas saloon operated by one Joe Krueger. An elderly sot known as "Old Blue" was a familiar barroom loafer. He was sitting in the rear room of the groggery, half-stupefied by liquor. Exhilarated by their booze, the young men had an argument as to which of their number was the best marksman. John Younger bet the drinks that he could shoot a pipe out of the mouth of Old Blue at ten steps. A companion accepted the bet. The drunkard was given two glasses of whisky, with the promise of all he could drink if he sat still and let Younger take a shot.

Younger counted off the steps and took position, raised his revolver and fired. Probably both he and his target were shaky on account of liquor. The bullet grazed the end of Old Blue's nose, causing blood to flow. Partly sobered by the scare, the target was indignant, not to say angry. Next day he caused a warrant to be issued, charging attempted homicide against John Younger.

Capt. S. W. Nichols was sheriff of Dallas County. He was from Missouri and had won his military title in the Confederate service. The sheriff served the warrant on Younger, who asked permission to eat breakfast before submitting to arrest. Nichols unwisely granted this request, but stayed by to watch Younger's boarding-house. After he finished breakfast Younger slipped out by the back way to a livery stable and was ordering a horse saddled when Sheriff Nichols saw him and commanded him to give himself up. Younger ran. The sheriff fired, missing.

Younger found himself in a blind alley. Back against a wall, he confronted the sheriff and a citizen who had deputized himself to aid in the young Missourian's capture. Both sheriff and citizen fired at Younger, who drew his pistol and put a bullet through the heart of Sheriff Nichols. Younger fired again, wounding the citizen, who sent a charge of birdshot from his shotgun into Younger's shoulder.

Younger escaped, by appropriating a horse he found

hitched to a fence. A posse pursued him for miles. He is said to have made his way up to St. Clair County, Missouri, and a little later he went to California. Seeking employment vainly in Los Angeles, he communicated with his brother Cole, who sent him money for transportation back to Missouri.

Detectives learned that one of the Younger brothers was aboard an eastbound train. Near Laramie, Wyoming, there was a sharp pistol duel between John and a Pinkerton operative, on trainboard. The detective got a shot in one arm. Younger leaped from the running train, spraining his right ankle. He limped for miles, until the driver of a freight wagon gave him a free ride into Denver. There he took train for home. Having no ticket, he was put off trains by one conductor after another. He walked several hundred miles. When he reached Jackson County he resembled the sorriest tramp in the industry of hoboing.

In a letter signed with the full name of Thomas Coleman Younger and undoubtedly written by that individual, the elder brother took occasion to defend John's record and his own. This communication, a long one, was addressed to Lycurgus Jones, a brother-in-law of the Youngers, living in Cass County, Missouri. It was published Nov. 26, 1874, in the Pleasant Hill (Mo.) *Review*. The theological trend of Coleman's thoughts is evinced in a paragraph relating to the slain brother:

"Poor John! he has been hunted down and shot like a wild beast, and never was a boy more innocent. But there is a day coming when the secrets of all hearts will be laid open before that All-Seeing Eye, and every act of our lives will be scrutinized. Then will his skirts be white as the driven snow, while those of his accusers will be doubly dark."

CHAPTER XIV

EARLY in 1874 a young college graduate named Wallace, whose shingle as a lawyer was hanging out in front of a modest office at Independence, Missouri, was earning his livelihood chiefly as a newspaper reporter whilst waiting for the clients who came along later. He wrote local news stories for the Kansas City *Times* and the Independence *Sentinel*. One morning in March, Will Wallace heard of some excitement a few miles out on the road leading to the Blue Mills ferry on the Missouri river.

Wallace hastened to the spot and discovered the makings of a mystery story that promised well. A man about thirty years of age had been shot to death and left lying in the road. He was dressed roughly, like a farmhand. But his hands were soft and smooth; no callouses, nothing to indicate that he had done any kind of manual labor. To the contrary, the bullet victim appeared to have been in such circumstances that he was able to take excellent care of his person. But the old jeans pants and coat, the old blue-check shirt, the old slouch hat—why such apparel?

Will Wallace turned up the right sleeve of the shirt and found, a few inches above the wrist, the initials "J. W. W." neatly tattooed. These facts and such

145

other scant information as he picked up he reported to his newspapers. It was all in the day's work for Wallace, who could not be aware that he was reporting the beginning of a murder mystery, intimately relating to the career of the Missouri outlaws, which time never can solve completely; nor that he, as prosecuting attorney of Jackson County, was to become some years later the active and successful Nemesis of the James Boys' Band, so called throughout the country.

Staff men from the Kansas City papers presently proved that "J. W. W." was the late John W. Witcher, a Pinkerton detective from Chicago who had come into the Jesse James country with the purpose of going direct to the Samuel farmhouse in Clay County, home of the mother and the stepfather of the James boys, where he hoped to pose as a farm laborer and capture the dreaded outlaws.

William Pinkerton, some time earlier, had visited Kansas City and established a branch of the celebrated detective agency, with the special object of running down the Jameses, the Youngers and their associates in outlawry. Young Witcher, regarded as one of the most astute of the Chicago operatives, had requested that he be assigned to the task of daring the lions in their lair. He outlined his plan; the Pinkerton executives approved it. The considerable error committed by the unfortunate young detective lay in his assumption that Frank and Jesse James were, after all, just a couple of rural bad men of average mental caliber, and that he could fool them with comparative ease.

Witcher went first to Liberty, the county seat, where

he visited the Commercial Bank and made a cash deposit. He had a talk with the president of the bank, to whom he stated his plan of procedure against the outlaws.

"Young man," advised the banker, "you'd better not try it. It won't be safe for you. You do not know those James boys as we know them, here in Clay County."

"Oh, I guess I'll try it, nevertheless," said Witcher, smilingly.

Then the detective called upon Col. O. P. Moss, a former sheriff of the county, and revealed his identity and his intentions.

"Mr. Witcher," the ex-sheriff warned him, "you don't know at all what you are going up against. I do; I know the resources of those James boys; they are not in any sense to be looked upon as ordinary criminals. You are not going out after a pair of city crooks, mind you. No—you are about to undertake the capture of two of the keenest-minded young men in America. Those boys are not asleep, I warn you! They never sleep, in the sense of being confident of security. If they happen to be at home, or either of them, your life won't be worth fifteen cents if you go out there disguised as a farmhand; they'll see clean through you. I repeat, you can't fool Frank or Jesse James."

Nevertheless, young Witcher thought he could. Proceeding to the local hotel, he exchanged his city clothes for the outfit of a farm laborer. With a Smith & Wesson revolver concealed on his bosom, he took the afternoon train for Kearney, ten miles from Liberty and about four miles from the Samuel homestead.

In the meantime the Pinkerton man had been shadowed by a very private detective who lived in Clay County and was a particular friend of the Jameses. This unofficial sleuth mounted a swift horse and rode to the Samuel farm, where Jesse James was visiting his mother. He told Jesse all about the young stranger who was using such open-work detective methods.

Leaving the train at Kearney, Witcher walked out the road toward the farm. It was late in the afternoon, almost dusk, when suddenly he was challenged by a man who stepped out of the bushes with a big six-shooter in his right hand.

"Who are you, and where are you bound for?"

"I'm out looking for work on a farm," Witcher replied. "Can you tell me where I might be able to find a job in these parts?"

"You don't want any job—you've got one already, with that damn Pinkerton outfit," said the man with the drawn weapon, smiling sardonically.

"I don't know what you're talking about," the detective said. "I'm a poor man out of work, and——"

"And you're looking for the James boys, hey? Well, here, take a look at one of 'em—Jesse James!"

Witcher winced, but kept up his pretense. Jesse James signaled. Two other men stepped into the road.

"Search him," Jesse ordered.

One of the men extracted Witcher's weapon from its place of concealment. Jesse's eyes blinked angrily.

"A farmhand with a loaded weapon on his chest!" he snarled. "Let me see your hands."

Jesse felt of one of Witcher's palms—soft and smooth.

"A hell of a farm laborer you are! A poor man, hey? You put some of Mr. Pinkerton's money in the bank at Liberty, didn't you? And you left your fine clothes at the hotel. Where are you from—Chicago?"

"I'm from Indiana," responded Witcher, who was a native of the Hoosier state. "Now I can't see why you don't let me pass on, for I'm not trying to harm you or anybody."

The three men consulted briefly.

"Better finish him, right here," suggested one.

Witcher began to plead for his life. He told his captors that he had a young wife at home, and for her sake he begged them not to kill him. Jesse James, who was going to take unto himself a young wife within a few weeks, is said to have been touched by this method of appeal. Such was the statement made by members of his band about eight years later, whose confessions provide the raw material for this record of the meeting on the road out of Kearney.

"Well, don't let's do it here, anyhow—not on my side," Jesse is supposed to have said. "My side" meant the Clay County side of the Missouri river.

Late that night the elderly man who operated the ferry at Blue Mills was awakened by some men on horseback; the hour was about 2 A.M. The party wanted to be ferried across the Missouri. The ferryman noticed that one of the four men was bound, hands tied behind, feet secured by a cord under the horse's belly.

"Who's this fellow—why's he tied up this way?"

"He's a horsethief; we're out after a gang of 'em and have just caught one."

The old ferryman then spoke directly to the bound man, who made no reply, though he gave his questioner an appealing look in the dim flare of the lantern.

"Gagged, by golly!" exclaimed the ferryman. "You-all must be afeard this here hossthief'll holler and skeer your hosses."

The party was ferried across. The rest of the episode, so far as facts are known, has been told earlier in this chapter. Frank James, according to the stories told by members of the later James Boys' Band who confessed to Prosecuting Attorney Will Wallace in 1883, was not of the trio that captured and killed Detective Witcher. The two companions of Jesse James on that night remain anonymous; various alleged identities have been applied to them without proof of any.

Some months prior to the Witcher tragedy another and a wiser Pinkerton man had appeared in the Samuel neighborhood. This fellow, who called himself Jack Ladd, hired out as a farmhand to Daniel Askew, who operated a large farm not far from the one on which the Jameses grew up. He was a capable farm laborer— probably native to the soil. Every day he worked in the fields or elsewhere, according to his employer's directions. On Sundays he donned his best clothes, a cheap hand-me-down suit, and went to church with the Askew family. He took part in the neighborhood social affairs. He talked the dialect of the countryside and was a popular fellow. He became acquainted with Dr. and Mrs. Samuel and, limitedly, with Frank and Jesse James.

At long intervals the boys visited their mother, to

whom they were deeply devoted, even as was she to them. Jack Ladd was not suspected by the Jameses or by any of their friends of being anything other than an ordinary farmhand—old Dan Askew's hired man.

In one month the Pinkertons had lost three men— Captain Allen (or Lull) of Chicago, Edwin B. Daniels, of Osceola, Missouri, recruited for special service, and Witcher of Chicago—two slain by two of the Youngers in a road battle, one captured and killed by Jesse James and two unidentified men. Only one of the outlaws, John Younger, the least conspicuous of them all, had gone to the tally of the Pinkertons. They determined, if possible, to make the score even by killing the two Jameses. Their plans were laid with commendable cunning, from the sleuth viewpoint. None of the Witcher business of showing the hand before playing the cards! The detectives kept their mouths shut.

Jack Ladd had seen both of the Jameses at home on the 20th and the 21st of January, 1875. He so reported to the Kansas City branch of the Pinkerton agency, where William Pinkerton and five selected operatives from the Chicago headquarters are said to have been on hand, waiting for a chance to avenge the death of Witcher. Ladd said he had reason to believe "the boys" would stop with "the old lady" for a week or so. On the afternoon of the 25th it was reported by spies for the Pinkertons that Frank and Jesse had been seen since noon in the yard of the old home. That night the Pinkerton operatives, accompanied by several men supposed to be residents of Clay or Jackson, surrounded the Samuel farmhouse, arriving about midnight. All the occupants of the house were in bed, asleep. Neither

Frank nor Jesse was there. With Dr. and Mrs. Samuel and the three Samuel children were an old negro woman and a small negro boy.

Archie Payton Samuel, half-brother to the James boys, was just eight and a half years old, the baby of the family. Jesse and Frank, who always liked children, were very fond of little Archie. Though they had been hiding out most of the time since he was born, they had played and romped with him many a time on their visits home.

The farmhouse had an old-fashioned combination kitchen and dining-room. There was a huge open fireplace, where a big backlog with a banked fire in front was smouldering. Leaning against the jambs of the fireplace were several tobacco sticks—split oaken timbers an inch in diameter and about three feet long, used in supporting "hands" of tobacco in the curing process. These were made to do duty as fire pokers. The windows of the house had green shutters opening on the outside. "The little white house with the green shutters"—a picture of rural simplicity which became that January night the seat of a tragedy that shocked the sensibilities of millions of people who read about it in the newspapers. Incidentally, the tragedy made many new friends for the hunted James boys.

Four men of the investing party approached the house, each bearing a big ball of cotton waste soaked with kerosene and turpentine. They forced open the shutter of a kitchen window and were raising the sash when the old colored aunty, sleeping in that room, was aroused by the noise. She gave a shrill shriek, awakening the whole family.

One of the men outside tossed through the window one of the balls of saturated waste, to which a lighted match had been applied. The highly inflammable fluids caused it to burn brightly, lighting up the large room.

The entire family had rushed into the kitchen. Dr. Samuel and his wife picked up tobacco sticks and began rolling the blazing ball toward the hearth with the object of getting it into the fireplace before it set the house on fire. Suddenly through the window came another ball of similar size and appearance. Covered with burning waste like the other, it fizzed and spluttered. It must be put into the fireplace at once; but—

We may let Dr. Samuel, the oldtime country physician and farmer, tell a part of the tale, as quoted from a chronicle of the time:

"The second fireball was not like the first, though it looked like that one: it was a bombshell. It was thrown into the room while the fireball was still blazing. It was light enough in the room for any person not over thirty yards off to have distinguished our faces. The detectives were not thirty feet distant.

"Thinking the bombshell to be another fireball, my wife at first tried to push it up onto the hearth but finding it to be much heavier than the first one she said, 'Doctor, try and see if you can get it to the hearth.'

"We had used tobacco sticks to get the fireball off the floor and put out its fire. I still had a stick in my hand, but found it too light to move the shell. I then got the shovel and began to push it toward the hearth, and just as I had succeeded, the shell exploded.

It seemed to me all at once that the room grew black as night. I was blown against the ceiling, and heard a tremendous report.

"Outside I heard several hurrahs; then the groans of my little boy and the agonized cries of my wife, who told me her right arm was blown to pieces. To add to the horror of the scene, the detectives began cross-firing past the house. Then they left, one man calling out, 'Hurry up, boys, for we'll have to come back again just to keep up appearances.' As soon as they started I went to the door and screamed for help, and at last some neighbors came."

Upon a single couch the neighbors found the mother of Frank and Jesse James and her little son Archie. The right forearm of Mrs. Samuel was mangled. In the boy's left side a piece of the bomb had torn a frightful hole, through which his lifeblood was gushing. Archie died before dawn, after suffering most frightful agony. The negro woman had aided Dr. Samuel, before the neighbors called in other surgical aid, in staunching the flow of blood from the arm of Mrs. Samuel, which had to be amputated. The little negro lad also had suffered a wound, happily but slight, from a fragment of the shell.

About one-half of the big hand-grenade lay upon the floor intact. The rest of it had been flung in fragments about the chamber, damaging furniture and utensils when missing human flesh and bones.

At dawn one of the neighbors picked up, just outside the house, a clew dropped accidentally by one of the detectives. It was a big revolver on the handle of which were carved the initials "P. G. G.," standing for "Pinkerton's Government Guard." The fellow who dropped that weapon may have kept his mouth shut, but wouldn't you be inclined to insinuate that he had lost his head?

The Pinkertons and their companions—or would you say accomplices?—did not come back; not even "to keep up appearances." Jack Ladd, able farmhand, never returned to Dan Askew's: he disappeared forthwith from Clay County and from history, human and inhuman, as Jack Ladd. No doubt he reappeared elsewhere and under his real name drew his pay check as a Pinkerton.

Clay County people called the bomb-throwing episode "the crime of the century."

Newspaper comment upon this affair was not complimentary to the Pinkerton agency. In fact, editors throughout the United States vied with each other in expressing the utmost condemnation of the men who were "guilty of the inexcusable and cowardly deed."

The writer of this true tale of blood and terror met Mrs. Zerelda Samuel at her home, many years after she lost her right arm and her youngest child. Dr. Samuel had gone to his long rest, after a life of turmoil and trouble which the kindly old Kentucky-born country doctor did not deserve of fate. The aged widow, extending her left hand in greeting, impressed her visitor as a notably pathetic example of man's inhumanity to woman.

The mother of the James brothers was a woman of infinite sorrows, of wellnigh infinite capacity for suffering. She was a strong woman—in body, in mind, in soul. Certain vile scribblers have uttered against her good name slanderous statements for which they deserve nothing less than castigations with cat-o'nine-tails whiplashes.

Knowing perhaps as much about Zerelda James Samuel and her people as any other writer who has penned a line about the family has known, I take occasion to set down here the matured conviction that she was a woman thoroughly good and noble—the one wholly heroic character of the whole unhappy outfit.

CHAPTER XV

ABOUT six weeks after the bomb-throwing episode, and as a direct consequence of that crime and the public reaction which it created, the celebrated "outlaw amnesty bill" was introduced in the Missouri legislature. The Hon. Jefferson Jones, known more familiarly as Gen. Jeff Jones—an alliterative euphony worthy to compete with that of the Jesse James combination itself—was the author of that remarkable piece of proposed legislation. General Jones represented the granite-grounded Democracy of Callaway County in the lower house.

Virtually throughout Missouri there was a general feeling that the border-bandit activities were in large measure a continuation or outgrowth of the Civil War. Intelligent citizens of open minds did not look upon the outlaw deeds of these men as upon crimes committed under ordinary circumstances. The interpretation of their activities was based upon a competent knowledge of conditions on the border which had upset normal human relations. A group of outlaws who were not bad men inherently had become bandits: under happier environment the same men might have developed into respectable preachers or respected plutocrats. Many Missourians, believing that the robbers would make good with society if they had a chance to turn about and get a new start along the right road, were ready to forgive if not to forget past transgressions.

This attitude crystallized in the measure fathered by Jeff Jones of Callaway, which in part was as follows:

"Whereas, by the fourth section of the eleventh article of the Constitution of Missouri, all persons in the military service of the United States, or who acted under the authority thereof in this state, are relieved from all civil liability and all criminal punishment for all acts done by them since the 1st day of January, A.D. 1861; and

"Whereas, by the twelfth section of the said eleventh article of the said constitution, provision is made by which, under certain circumstances, may be seized, transported to, indicted, tried and punished in distant counties, any Confederate under ban of despotic displeasure, thereby contravening the Constitution of the United States and every principle of enlightened humanity; and

"Whereas, such discrimination evidences a want of manly generosity and statesmanship on the part of the party imposing, and of courage and manhood on the part of the party submitting tamely thereto; and

"Whereas, under the outlawry pronounced against Jesse W. James, Frank James, Coleman Younger, James Younger, Robert Younger and others, who gallantly periled their lives and their all in defense of their principles, they are of necessity made desperate, driven as they are from the fields of honest industry, from their friends, their families, their homes and their country, they can know no law but the law of self-preservation, and can have no respect for and feel no allegiance to a government which forces them to the very acts it professes to deprecate, and then offers a bounty for their apprehension, and arms foreign mercenaries with power to capture and kill them; and

"Whereas, believing these men too brave to be mean, too generous to be revengeful, and too gallant and honorable to betray a friend or break a promise; and believing further that most if not all of the offenses with which they are charged have been committed by others, and perhaps by those pretending to hunt them or by their confederates; that their names are and have been used to divert suspicion from and thereby relieve the actual perpetrators; that the return of these men to their homes and friends would have the effect of greatly lessening crime in our state by turning public attention to the real criminals; and that common justice, sound policy and true statesmanship alike demand that amnesty should be extended to all alike of both parties for all acts done or charged to have been done during the war; therefore, be it resolved by the House of Representatives, the Senate concurring therein:

"That the governor of the state be, and he is hereby, requested to issue his proclamation notifying the said Jesse W. James, Frank James, Coleman Younger, Robert Younger and James Younger, and others, that full and complete amnesty and pardon will be granted them for all acts charged to or committed by them during the late Civil War, and inviting them peacefully to return to their respective homes in this state and there quietly to remain, submitting themselves to such proceedings as may be instituted against them by the courts for all offenses charged to have been committed since said war, promising and guaranteeing to them and each of them full protection and a fair trial therein, and that full protection shall be given them from the time of their entrance into the state and his (the governor's) notice thereof under said proclamation and invitation."

Truly a human document unique, if ever such hath been!

When the measure came up for its third reading, General Jones delivered an impassioned appeal to his fellow-statesmen to vote for its passage. On the Republican side of the house there appeared to be no great opposition. But for the action of a Democratic member who tossed a party bombshell into the arena, the probability seems to be that it would have been adopted by the house and sent to the senate. This member arose and read a message from Gov. Silas Woodson, promulgated a couple of years earlier, in which that executive made special denunciation of the identical outlaws named in the Jeff Jones resolution. That turned the tide against the amnesty bill and it was defeated, the vote being close.

Had the measure been enacted, there is no reason whatsoever for believing that any of the men named therein would have accepted its terms. To surrender

and stand trial for acts committed, or alleged to have
been committed, by them since the war, would have
meant hanging or life imprisonment. Nobody was
more keenly aware of this fact than were the outlaws
themselves. Jesse James probably enjoyed a good
laugh over the Jeff Jones effort; though it is not to be
doubted that he and the rest of them felt grateful to the
Callaway statesman and his followers. The five men
specifically invited "peaceably to return to their
respective homes" felt that the agitation in favor of the
limited amnesty thus proposed was considerably to their
advantage. Public discussion had revitalized the
earlier sentiment that they were "victims of circumstances" and were persecuted men.

Jeff Jones had accomplished for Jesse James and his
associates nothing that tended definitely toward
rehabilitation; but the Hon. Jeff had handled the
hand-grenading Pinkertons with neither gloves nor
tobacco sticks. He had assailed the bomb-throwers as
wanton murderers of women and children; and he had
pointed out the indubitable fact that not even Quantrill
the Bloodthirsty, under whose tutelage the outlaws
had taken first lessons in violence, ever under any
circumstances had made war upon women or children.

Defeat of the amnesty bill was followed, after a quiet
interval of about a month, by another tragedy in Clay
County. This was the assassination of Daniel Askew,
in whose employ the Pinkerton operative known as
Jack Ladd had worked as a farmhand. The general
public suspected the Jameses of having killed or
instigated the killing of Farmer Askew as a matter of
vengeance, and the tide turned against them.

On the evening of April 12, at about 8 o'clock, Askew emerged from his house and went to a spring 150 yards away, to fetch a bucket of water. It was a moonlit night. Askew returned to the house, set the bucket upon a shelf on the porch, and dipped out a cup of water. As he was lifting the cup to his lips the crack of rifles was heard. The farmer received three wounds, one bullet penetrating his brain. The assassins, local tradition has it, were hidden behind a woodpile.

There is a tradition that a few minutes after this assassination a citizen passing along a road not far from the Askew farmhouse met three armed men whom he recognized as the two Jameses and Clell Miller, and that one of the former announced:

"We've just been over and killed old Dan Askew, because he was in cahoots with those damn Pinkertons who threw the bombshell into our house."

Frank James said, long afterward, "If I had known, or even strongly believed, that it was Askew who led the party to my mother's, I would have killed him at the first chance; but I never believed he could be such a fool, and I ascribed the guilt to Jack Ladd, his hired man."

Friends of the Jameses insisted that Frank and Jesse were out of the state at the time of the Askew assassination. Absence of definite evidence keeps alive the query, Who killed Dan Askew? Well, who struck Billy Patterson? The two mysteries may be shelved together; but in the Askew instance the inference is considerably more substantial than in the case of the late Billy Patterson.

Exactly a month after the slaying of Askew there was

a stage robbery in Texas which bore striking resemblance to a James-Younger job. The fine old Spanish-American city of San Antonio then had no railway connection with the world. The stage line from Austin, the state capital, was the principal avenue of access and exit.

On the evening of the 12th of May five masked men loomed out of the deepening dusk and stopped the stage bound for "San Antone" at a point about twenty-three miles southwest of Austin. Eleven passengers, three of whom were women, were aboard. The big coach was drawn by four horses.

Two of the holdup men took position on one side of the coach, two on the other, the fifth at the horses' heads. The driver and his passengers alighted under cover of sixshooters and were lined up beside the coach. Two of the robbers passed along in front of the line, one holding open the mouth of a wheat sack. The other dropped purses, watches and other personal articles of value into the capacious maw as each victim contributed. This receptacle seemed grotesquely large for the limited personal loot; but when the freebooters opened two or three trunks belonging to passengers and extracted other valuables from their contents, and also cut open the mailbag and added a bundle of registered letters to the growing plunder, the sack turned out to be no bigger than its uses required.

The bandits were polite, presence of the ladies apparently keeping their language genteel. They were also, it appears from the more or less hazy record, facetious fellows. For an hour or so they kept the travelers stationary, but two or three of them tried to entertain their victims by cracking jokes and opening up conversations of a decidedly one-sided jollity.

One of the travelers was Bishop Gregg of the Protestant Episcopal church, living in Austin. The bishop did not seem at first to comprehend the situation.

"You must give up your watch and your money, parson," said one of the robbers.

"What—do you mean to rob us?" inquired the bishop, with the accent strongly on the rob.

The robber laughed.

"We mean to relieve you of your surplus funds and your useless jewelry. You can call it robbery if you look at it that way, but we hardly care to apply so harsh a term to our business."

The bishop finally understood.

"I am a minister of the gospel," he told his adversary, "and I beg you to permit me to keep my watch; it is a present from an old friend."

"I recognized your calling, from your cloth," said the robber. "We don't really like to compel a parson to do our bidding, but we are poor men for the time being, sir, and the world owes us a living. As to your watch, you really don't need it; your Master, the Nazarene, never owned one. And as the good Book commands you, when traveling, to take along neither purse nor scrip, we propose to put you in good standing with the Lord. Therefore, parson, shell out!"

Bishop Gregg gave up cash and timepiece. Another passenger was a noted banker and capitalist of San Antonio. He was George W. Brackenridge, president of the First National Bank. Later he donated to the city of San Antonio the land which comprises the celebrated and beautiful Brackenridge Park, wherein thousands of tourists take their ease every winter season. Brackenridge surrendered watch and wallet, the latter containing about $1000. Outlaw income from this robbery, including personal property and money and the cash taken from registered mail, was estimated at a total of approximately $3000.

The highwaymen also cut loose the lead team of horses and took the animals along when they mounted their own steeds and galloped away. The stage was many hours late when it pulled into San Antonio, about eighteen hours after the holdup, and the two horses that did double duty were wellnigh worn out. It was not until the stage reached the city that news of the robbery could be sent out. Pursuit was futile.

In that section of Texas at the time was one Jim Reed, of evil repute. He was suspected of complicity in the stagecoach affair and was trailed by detectives. There was shooting from both sides, Reed receiving a fatal wound. An alleged confession was made public after his death, in which he implicated Frank and Jesse James, Cole and Jim Younger and Clell Miller as participants with himself in the stage robbery. Driver and passengers reported only five men in the party of highwaymen. If Jim Reed was of the gang, one man must have made himself invisible. According to his alleged confession, Reed also took part in the robbery of the Iron Mountain train at Gadshill, Missouri, nearly a year earlier.

In those times it was the common fashion to accuse the Missouri outlaws of being guilty of almost every act of outlawry that took place anywhere within the area of a dozen states. Friends of the Jameses declared hotly that the Jim Reed confession was faked by the detectives. Jesse James, they averred, was in Kansas City when the San Antonio stage was robbed. Who knows—now?

CHAPTER XVI

THE FATAL DRUNK OF BUD MCDANIELS

B UD McDANIELS now re-enters the outlaw epic,
presently to make final exit by the bullet route.
We swing back to the end of 1874. Seventeen
days after publication of Cole Younger's letter of self-
defense, an express train bound from Denver to Kansas
City on the Kansas Pacific Railroad was held up and
robbed near Muncie, Kansas, about five miles west of
Wyandotte, the beautiful Indian name of which some
Vandal influence succeeded a few years later in having
changed to Kansas City (Kansas). The scene of this
robbery was less than ten miles from the old Union
Depot at Kansas City, Missouri, the heart of the Jesse
James country. This proud and progressive metropolis
now calls itself, through Chamber of Commerce and
other enterprising agencies, "The Heart of America."

Tradition names as the six men who committed the
Muncie crime Cole and Bob Younger, Frank and Jesse
James, Clell Miller and Bud McDaniels. The latter
was the only one who suffered for it.

McDaniels was a resident of Kansas City, working
intermittently as a railroad switchman. He was not
noted for anything resembling respectability. Through
some mysterious source, Bud is supposed to have
learned that a shipment of gold dust from the Colorado

mines was to be aboard the express car of the train that left Denver on Dec. 12. At 4:45 P.M. next day the train was stopped about a mile east of Muncie, railroad ties having been piled up on the track.

Six masked men, whose horses were hitched in plain view of trainmen and passengers, carried off the affair in familiar border-bandit fashion. They uncoupled the express car and compelled the engineer to pull it a short distance from the beheaded train. The loot in this instance was richer than usual. The virgin gold and the coin and currency mounted well into the five-figure total. Some jewelry also was taken from the express car, which turned out to be unlucky for Bud McDaniels.

A couple of dozen men rode out from Kansas City, headed by the sheriff of Jackson County, in pursuit of the bandits. Through Westport, now a part of Kansas City, they were trailed to a point on the Blue river; there the trail vanished. Officials attributed the Muncie job to the James-Younger outfit, but none of the regular members was apprehended.

Bud McDaniels couldn't stand his prosperity. He had a lady-love in Kansas City, to whom he boasted that he had come into possession of a fortune. Two or three days after the holdup, Bud hired a horse and buggy at a livery stable and called at his girl's home to take her out for a romantic ride. She was absent— gone with a man possibly handsomer than Bud. Her best fellow showed that he was much miffed. It was an unheard-of thing, for one's best girl to cut him for another fellow just when he had acquired the cash to show her all sorts of good times.

Bud drove his rig to a saloon, to another and yet another, and by nightfall he was drunk. He soon began to drive rapidly and recklessly. Police arrested him as he was whipping his horse through one of the downtown streets. He was locked up on a police-blotter charge of reckless driving, plus intoxication in public. Before the police put him into a cell to sleep off his drunk they searched him, according to routine procedure. More than $1000 in cash, two large six-shooters and some pieces of jewelry comprised the yield.

The jewelry was identified as a part of the plunder from the express car at Muncie. McDaniels said he had bought it to give to his girl.

"But she's gone back on me," complained Bud, "and I don't care a cuss who gets the jewelry now. I've got no use for such trash."

Investigation showed that Bud had been out of the city at the time of the train holdup. He was taken to Kansas. After preliminary hearing he was placed in jail at Lawrence. The grand jury indicted him for alleged complicity in the train robbery. He escaped from a deputy sheriff who was taking him to the courthouse for trial.

About a week later Bud McDaniels dropped definitely out of the story, being shot to death near the Kaw river by officers who recognized him and whom he resisted. He had denied connection with the robbery and, as it followed naturally, refused to give any information as to the identity of the robbers.

Now enters into the epic tale another McDaniels, brother to Bud. This was Thompson McDaniels, known as Tom. He also presently was to make tragic exit. Nearly a year after the Muncie affair the Missourians transferred their activities to the Middle East. Up to that time daylight bank-robbery had been confined to the Middle West. Now the industry assumed to have been invented by the one-time guerrillas of the border found itself transported to West Virginia for one day's operation. Huntington was the town chosen.

If any of the Missourians were on hand there, they were a long way from home, which may account for the fact that the bank at Huntington was robbed by only four men. Frank James and Cole Younger were the only members of the old group who were suspected of complicity, and no definite proof against either was adduced.

Tom McDaniels, who was sojourning temporarily in Virginia or West Virginia, and a man known both as Jack Keene and Tom Webb were the other two in the quartet. Keene lived in West Virginia. Wearing long linen dusters, the four men rode into Huntington and drew rein in front of the bank. Two dismounted and went inside. The others remained in their saddles and began firing pistol shots into the air to clear the streets. The date was Sept. 1, 1875.

Cashier Robert T. Oney opened the bank safe when ordered to do so. One robber kept him and a citizen present under menace of a cocked weapon. The other collected several thousand dollars from safe and cash-drawer. They rushed out, whistling shrilly for their accomplices, who brought up the two led horses. The bandits fired a few more shots as they dashed out into the country.

The pursuit following this raid was one of the most exciting in the records of American man-hunting. Twenty men, well armed and well mounted, rode out from Huntington on the trail. From several other points posses joined in the chase. When one posse lost the trail, another found it. There were several pistol fights with the fugitives, who found things so hot that they abandoned their horses more than once, stealing new mounts wherever they found available horseflesh. Their general route was to the southwest, through the mountains of West Virginia and eastern Kentucky.

About ten days after the robbery two young farmers, brothers named Dillon, living in the neighborhood of Pine Hill in the Kentucky mountain region, read newspaper accounts of the chase and found reason to believe that the bandits were headed straight in their direction. The Dillons oiled and polished two old army muskets, which they loaded with slugs calculated to tear paths through meat and bone. They kept close watch of the roads and trails near their home.

One moonlit night, two weeks after the bank raid, the Dillons saw the figures of four men stalking toward them through the woods. The handles of sixshooters were visible, sticking out from under the men's coats. The Kentucky mountaineers with the army muskets waited near the road. When the four strangers reached the road they separated, two walking away from the hiding place of the Dillons, two advancing in that direction.

"Halt! Throw down your pistols," the musketmen cried as the two figures came near.

They "threw down" their pistols by leveling them and firing at their challengers, who fired each one shot in return. The two strangers made off into the bushes. The Dillons went home. Throughout the rest of the night one kept alternating watch as the other tried to sleep. Both were up early. They went to the spot where the brief duel had taken place.

"I'm sure I hit one of 'em," one Dillon had said to the other a score of times since the duel.

"I'm sure I hit one, too," the other Dillon had contended as many times.

"Well, one of us did, sure thing!" exclaimed a Dillon as the two brothers saw leaves on the ground stained with blood. Similar stains led them to a cornfield hundreds of yards away. There they found a man lying on the ground, between the rows of corn, with a terrible wound in his side. The slugs had done the full duty expected of them.

The young mountaineers carried the wounded man to their home, laid him upon a bed and called in the nearest doctor. The patient was delirious. He cried out frequently for "Bud." In moments of consciousness he told the watchers:

"I'm dying. Where are my friends?"

He was asked to tell the names of his friends. He replied, indignantly:

"I never betrayed a friend yet, and I won't now."

He died with sealed lips. In his coat pocket were two photographs. One was identified by detectives as the likeness of a man named Robert Ricketts.

"Tom McDaniels," said Ricketts, when located, "is the only man who has my picture."

The other photograph was identified as that of a young woman who had been courted by Thompson McDaniels when the outlaw was seeing better and nobler days. She is said to have received, some days after his death, a letter enclosing a piece of black crepe, evidently sent by one of the unnamed friends of McDaniels. A seal ring found on a finger of the dead man was identified as one which Tom McDaniels had worn for years.

Cashier Oney of the Huntington bank arrived at Pine Hill shortly after the death of McDaniels and identified him as one of the two men who had entered the bank, held him up and taken the money. Oney returned home by way of Louisville. In that city he received a telegram from Pine Hill, signed by W. R. Dillon, one of the brothers who fired upon the outlaws. It was dated Sept. 20, and read:

"The other three entered the house and had the coffin opened. Said he did not look like he did before. One of them was crying. They asked for me and then went into the cornfield. I was at the house about five minutes after they left. I look for a desperate attack today."

The telegram was given to the press through the Louisville *Courier-Journal*, which first published it. In the absence of the Dillon brothers three strange men had visited the house and requested the privilege of looking at the corpse. Only Mrs. Dillon and a few other women were present, no men being on hand. They declined at first to permit the visitors to see the body, explaining that the coffin-lid already had been screwed down. The largest man of the three, who was well dressed and appeared to be a person of some culture, explained with great politeness that it was necessary for them to view the remains.

"And, madame," he added, "our request must be granted."

The women escorted the strangers into the room where the coffin rested upon two chairs. With a screwdriver the lid was unfastened. Mrs. Dillon held it up whilst the three men gazed earnestly at the face of the corpse. The big man wept, his tears falling upon the dead face.

"Where is the man who killed him?" one of the visitors inquired.

"We don't know," the women replied; "he's nowhere around here, anyhow."

"Thank you, madame," said the big man to Mrs. Dillon, wiping his tears away with a handkerchief. "We bid you all good-day."

The three departed. The women saw them walking through the cornfield. Some time later the man known as Keene or Webb was captured by detectives in Fentress County, Tennessee. He had a large sum of money, the source of which he was unable to explain. He was taken to Huntington, identified as one of the bank robbers, indicted, tried, convicted, and sentenced to serve twelve years in the West Virginia penitentiary.

Friends of the Jameses and the Youngers insisted that the two uncaught robbers belonged to a Kentucky mountain gang that had given the people of the eastern part of Kentucky and of West Virginia a series of scares by their desperado deeds. The identification of the late Thompson McDaniels made the matter look suspicious as to the other Missourians mentioned.

CHAPTER XVII

"THE MAN JESSE JAMES HELD UP"

WE reach now the apogee of the James-Younger confederation's outlaw supremacy in Missouri. Ossa on Pelion piled makes perihelion at last. Also, Alpha climbing step by step reaches Omega and takes a tumble—that being the end.

The last affair in freebootery from which "the boys" of both families rode away unscathed was a success measurably brilliant. Boys they were no longer, nor even youths. Frank James and Coleman Younger were past thirty-two. Robert Younger, youngest of them all, had reached his twenty-third year. Both the Jameses had become married men—family men—and both were what moralists are apt to describe as "good family men." It is a remarkable fact that not even the most shameless fictionists have insinuated the slightest deviation upon the part of either Jesse James or Frank James from the straight path of marital faithfulness. In the matter of being true to their wives they appear to have been of such quality as to satisfy the most exacting advocate of the so-called single standard. Freebooters they were, upon occasion, but philanderers never, so far as the record runs.

All of the outlaws were, as any strict stickler for

conventional comportment might suggest, old enough to know better than to rob trains or banks as a means of livelihood. For men of their years they had enjoyed —if one may say it thus—an extraordinarily wide and varied experience in active life. Much had they traveled, many states and cities had they seen, and many successful campaigns had they carried out in their own peculiar fashion. But the border bandits had been riding to a fall, though the fall was not quite yet. One more victorious campaign was to be theirs.

As the Rocky Cut holdup this affair was known for some years, but we shall call it simply the Otterville train robbery. Not long after this high tide of riding out of Nowhere, robbing, and riding back into Nowhere, the two-family confederacy was to split in twain upon crimsoned shards in a distant state, the Younger section retiring permanently from the field. The robbery of the Missouri Pacific train near Otterville, Cooper County, Missouri, July 7, 1876, was exactly two months before the violent smashup.

This campaign is important in the chronicle because for the very first time we are able to say definitely who were the eight men comprising the raiding force. Here at last do we hammer in the brass tacks of fact. Rumor, suspicion, probability—all these take to the winds now. Names leap forth from Rocky Cut which we may hang as crimson rosettes upon the tablets of authentic history.

The men who robbed that train were Jesse Woodson James, Alexander Franklin James, Thomas Coleman Younger, Robert Younger, McClellan Miller, William Stiles, Samuel Wells and Hobbs Kerry. Stiles has appeared heretofore as Bill Chadwell and Wells as Charlie Pitts. It is high time that their real names be bestowed upon them for permanent recollection, if that be in any wise desirable; for the Messrs. Wells and Stiles shortly are to disappear forever from this narrative and from the living herd of humans.

Fortunately we have with us a man who saw that train robbery from the inside. Make the acquaintance of Mr. Louis Peter Conklin of Chicago, "Pete" Conklin to his friends, for more than half a century a faithful baggagemaster on railroad trains in the Middle West. He is a native of St. Louis. For nearly fifty years Pete Conklin has passed amongst trainmen as "the man who was held up by Jesse James." Jesse James, everybody admits, held up many men; but our Mr. Conklin gets the honor of the definite article when he is introduced as, presumably, the sole survivor of the Otterville holdup.

In a recent interview Mr. Conklin told your outlaw author the story of that affair as he remembers it—and his friends aver that his memory is of letter-file accuracy. Passages in Pete Conklin's own words will be used in telling most of the story of this high-tide train raid:

"How do I know it was the James and Younger gang that held up my train away back there in '76? Well, it's a rather long story, but if you care to listen I think I can convince you that it was they who robbed our train and rode away. I doubt if people of this generation know anything about Hobbs Kerry. Nevertheless, it was Kerry who supplied the names of the other seven after having confessed his part in the job. From his testimony, and from what I have learned since 1876 about the Jameses and the Youngers, and also from what happened to the Youngers and to Clell Miller, Bill Chadwell and Charlie Pitts a couple of months after the Otterville affair, I have no doubt as to the identity of the eight robbers.

"The train left Kansas City at 4:45 o'clock Friday afternoon, July 7, for St. Louis. I came along as baggagemaster. We carried a combination express and baggage car, a smoker, several day coaches and two Pullman sleepers. All the coaches were fairly well filled with passengers. At Sedalia, thirteen miles west of Otterville, we took on an express car from the Missouri, Kansas & Texas, or 'Katy' road, and it was coupled in next to our express-baggage car. The Katy car was locked, nobody riding in it. The car in which I worked had front and rear platforms, and both side and end doors.

"In the car with me was John B. Bushnell of St. Louis, messenger for the United States Express Company. Bushnell had two safes in his care. One belonged to his own company, the other to the Adams Express Company. Both, of course, were locked, though Bushnell had no key to the Adams safe, which was simply being carried through as special express.

"It was a beautiful moonlit night, rather hot. After I finished handling the baggage taken on at Sedalia, I sat down in a chair near one of the side doors, to cool off. I was admiring the scenery when, rather suddenly, about 10 P.M., the train came to a stop near the western end of the wooden bridge across the Lamine river, a mile or so east of Otterville. This was in a place called Rocky Cut, the name of which explains its character. First thing I knew, somebody fired a shot. Later I found that the bullet had struck the door frame a few inches from where I had been sitting. I jumped out of my chair and took to cover. Outside were several men, shouting and shooting.

"Pretty soon three men climbed into my car. Bushnell, aware that a robbery was on the immediate program, went back in the train and handed the brakeman the key to his safe. The safe had no combination lock. When the robbers entered the car they searched me for weapons and told me to stand up to one side, which I did. Their big guns didn't look nice to young Pete Conklin. They brought in the engineer and fireman and lined them up with me. Some of them had climbed into the cab and got the drop on the engine crew.

"Each of the three robbers in the car, and also one who stayed just outside and fired a shot now and then, to scare us, wore a red bandanna handkerchief tied around the lower part of the face. All had sixshooters; looked like those big old Colt's navies that were in such general use then.

"I have always believed that the man just outside the car was Frank James and that two of those who came into my car were Jesse James and Cole Younger. I saw Frank James frequently in St. Louis, after he came in and was acquitted, and from descriptions of Jesse and Cole I formed the belief that they were two-thirds of the trio that worked in my car for an hour that night.

"One of these three men demanded that I give him

the key to the safe. I told him I didn't have the key.

"'Get it, then, young fellow'—I was twenty-one—
'and be quick about it, or you'll get hurt!' he said.

"At the same instant he shoved the muzzle of his gun
against my ribs. That gentleman, I think, was the
renowned Jesse James.

"'I'm only the baggagemaster,' I explained.

"'Where's the express messenger, then?'

"'He's back in the train somewhere.'

"'Come with me and find him.'

"I went with him, for he still held his Colt in a
threatening position. Bushnell was found, but he told
the bandit he didn't have the key.

"'Find it!' was the sharp order.

"Bushnell was taken into one of the sleepers, where
the brakeman sat. Threatened with death, the brakeman handed over the key. The man with the big gun
then marched us all back to the baggage car. As we
walked through the train we found that several other
armed men were posted outside, on each side of the
train. Now and then one of them fired a shot. From
time to time they uttered loud oaths.

"The newsboy, or train butcher as he would be called
today, was a lad from St. Louis named Lou Bales.
Lou was a nervy little cuss. He carried a little firearm
that made a squeaky sound when it was fired off. He
was game—probably had more courage than discretion.
When he saw a large man standing up the rocky side of
the cut, shouting and shooting, Lou turned loose at
him, firing two shots.

"'Say, boys, just listen to that little feist pup bark
at us!' laughed the big bandit.

"The feist pup barked no more, for Lou Bales was taken in hand by some passenger whose discretion exceeded his valor.

"As the robber was marching Messenger Bushnell up front, the negro porter in one of the Pullmans remarked to the passengers who happened to be awake:

"'If any o' yo' gents got a weepon, now's the time fo' yo' to take a crack at that fellah in the back o' his haid.'

"'Hush up, you black fool! Do you want to get all of us killed?' admonished a passenger.

"The porter hushed up, instantly. Once back in our car, the robbers got busy. The U. S. Express safe was opened with the key, and the cash was taken out and placed in a long wheat sack by one of the outlaws. Then the leader of the gang—Jesse James, say I—turned to the Adams Express safe.

"'Here—where's the key to this?' he demanded, looking fiercely at Bushnell. We could see only his eyes and forehead, but those eyes were fierce, all right; they were blue eyes, and blinky eyes.

"'I don't know,' the messenger replied, explaining in some detail that the safe was being shipped through, locked. Finally the robbers seemed to conclude that he was telling them the truth, as in fact he was.

"One of the men, a wiry fellow of medium size who seemed to have a lot of initiative, skipped ahead to the engine tender. I think he was young Bob Younger. He got the fireman's coal hammer, or pick, and brought it into the car. He tried to break the hinges of the safe door with the hammer, but failed. Then he gave the door several sharp, digging blows with the pointed end of the pick. This had little or no effect.

"A bigger bandit, with a fist like a ham, seized the pick and dealt several blows. This man, from his superior size and strength, I have no doubt was Cole Younger. At last he made an opening in the metal. After a dozen or more of hard licks he stopped and tried to thrust his hand through the ragged hole. I fancy he lost some of his skin.

"The smaller fellow brushed him aside.

"'I wear a No. 7 glove and can get my hand in where yours won't go,' he said.

"The fellow stuck in his hand as far as he could and found a leather pouch containing money. He had to take a knife and cut open the pouch, it being too big to pull through the hole. He got the money, though, and it went into the wheat sack with the packages of currency from the U. S. Express safe.

"All this hard work on a hot night made the robbers thirsty. One of them asked me where the drinking water was kept. In those days water aboard trains was served from buckets. I indicated the location of our water bucket. The bandit ordered me to sample the water. I took two good swigs of it myself, for I— well, my mouth was feeling what you might call kind o' dry. The robber, satisfied that we had not poisoned the supply, drank heartily. His companions did likewise. They all seemed to be fond of the innocent drink.

"The man guarding the outside of my car—or Frank James, to be personal—was getting impatient.

"'Hurry up, in there!' he would call out. 'What's the matter? Won't that fellow give you the key? Shoot the son-of-a-gun, then!'

"But the inside workers continued about their business, calmly enough to keep their heads. The man who seemed to be the leader of the gang—Jesse James, as I figure—asked me what was in the other express car. I explained that it was a car from the Katy and I didn't know what was in it. He insisted that I unlock the door and take him into that car. The key to my car fitted the lock, so I opened it on demand and threat —oh, that overgrown Colt! We went in, and the robber looked about. Satisfying himself that there was nothing the gang could use to advantage, or get without too much delay and danger, he returned to the other car—with me.

"The robbers now were about through with their work, but one of them suggested that they go back and hold up the passengers. 'I want to get me a good super,' he said, meaning a watch. 'No,' said the leader, 'we've been here long enough. Other trains will be along soon. We must get away now. All out!'

"They loped out and were off in a jiffy. But just before they left, one said to me, 'Now, young fellow, you'd better go to the rear of the train and remove some ties we put on the track there; might cause trouble if you don't.' With others I went to the rear and lifted off a few ties they had placed there after the train stopped.

"I could hear their horses stamping, but I could not see the animals out in the trees. After a parting shot they all disappeared, and the night became as silent as a tomb. They had been there just one hour, by my watch.

"But hold on—I've forgotten something, something

important, I guess. Just as they were getting away, the leader turned around and called out:

"'Well, if you see any of Allan Pinkerton's men, tell 'em they'd better come and catch us.'"

It was the defi of Jesse James.

According to contemporary accounts there were but three firearms aboard the train, other than those borne by the bandits. These were the "feist pup" of Lou Bales, a revolver carried by the brakeman and appropriated by Jesse James just before Jesse got the safe key, and a "four-shooter" in possession of a gallant girl from Texas whose name is lost to fame. She is said to have flourished her weapon and to have announced:

"If anybody tries to rob me I'll put four bullets through him quicker'n he can say Jack Robinson!"

Eli Lewis, traveling agent for the Santa Fé Railroad, was in the rear Pullman with J. D. Brown, general ticket agent for the "Katy" line. The porter woke Lewis up in the midst of the mêlée. Lewis, in the lower berth, was pulling on his boots—those old long-tom fellows such as grandpa used to wear—when the bold bandit was passing through the aisle looking for the brakeman who had the safe key. His head came in sharp contact with the robber's elbow.

"I thought I was shot, sure," confessed Lewis, later.

There was a preacher aboard—the Rev. J. S. Holmes of Bedford, Westchester County, New York. He prayed loudly that all might be spared, and that if any must be killed, the unfortunate one or ones might repent in time to be saved. Then he sang church hymns. Jesse James probably would have liked to join in the singing, for he was familiar with all of the old-time church songs. He had sung them fervently himself, when he was a Baptist in good standing.

In the smoker rode a long, lank Hoosier. Emulating the example of some other passengers, he got under the seat. His legs were too long to be accommodated altogether in hiding. One foot stuck out into the aisle. Herding Bushnell, the brakeman and Pete Conklin to the rendezvous up front, Jesse James stumbled over the Hoosier's big and booted foot.

"Oh, Mister!" pleaded the gentleman from Indiana, his voice issuing from beneath the seat like a wail from a grave, "please don't shoot me! I didn't mean to trip you up, Mister! I swear I didn't! I wouldn't 'a' did it for anything! I beg ten thousand pardons, Mister!"

Jesse James, having righted himself, laughed heartily, and marched on with his captives.

The train again in motion and the outlaws gone, passengers began retrieving their valuables from the places where they had hidden them. One man had reached through a ventilation aperture and laid his money and jewelry on the roof of the coach. He complained loudly that he had been robbed; but it was only the midsummer night's breeze that was the bandit in that instance.

Conductor Tebbets wired news of the robbery from Tipton, Missouri, to the St. Louis police and to the Missouri Pacific officials at headquarters in St. Louis. Posses promptly went in pursuit from several points in mid-Missouri. As usual, nobody was caught. Several weeks afterward, the major excitement having subsided, Detective Sergeant Morgan Boland of the St. Louis police department asked permission of Chief of Police James McDonough to go down into southwestern Missouri on a still hunt for one of the men who had robbed the train in Rocky Cut. Boland had been doing some quiet investigating. The chief gave him leave of absence.

Boland proceeded to Granby, Missouri, where lead mines had been operated for many years. It was from the Granby mines that Gen. Sterling Price's army of Missouri Confederates got lead for moulding into the bullets used on more than one great raid from Arkansas far up into Missouri. Boland became friendly with a few of the lead miners and learned many things about one of them, Hobbs Kerry, who recently had been doing some high living.

Kerry seemed to have come into some sudden cash. Boland met him, got chummy, and the man with the homely Celtic name and the simple mind boasted of having taken part in the train holdup with the great bandit Jesse James. Kerry's part, he stated, was the modest task of minding the horses whilst the other fellows robbed the train.

Hobbs Kerry was taken to Boonville, capital of Cooper County, and he made a full confession. In consideration of his having named all of the notorious Missouri outlaws save Jim Younger, who was not in the Otterville affair, Kerry got off with only two years in the penitentiary.

Hobbs Kerry was a raw recruit and considerably much of a crackbrained simpleton. The bandit confederation made a mistake of judgment in enlisting him.

On their next raid, which was the most sensational and one of the most sanguinary in the world's annals of out-lawry, they took along only tried men, true to their criminal cause.

CHAPTER XVIII

NORTHFIELD was Farthest North for the confederated Jameses and Youngers. It was both their Gettysburg and their Waterloo. The Missouri rough riders had been riding hard and far, and frequently, for about ten years; and now they rode their farthest ever—and to their fall, six of the eight. For our hardy bandits of the border had become foolhardy. Their avocation of riding, raiding, robbing and riding away had hardened their muscles, and surely it had not weakened their hearts either physically or otherwise. Bold men always, success in boldly desperate deeds had made them bolder than ever. Apparently they had come to believe themselves an impregnable as well as portable fortress of offense and defense.

The Otterville victory had provided them with plenty of ready money, nearly $2000 apiece. Beside that, it had been so easy, down in poor old Missouri. But for the present, if they operated at all, it must be in some fresh domain afar. Otterville was quite too recent. Moreover, they must see to it that their personnel be perfect, in so far as perfection may dwell in bandit bosoms. There must be no more Hobbs Kerrys in the outfit. Every man must be thoroughly dependable.

Only those of proved 100 per cent daring and devotion could pass muster for the forthcoming campaign.

Jim Younger had been sojourning somewhere in California. He was notified that his furlough was up; he must return to the service. Jim didn't relish returning; he was rather much of a perfunctory bandit, after all; a quiet-spoken, unshowy man, of genteel appearance and of gentlemanly demeanor in the main, he had drifted into outlawry rather than ridden into it at full tilt. Jim was enjoying the simple life in his California retreat and liked it far better than he liked outlaw duty. He had an honest job and was working faithfully. He protested at first but in the end was won over and resucked into the maelstrom of the fate which menaces all men who pursue such an avocation.

So back to old Missouri came Jim Younger, to Jackson County, where he rejoined the command. About the middle of August (1876) the reunited confederation moved upon Minnesota. The personnel now comprised the two Jameses, the three Youngers, Clell Miller, Samuel Wells (alias Charlie Pitts) and William Stiles (alias Bill Chadwell)—eight oldtimers in horse and revolver work. In all-around outlaw efficiency this band probably never has been equaled in America or anywhere else. Every unit in the octet was a 100-percenter.

Stiles had lived in Minnesota, where he had relatives and a record as a horsethief. He knew the lay of the land in southern Minnesota—the towns, the roads, the lakes, the rivers, the bridges, the banks. He could lay out the itinerary of a campaign against a chosen town, with entrances and exits, the local topography, the geography and topography of the get-away routes. He was accounted, therefore, a most valuable member of the invading force.   All the others were adventuring in strange new fields: Stiles was returning to home pastures.   Though not the commanding general of the expedition, he was the commissioned guide and pilot.

The outfit had determined to raid and rob a bank somewhere in southern Minnesota, the Bill Chadwell country, but no particular institution of finance had been selected when the eight left Missouri for the North, where, incidentally, three of them were to remain as corpses quick-prepared, one was to die in prison, a fifth was to take his own life after serving twenty-five years, and a sixth was to be permitted to quit Minnesota only after a quarter of a century's perfect-behavior record in the state penitentiary.

The Missourians rode splendid horses into Minnesota, mounts which probably they had picked and paid for; they always preferred purchasing to stealing when they had the cash.   Each man wore a long linen duster. That was a garment common to travelers by dirt roads in those days.   It helped to keep the clothing free of dust and mud.   In the case of our energetic Missourians it served also the purpose of concealing the handles of sixshooters which otherwise might have peeped out from under suit-coats.   The dusters were of generous cut, so that two or even three revolvers and the requisite equipment of cartridge belts did not make so much of a knobbiness as to reveal the interesting fact that eight arsenals on horseback were moving forward beneath the floppy yards of yellow-brown linen.

Under their dusters the outlaws were dressed like

prosperous business men. Most of them knew well enough how to play that part. They were men of information, readers of the daily press, capable of discussing politics, agriculture, or even religion, with engaging charm. Coleman Younger's specialty, by the way, was theology. That of Frank James was the Elizabethan drama. Younger had also a fondness for historical research, and James could hold his own in any casual conversation on literary topics. A local pastor or a high-school principal would pronounce these two men well-read, at least considerably beyond the average.

Younger, with his six-foot-plus of stature and his 200-pound-plus of avoirdupois, was an upstanding and outstanding individual; and his physiognomy suggested that of a bishop or a benevolent captain of commerce rather than that of a bandit, whilst his well-modulated voice and his keen intelligence made his conversation agreeable to persons of polite cultivation.

Miller, Wells and Stiles were of rougher aspect, physically and mentally, than the others. They had grown up in rural surroundings similar to the early environment of the other bandits, but they came of families by no means so well-descended. Of coarser fibre than the others, they looked coarser, and they talked and acted more like men who had been habituated since early boyhood to companionship of the lowbrow type and to rough usages of life and language. They were essentially desperadoes, men quick on trigger and not of the sort to be borne down by remorse for straight shooting. But in the company of the theological Cole and the Shakespearean Frank, and under their influence, the three outsiders could be depended upon to observe orthodox conventions when in presence of persons of good standing in civic life.

Such, then, was the apparently innocuous outfit that rode into southern Minnesota late in August of America's centennial year. The outlaws did not ride about the state in a single group. They were divided into scouting parties. Two or three would canter into a town, put up at a hotel, chat with drummers or with townspeople, and make themselves agreeable. They pretended to be cattle and horse buyers, or grain dealers, or real-estate speculators, or civil engineers looking out prospective railroad routes—whatever the immediate occasion suggested as most likely to be accepted.

Nobody seems to have questioned their pretensions. They were taken for what they claimed to be. In the small cities and towns, and at farmhouses where some of them stopped now and then, they made favorable impressions. Some of them went as far northward as Minneapolis and St. Paul, in which populous cities their personalities floated serenely along the general stream. Passing under assumed names as well as assumed occupations, the incognitos of the Missourians were invulnerable. Southern Minnesota was glad to see them. They paid their way and were not niggardly in spending money.

For a fortnight these men traversed the roads of several counties, visiting such towns as Red Wing, St. Peter, Mankato, Lake Crystal, Madelia (historic in this connection), St. James, Garden City, Janesville, Cordova, Waterville, Millersburg, Cannon City and—

Northfield. Wherever they went, they visited the banks, usually on pretext of getting large bills changed. A hundred-dollar bill was a commonplace with these free-booters, shortly after a successful raid.

They made inquiries as to local conditions, crops, general prosperity, good roads; they familiarized themselves, under tutelage of Comrade Stiles, with rivers, lakes, bridges, thickets, forests, having eye always to lines of retreat. They were as pioneers for a military expedition. However, as it turned out, their generalship in the Minnesota campaign was exceedingly inefficient, save on the retreat.

Mankato appears to have been their first selection as a place where they might raid a bank, gather plenty of money in their wheat sack, and get away. Five of them visited that town on Sept. 2, some putting up for the night at one hotel, others at another. Two or three called at the First National Bank, where one got change for a fifty-dollar bill.

A Mankato man who happened to know Jesse James "by sight," so he averred, notified the police that the notorious Missourian was in their midst. But the local guardians of the people refused to believe that their modest home town had been honored with a visit from such a celebrity. Jesse James probably was the last man they would expect to see there. However, the strangers were under police observation that night. Next day, which was Sunday, a casual surveillance was kept up; but so innocent were the actions of the hotel guests, in appearance at any rate, that the police were not impressed particularly with the probability that Jesse James was one of the visitors.

It is to be assumed that the Mankato guardians were careful not to let the men suspect that they were suspected. In any event, they were not molested. It appears also that the bank officials entertained no fear of robbery, for about noon on Monday the visiting horsemen appeared in full force in front of the First National and created no excitement. Idle citizens who were watching the progress of repair work on an adjoining building noticed the horsemen. The riders observed that they were being observed. They rode away, but later in the afternoon they returned. The same citizens were on hand. Evidently believing that their purpose was suspected, the Missourians rode out of Mankato.

It was said later that the Mankatoans' admiration for the excellent horse-flesh ridden by the strangers was the sole occasion of their taking notice of the group which visited the vicinity of the bank twice.

Stiles, who had lived in Rice County, knew that the First National Bank at Northfield, in the northeast corner of that county, was a prosperous institution. This was one of the banks that had been visited by some members of the party in the campaign preliminaries. Northfield was a pleasant little place of about 3000 people, about 40 miles east and slightly north of Mankato, in the midst of a rich farming country. The Cannon river bisects the town, a bridge connecting the two sections. East of the bridge is a part of Northfield known as Bridge Square. The principal business thoroughfare, Division Street, runs along the eastern side of the square.

At the intersection of Bridge Square and Division

Street stood, in 1876, a stone building called the Scriver block. The upper floor was used for offices. Downstairs were two stores. The First National Bank occupied temporary quarters at the southern end of the building, the front entrance being on Division Street. A hotel, two hardware stores, a drugstore and other places of business on Bridge Square were in the vicinity of the bank.

This quiet small-town business center became, on Thursday, Sept. 7, the battleground of the Missourians' Waterloo. It became, incidentally, very far from quiet. There were cries of "Murder! murder! robbers! robbers!" There were shouts of warning from citizen to citizen. There were oaths and other outcries from the invading eight, with "Get in! get in! get inside, quick!" as the prevailing tenor of the commands from bandit to citizen. There were pistols popping, shotguns crashing, rifles cracking. Minnesota and Missouri were in deadly duel.

On that afternoon the outlaws rode into Northfield in three groups, having met for final consultation in a piece of woods about five miles to the westward. At that meeting each man was given to know precisely what part he was expected to take in the Northfield job —emergencies, of course, not being lost from the reckoning. The octet divided into three sections. Three men were to enter the bank and get the money—if they could; two were to sit their horses on Division Street, opposite the bank, and keep too-curious people away; three were to occupy posts on Bridge Square as a rear guard, the gang intending to make its get-away by crossing the bridge over Cannon river.

The three who were to rob the bank rode across the bridge about 2 o'clock, crossed the square, dismounted in front of the bank and threw their reins over hitching-posts. These men were Sam Wells, Bob Younger and, it is believed, Jesse James. They walked in a leisurely way to the street corner and sat down upon some dry-goods boxes in front of a store. Nonchalantly, in appearance, they began whittling the pine boxes.

In a short time Cole Younger and Clell Miller rode up Division Street. The three whittlers pocketed their knives, arose, walked slowly to the bank entrance and went inside. Leaving his horse unhitched, Clell Miller walked to the door of the bank, which the other three had left open. He closed the door and sauntered back and forth on the sidewalk, keeping an eye on the door.

Cole Younger's saddle-girth seemed to be troubling him; anyhow, he got off his horse, in the middle of the street, and pretended to be tightening the girth. He was an excellent actor, but this particular bit of acting failed to go down with the Northfield male element, which already had begun to suspect that the play was a bad one.

One of the spectators who didn't like the prologue was Henry M. Wheeler, a youth of twenty-two who was at home on vacation from Ann Arbor, where he was a senior medical student in the University of Michigan. Henry's father conducted a drugstore on the east side of Division Street. The college student had been sitting under an awning in front of the pharmacy when the horsemen rode up. He arose and walked along until he was opposite the bank and the bandits.

Another spectator who was not impressed with the genuineness of the acting was J. S. Allen, a hardware merchant. When he saw the three strangers enter the bank he tried to follow. Clell Miller seized him by the scruff of the neck and ordered him to stand back, get away, go inside somewhere else.

"And if you speak a word," said Miller, fingering a large revolver, "I'll kill you!"

Nevertheless, Allen jerked loose, ran around the corner to his store, and shouted so loudly that he was heard all up and down the square:

"Get your guns, boys! Get your guns! Those fellows are robbing the bank!"

Henry Wheeler, who had heard a pistol shot from inside the bank, also was shouting loud alarms. Cole Younger and Miller remounted and ordered young Wheeler to "get inside," firing a shot or two over his head to frighten him. The future physician and surgeon was not of the frightening breed. Nor did he get so excited as to lose presence of mind.

Whilst Younger and Miller were riding up and down, yelling for everybody to get in, and firing right and left, and the three bandits from the bridge side were dashing into the square and beginning tactics similarly violent, Wheeler dashed into the drugstore to get his gun. He was a huntsman and kept a competent fowling-piece. Suddenly he recollected that he had left the weapon at home, some blocks away. He ran on through the store and into the Dampier Hotel, where he found an old army carbine, a relic of Federal use against Southerners of the Sixties, including possibly some of the ex-guerrillas now invading Northfield.

Three paper cartridges were the only ammunition to be found. Wheeler loaded the carbine with one of these, pocketed the others, ran upstairs and posted himself at a front window overlooking the scene of the outdoors excitement.

Anselm B. Manning was a business rival of J. S. Allen, being another hardware merchant. But Allen forgot all about business, save that immediately in hand, as he rushed past Manning's store toward his own after he got out of Clell Miller's clutch.

"Get your gun, Manning! They're robbing the bank!"

Manning had a breech-loading rifle in his store window. From his desk he took a box of cartridges. Loading as he ran, he reached the scene of battle in a jiffy. Standing in the open street, he met a shower of bullets. They whistled all about him. Manning was cool and calm.

Allen reached his own store, where he had in stock a number of rifles and shotguns. He began loading them rapidly, passing them out to citizens who could use them. Elias Stacy accepted one and used it well in the subsequent proceedings. Others also made good use of the Allen arsenal stock.

But it was a shotgun in the hands of Stacy, provided and loaded by Allen, that drew first blood from a bandit. Just as Clell Miller was mounting his horse to help Cole Younger drive Henry Wheeler away, Stacy fired at Clell. The gun was loaded with small birdshot. Miller was knocked from his saddle, but he got back at once, his head and shoulders peppered with birdshot.

"Why, this is the very fellow who grabbed me and

threatened to shoot me at the bank door," said J. S. Allen, after the battle.

Allen was inspecting the peppered countenance of a corpse; but it was not birdshot that had killed Clell Miller of Clay.

CHAPTER XIX

L ET the battle scene shift now from the open street and the square to the interior of the First National Bank of Northfield. When the three robbers entered the bank they found the bookkeeper, Joseph Lee Heywood, at the cashier's desk, substituting for Cashier G. M. Phillips, who was away on an extended trip. A. E. Bunker, teller, and F. J. Wilcox, assistant bookkeeper, were engaged in routine duties. Only these six—three armed robbers and three unarmed employes—were present. There was, to be sure, a ladylike little pistol on a shelf under the teller's counter; but Bunker, luckily for himself, was not in touch with this weapon at the moment of his surprise by the "hands up" command from one of the three who already had man-sized sixshooters pointing directly at his head.

Before Bunker was able fully to comprehend the situation the three had climbed over the counter, a makeshift affair not intended for permanent banking use. The man who had uttered the order then coolly notified Bunker and his companions that the purpose of the invasion was to rob the bank.

"And don't any of you fellows holler!" he added.

"We've got forty men outside, and it'll be no use to holler. It'll be dangerous if you do."

He flourished his revolver by way of emphasis. The other two indulged in similar flourishing. Each had his eye and his aim on a bank employe.

"Are you the cashier?" the spokesman inquired, turning toward Heywood.

"I am not," replied Heywood.

In the literal sense this was true. Bunker and Wilcox both replied negatively to the same question put in turn. The robber turned back to Heywood, who sat at the cashier's desk.

"I know you're the cashier," he said, angrily. "Now you open that safe, damn quick, or I'll blow your head off!"

The door of the vault, in which the safe was visible, stood open. Sam Wells rushed to the vault and stepped inside. Heywood arose, walked rapidly to the vault and tried to shut Wells inside. Before he could slam the heavy door shut he was seized by both Wells and the leader of the robbing squad.

"Unless you open that safe at once you'll be shot dead!" cried the leader.

"I can't open it—the time lock is on."

"You're lying!"

Repeatedly they demanded that Heywood open the safe. They pulled him back and forth about the big room, cursing him.

"Murder! murder!" Heywood shouted.

The leader struck him on the head with a heavy revolver. Heywood sank to the floor.

"Let's cut his damn throat!" cried Sam Wells, who

opened his pocket knife and made a slight cut in the neck of the fallen man. At least a semi-cutthroat was Wells of Jackson County! Then the pair caught Heywood under the armpits and dragged him back to the door of the vault, again insisting that he open the safe.

From time to time the desperate men turned to Wilcox and Bunker, ordering each in turn to unlock the safe. Both replied that they could not unlock it.

Heywood lay upon the floor near the vault, hardly conscious. Wells bent low and fired a shot close by the acting cashier's head—the first shot fired inside the bank. This was done in the hope of inducing Heywood to unlock the safe. The bullet passed through a tin box in the vault, containing valuables left by a special depositor.

Bob Younger was keeping watch on Bunker and Wilcox. He made them get down under the counter, on their knees. Bunker then thought of the pistol on the shelf. He was edging toward the place where it lay, at a moment when Younger had turned his back. Wells, who seemed to see in every direction at once, divined Bunker's intention. Leaping forward, he seized the pistol, which he stuck into one of his pockets.

"Huh! you couldn't do any harm with this little derringer, anyhow," he said.

Bunker arose to his feet. Bob Younger was on guard again.

"There's money here, somewhere, outside the safe," he said. "Where do you keep it? Where's the cash till?"

On the counter was a box containing some fractional

currency. The teller pointed to this. Drawing from under his linen duster the inevitable wheat sack, Younger began to stow away the loose change—a pitifully small quantity of loot; and that was all the outlaws got from the bank. In a drawer under the counter, close to the robber's hands, reposed in safety $3000 in paper money.

Bunker, who had been ordered to get back beneath the counter, still stood up. Younger told him to get down and stay down.

"There's more money somewhere here. Where do you keep it? Show me where, or I'll kill you!"

However, he did not kill Bunker. Robert Younger probably never killed any man; there is no record of his having done so. He tried hard that day to kill a man, however—an armed man outside the bank.

Bunker made a dash for liberty. He ran through the bank directors' room to the rear door, which was closed, with inside blinds which were fastened. He hoped to reach Manning's hardware store, across the alley, and give the alarm, for as yet he was not aware that Manning, Allen, Wheeler, Stacy and several other citizens already were exchanging hot shots with the five bandits outside.

Sam Wells leaped again to the breach. Bunker was close to the rear door when Wells fired at his head. The bullet went through the door-blind. Bunker burst open the blind and the door, and dashed down the steps outside. Wells pursued him, firing a shot which passed through the teller's right shoulder. The wound was severe but not fatal. Bunker made for a surgeon's office in the adjoining block. He was out of the battle.

Sam Wells got back into the banking room just in time to hear one of the bandits outside the bank shouting that the game was up.

"Come out, boys! come out. They're killing all our men!" was the warning Wells and his two companions heard. The three escaped by way of the teller's window and the front door. Heywood, still dazed from the terrific blow on his head, had managed to get to his feet. He was groping his way toward his desk just as the last of the departing desperadoes was climbing through the teller's window.

This man turned and shot Heywood through the head. The faithful acting cashier dropped to the floor, stone dead. It was a deliberate murder, inexcusable even on the ground of self-defense, for Heywood was unarmed and was virtually helpless from his hurt.

They were not killing all of the raiding party's men, but they were killing just as many as they could. The Northfield defenders had been apt and able. For amateur fighters they made magnificent records. Their marksmanshp turned out to be far better than that of the notorious Missourians who had been regarded as dead shots. As for the Minnesotans, the deadliness of their execution on the edge of the instant was and remains an unsurpassable tribute to the steadiness of their nerves at a time of sudden and violent excitement.

Those Northfielders knew what they were after, and they went straightway and got it. They did not know at the moment that they were beginning to decimate the ranks of the hitherto invincible border bandits, to split in twain the James-Younger confederation of crime; but they did know that they were "getting" some of the most desperate freebooters that ever had raided a bank, and that knowledge no doubt gave them great joy of the battle.

First to fall in the street fight was an innocent aid to the outlaws—one of their splendid saddlehorses. When Merchant A. B. Manning arrived with loaded rifle and stood with bandit bullets zipping past his ears, he saw the horses belonging to the men who had gone in to rob the bank. Above the horses' backs were visible the heads of two highwaymen.

Manning took aim quite deliberately at the head of a selected outlaw, who ducked behind a horse before the merchant was good and ready to pull trigger. Keeping his rifle leveled and changing his aim slightly, Manning shot the horse nearest him. He had realized, on the instant, that a horseless rider would have upon the invaders a weakening effect as valuable to the local cause as would a riderless horse.

Manning stepped around the corner to reload. The breech-lever jammed. The merchant ran into his store, got a ramrod, ejected the empty shell. Returning to the street corner, he fired at one of the robbers who was near the door of the bank. The bullet struck a post and glanced off, finding for second target Cole Younger and inflicting one of the several wounds which the biggest of the bandits received that day. Cole Younger was such a stalwart that he was hard to miss. Physically, at any rate, Cole was not cut out for a bullet-inviting freebooter; there was too much of him.

The coolheaded Manning reloaded, the ejecting lever working all right again. Glancing around the corner of the building, he saw William Stiles, sole Minnesotan of the outfit, sitting in saddle about eighty yards away. Manning was taking no pot shots. He intended that every bullet should count. "Tally!" was the song of his missiles. So deliberate was the man in drawing a bead on Stiles that some fellow-townsmen standing not far away grew impatient, almost indignant.

"Get him! get him! Shoot, man, shoot!" they urged.

Manning took his time. Stiles evidently was posted there on sentry duty; his horse was at a standstill. The merchant's bullet went through the bandit's heart, and the "Bill Chadwell" of several desperate forays cashed in at last, in his old home county. Relieved of his burden, Stiles's horse ran gaily to a livery stable, the subsequent proceedings interesting him no more; the horse was looking for hay. Manning stepped back, reloaded, stepped forward, and watched his chance to get another outlaw.

All this time—and it was but a very few minutes, at that—young Henry Wheeler was busy with the old army carbine he had borrowed. From his second-floor window in the Dampier Hotel he surveyed the scene, a cool and collected youth. Jim Younger was riding past. Wheeler fired at him and missed. Younger heard the bullet hit a spot beyond him and turned to gaze at that spot. Then he turned about to see whence the missile came. Several citizens were firing at the robbers, and Younger failed to discover the medical student at the window.

Wheeler next observed Clell Miller, bleeding from Elias Stacy's charge of birdshot but still in his saddle and perfectly good for further fighting. The future physician had rammed the second of his paper cartridges down the throat of the old carbine and now aimed coolly at Miller. The bullet that had been intended for some Confederate soldier a dozen or more years earlier and had been preserved as a relic of the Civil War, found now a vital spot in the body of the oldtime Quantrill guerrilla from Clay County, Missouri. Penetrating his right shoulder, it severed the great sub-clavicle artery. Clell Miller died almost instantly. Tumbling from his saddle, he lay crumpled upon the ground.

Henry Wheeler's third cartridge, and last, had fallen to the floor; the paper covering burst, and the powder was spilled. Eager for more of the same kind of shooting, Wheeler turned to go downstairs in search of more ammunition. He met the hotel clerk coming up with a fresh supply. Wheeler again took position at the window.

Northfield citizenry was up and at it. Shotguns instantly and inadequately loaded were in the hands of James Gregg, Ross Phillips, J. B. Hyde and others. These men did the best they could with what they had to do with. Elias Hobbs, not having even a birdshot weapon such as the other Elias, Citizen Stacy, had used in peppering the now deceased Clell Miller, found somewhere an armful of loose rocks.

"Stone 'em! stone 'em!" shouted Elias Hobbs, and he stoned 'em. Two or three others also stoned 'em. Northfield, in this emergency, got back to primitive methods of warfare. The stones worried the des-peradoes but did little or no damage.

Henry Wheeler and Merchant Manning had not had enough of it. The six unslain outlaws were shooting at heads wherever heads were visible, and missing, save in one instance. Nicholas Gustavson, a Swede who understood little English, failed to "get in" when ordered so to do by one of the horsemen; he was shot to death. The raiders were firing also at windows and doors. Glass was crashing in the windows of the Dampier Hotel, and the casements of stores and offices here and there along the square were being shattered.

Henry Wheeler rammed home another paper cartridge and stood awaiting another chance to exercise his trigger finger. Anselm Manning, standing at his corner, saw Bob Younger running toward him. It was Bob's horse that was the victim of Manning's first bullet, and the young outlaw was afoot.

Manning proceeded to take deliberate aim at Younger. At the same moment Younger leveled his revolver at Manning. Each man moved aside to escape the other's expected bullet. Younger took refuge under the outside stairway of the building in which the bank was located.

Wheeler, at his window, saw Manning and Younger trying to get each other within range and, incidentally, trying to keep out of range. He could see Younger's right arm, with the big weapon gripped in the fingers, but the rest of the bandit's body was invisible. Wheeler fired. The bullet shattered Younger's elbow. Younger shifted his sixshooter to his left hand and kept on trying to get his chance at Manning.

Just then came a lull in the battle. Manning had dashed through a store with the intention of getting on the other side of Younger and driving him from shelter. Wheeler was reloading. The old carbine was renewing its gallant and militant youth, and the young collegian now had full confidence in the retired and re-enlisted weapon.

The surviving robbers had had more than enough of it. Miller's horse, like that of Stiles, had run away when his master was shot from the saddle. Bob Younger's mount being dead, there were but five horses for six men. The youngest of the Youngers, his right arm swinging useless, darted out from under the stairway and up Division Street, where the eldest of the Youngers sat in saddle. Cole helped Bob to climb up behind. It was an enormous burden for the horse, but the fine animal was equal to the demand. With the four other horses, each carrying a survivor of the engagement, he galloped down street and out of town, southward.

Wheeler was back at his window, Manning again out in the open. But the street showed so many citizens in the wake of the retreating raiders that neither of the marksmen risked another shot.

Church bells had been set ringing. The big bell in the cupola of Carleton College, of which institution the slain Heywood was treasurer, was clanging resonantly. From all points in the little city people were gathering in Bridge Square. Some were inspecting the corpses of Stiles and Miller. Others had entered the bank and were looking after the body of Heywood, whose devotion to duty had cost him life. Still others, a considerable group, were preparing to mount horses and pursue the six survivors. They felt that at least they should be able to capture or kill Cole and Bob Younger, taking into consideration their horse's handicap.

Though the shattered window-panes and the bullets imbedded in posts and walls proved—if such proof were needed—that the bandits had not been firing blank cartridges, not a single member of the citizens' impromptu shooting force had been hit.

The professional dead shots had failed miserably, the amateur sharpshooters had carried off all the honors of the day.

CHAPTER XX

DOWN in Missouri the business of pursuing the bandits after a raid had become more or less perfunctory. Though the Pinkertons always sleuthed about assiduously in the hope of catching or killing an offguard James or Younger, the general public had come to feel that it was an idle industry. The successive sheriffs of Clay and Jackson Counties, with their official staffs, though never altogether discouraged, agreed in the main with the general public.

"What's the use?" seemed to be the too-languid-for-utterance response to the beyond-state demand that the band be broken up. "If you want 'em caught, come in and catch 'em yourselves," was the challenge flung back at Outlanders; "but if you do come and try it, bring along your own coffins or the cash to buy 'em."

Missouri knew a wasps'-nest when she heard it buzz.

Up in Minnesota the case was different. For the first time Minnesota had experienced a charge of the light brigade from Missouri; and the Northern state made up its mind that this must be also the last time. Once was enough! Two of Northfield's innocent citizens had been slain by the invaders, the lives of many others imperiled by the poor marksmanship of the veteran pistolers. On the other hand, two brave Northfielders had taken gory toll of the marauders. Minnesota had proved that she also could shoot some. Missouri, the Fighting State, must be taught a salutary lesson, to the general if not specific effect that her trigger-finger was not to be taken as this great republic's pre-eminent digit in the doing of deeds of daring, desperado-wise or otherwise.

There was nothing of languor in the preparations of the Minnesotans, beginning at Northfield and spreading out over a large area west and south, to keep the remaining Missourians from getting back home. Determination, grim and relentless, was the watchword. Those fellows from the Missouri border had outraged and enraged southern Minnesota beyond forgiveness. They must be killed or caught—it made little difference which. In either event, extermination; for public sentiment was strong for the gallows in case of capture.

Now began a man-hunt unique in the annals of America. At its outset the Minnesotans under-estimated the task. They suspected from the start that they were after the James-Younger outfit; there was that man in Mankato who had recognized Jesse James. They knew that most if not all of the escaping six had been wounded by Northfield bullets. They knew, as they had high reason to know, the desperate situation of the men—that they would fight for their lives to the ultimate round of ammunition.

But the Minnesotans did not know the wellnigh superhuman resourcefulness of their quarry. They did not know to what height of superlative degree these frustrated bank raiders were able to suffer, to endure, in their efforts to escape death by lead or hemp. The pursuit began as a new sort of holiday pastime—not a picnic, to be sure, yet in the nature of a pleasurable outdoors recreational junket. As the days passed it grew into a proposition considerably more serious, and long before the end it had settled down into a near-military campaign undertaken in a state of unpreparedness.

Approximately a thousand men, according to contemporary estimate, took the field against the bandits. Not all of them were in the service simultaneously; but that many were on duty here, there and yonder in the southern section of Minnesota at some time or other in that astounding two weeks' chase. Some went out for adventure pure though hardly simple, some in the hope of winning the large rewards offered, and many others from a sense of civic duty.

Many were inefficient, hindering instead of helping. Others were timid and fearsome, abandoning the enterprise at first scent of probable peril. But hundreds of these Minnesotans were highly efficient man-hunters, and scores of them gave conclusive proof that they were not afraid to stalk even Jesse James himself, if given opportunity and ammunition.

Let us remember that the Northfield raid took place on Thursday afternoon, Sept. 7, which was just two months after the physically safe and financially successful train robbery near Otterville, in Missouri. Two months from high tide of prosperous outlawry to tidal wave of disaster and semi-annihilation! The time was not long, but the rough riders had ridden hard and far; and now they were riding hardly at all, and in slow, unshowy style at that; and at times they were walking, and limping, leaving trails of blood from their own wounds. Minnesota was so different from Missouri!

Because they found things "too hot" for them, as the survivors expressed it later, in the western direction which they had chosen beforehand as their route of get-away, the six bandits escaped from Northfield by the Dundas road. Dundas was a small village three miles to the south. The desperadoes were glad to find any route open. They were compelled also to abandon their plan to stop by the Northfield telegraph office and destroy the apparatus which presently would be sending out to all neighboring towns a warning to look out for six men on five horses.

It is of local record that the five horses tore down the Dundas road abreast. The old guerrillas were making their last cavalry charge. Other travelers, in either direction, were crowded off into the ditches. Before the bandits reached Dundas they held up a farmer driving a team of good horses. Bob Younger, nursing his shattered right elbow without the benefit of first aid to the injured, slid off the rear end of Cole Younger's steed, doubtless greatly to that overburdened animal's delight, and was helped aboard one of the barebacked horses unhitched from the farm wagon.

"Off again, on again, gone again!"

It so happened that the first pursuers from Northfield were mounted on the horses of the slain outlaws Stiles and Miller. These fine beasts tore out gladly after their comrades, carrying their riders in sight of the fugitives before the cavalry squad reached Dundas. It was two against six. The Northfield men found it difficult to hold back the eager animals. Wisdom dictated discretion, and the two pursuers waited for reinforcements. The squad rode on out of sight and got a start of several miles before the larger posse from Northfield reached Dundas.

Not far down the road from the point where Bob Younger found his mount the six horsemen stopped in front of a farmhouse.

"We're deputies in pursuit of horse-thieves," said a spokesman bandit, "and we want to borrow a saddle for this young man. He didn't have time to get his saddle when he joined us, and he has been thrown off and got his arm hurt."

The farmer cheerfully gave them the loan of a saddle, and failed to kiss it farewell. Off again, on again, gone again—for Bob the Bandit. Verily resourceful riders they! Through Dundas they galloped at race-horse speed, even the farmhorse keeping nose-by-nose with the trained saddlehorses; such is the inspiration of a noble example. Little old Dundas rushed to its windows and watched the road-filling line sweep past.

Below Dundas the raiders turned into a road leading westward. By 4 P.M. the town of Millersburg, where some of the outlaws had spent the night before the bank raid, witnessed their wild dash through its main street and out southwestwardly. The hotel man who had been host to one small division of the confederation stood upon his front porch and peered into the faces of the linen-dustered riders. He recognized those who had put up at his place, and vaguely he wondered why they were riding through town at such a hell-to-split pace and why there were twice as many men in the party.

Bob Younger certainly was having hard luck that day, despite his temporary pickup of horse and saddle. The impressed mount presently lost his ambition, stumbled, fell, and Younger's crushed elbow got another jolt. The fall broke the saddle-girth. Younger was helped up behind a member of the band who was considerably lighter than Big Brother Cole.

Off again, on again, gone again! Some miles farther along, another farmhorse was commandeered. Bob got aboard and had high hopes again. But this beast balked so stubbornly that after strenuous efforts to make him keep up with the cavalcade he was mustered out, and for the third time that dismal afternoon Bob Younger had to ride double.

Thrice before nightfall small squads of pursuers saw the fleeing robbers. Faribault, county seat of Rice, having been notified by wire, sent out a party. These men had entered a house at Shieldsville, about fifteen miles west of Northfield, for refreshments. Apparently they were not expecting the fugitives on that road, for they left their weapons outside the house. Whatever their faults, the Missourians never were guilty of such a carelessness.

Suddenly the six dashed up, drew water for their horses at the town pump near by, each man gulped down a reviving swig, and after firing a volley of bullets at the pump—which would have been killed instantly had it been animate—they tore away, westward.

The Faribault posse came within long range of the quarry some miles west of Shieldsville. Shots were exchanged. Everybody missed. Leaving the road now for the first of many times in the fortnight to come, the bandits galloped into the woods. It was no new experience for them to ride between trees and through underbrush. Hundreds of times had they done likewise when fighting under Quantrill, Anderson or Todd, in Missouri and eastern Kansas. The Minnesotans stopped at the edge of the timber.

The pursuers who encountered the pursued spread the news, and it became known to hundreds of armed men in that part of the state that the route of the Missourians was, generally speaking, of a southwestward trend. In that direction lay the old Missouri home—a long way off. By nightfall at least 200 men, in squads of five to forty, were scenting the trail. Before the end of the next day half a thousand were under arms in posses at various points, all keeping watch for the approach of the enemy.

The scattered army of chasers included the chiefs of police from Minneapolis and St. Paul, private and police detectives from those cities, Pinkerton operatives, mayors, sheriffs, deputies and many unofficial recruits. Some were on horseback, others afoot; some carried antiquated weapons, others were armed with the latest models of shotguns, rifles and sixshooters.

It being evident that the outlaws were making for the great forest region known as the Big Woods, abounding in swamps, lakes, thickets, ravines and underbrush, the general plan of the campaign was to throw out picket lines beyond, to prevent escape to the west or the south. Other units of the pursuing forces were to follow and find the fugitives, and to catch or kill them when driven to bay. Accordingly, men were posted at all bridges, fords, roads, trails and open places some distance beyond the approximate location of the fleeing party. This rim of pickets extended in a sort of semicircle for almost a hundred miles.

Six hundred, perhaps, after six! A hundred-to-one horserace and footrace chase! And the program continued, night and day, for two weeks, with a most thrilling fadeout at the end of the serial.

Adding greatly to discomfort of both pursued and pursuers was a heavy rain which began falling the night following the Northfield raid and continued, with occasional intervals of cessation, for a dozen days and nights. This drenched everybody who was in the open, made the roads wellnigh impassably muddy, softened the leafy soil in the woods, and swelled the streams that must be forded.

From their place of retreat in the woods near Shieldsville the robbers traveled slowly in the direction of Waterville, to the southwest. A ford of the Little Cannon river was guarded by three men who fired upon them. The fugitives retreated into the timber. Not long afterward they sent out a scout who found the ford abandoned by its guard. The six outlaws crossed the river and thus easily broke through the line. It was no Hindenburg that established the line in Minnesota.

The job of picketing had to be done over. Those in command threw their forces some miles farther west and southwest, forced marches being made through mud and rain. One posseman who had fought under Stonewall Jackson in Virginia and who now found himself boot and elbow with some of the Yankees he had marched against, recalled vividly the feats in forced trekking which he had performed under "Old Jack's" compulsion.

"It was just like this," so Johnny Reb remarked to his new comrades.

Again all points of possible egress were guarded with armed and eager men. Recruits arrived from hour to hour, being brought by special trains to points nearest the new picket line and proceeding thence by horse or by Shanks's mare to the places where they were to be posted.

In the midst of the lake and swamp country the robbers made a swap of horses. Two of their mounts were exhausted. At a lonely farmhouse they left these, taking in exchange two fresh animals. The farmer did not fancy the trade, but he yielded to persuasion of pistols. Later on the same day the Missouri experts caught another horse, in a pasture, and another bandit had a fresh mount. Near German Lake they went into camp that night, which was Friday and the second night from Northfield. They turned loose the three appropriated horses, all of which went home. Thus one unwilling farmer profited by the proposition, after all.

Rainfall continued through the night. The bandits had a most uncomfortable time of it. They spread saddle blankets over a clump of bushes and beneath this sorry shelter got a little sleep. Their three remaining horses they tied to trees. When they broke camp Saturday morning they left the animals tied. Now for the first time the six men set out on foot; Missouri cavalry became infantry. Three days later a party of man-chasers happened along and found one hungry horse still hitched to a tree; the other two had escaped, having gnawed through their halter straps.

It was a march most toilsome and slow for the fugitives on Saturday. During most of the day they sequestered themselves upon a damp little isle in a swamp. That night they traveled tediously, or rather they waded, and after daylight on Sunday they made camp a few miles south of the hamlet of Marysburg. At dusk they resumed their trek, making about nine miles by midnight—a march which even Stonewall Jackson, taking into consideration the condition of the men and the state of the weather, would have pronounced a fine performance.

About three miles from Mankato they found an abandoned farmhouse in a thick forest. Here they spent the rest of Monday night, all of Tuesday and Tuesday night, attending to their wounds and getting what rest they could. Meals were neither regular nor square. The swampy section of the Big Woods is a sorry place for foraging, even by such seasoned foragers as were these men who had learned the art under Quantrill and Bill Anderson.

They had been on the retreat five days, and they were less than fifty miles from Northfield.

When the tied horse and the gnawed halters were discovered, the commanders of the chase felt seriously blue. Everybody had been looking for a bunch of men on horseback, nobody for anybody on foot. There were plenty of posses afoot, out looking for the robbers. Very likely the Missourians had made themselves look like Minnesotans in pursuit of the invaders. Now they had three days' start, from the horse-tying camp.

Probably they had trekked through the wide-spaced line and were well out of Minnesota.

Many of the pursuers took that view and gave up the chase. After these had departed for their homes, those still in the service heard something that aroused a renewal of interest. After all, the birds had not flown so very far away: their wings were crippled, though not clipped.

CHAPTER XXI

THE GETAWAY OF THE JAMES BOYS

R ICHARD ROBERTS was the name of a gallant youth who stood guard at a picket-line post on a road near Lake Crystal. He had several comrades in his squad, but the others were less watchful than he. Tired of standing by the roadside, or squatting in the wet brush near by, they had retired to a place in the woods more nearly dry and were sleeping soundly on the night of Thursday, Sept. 14, a week after the Northfield raid and battle.

"Those devils have got away, Dick, anyhow," they had said to Roberts. "What's the use to keep up this job? It's a farce! Why, everybody'll laugh at us when we get home."

"All the same, fellows," said Dick, "I'll keep it up; that's what they put me here to do."

"Little Dicky Bobby, Sunday-school boy!" taunted one of the derelict guards. "Say your prayers, Dicky, before you go to sleep to night."

"You go to hell!" snapped little Dicky Bobby.

"We'll go to sleep—that's better."

So Richard Roberts, fit type of a future movie hero, stood by. It was a lonesome sentry job, there in the pouring rain, far from any human habitation. Dick himself didn't fancy it, but he was determined not to leave the road unguarded altogether. He was getting very drowsy when, late in the night, he heard a peculiar noise. It was the smacky sound made by the hoofs of a horse releasing themselves from vilely viscous mud. Young Roberts cocked his gun and stood at attention.

Some rods up the road, advancing slowly toward him the sentinel saw in the semi-darkness a horse, and on the horse a man—yes, two men! Standing in the bushes where he could not be seen by the double-riding cargo, Roberts waited until the equine craft had voyaged painfully down the waterlogged road to a point within a few rods of his station. This was an open place, and the young man observed that the man riding behind wore a white bandage around his right leg, outside the trousers.

"Halt!" the picket challenged. "Who are you fellows?"

At the same instant Roberts covered the forward rider with his rifle. The man jerked his reins and turned the horse's head out of the road, shouting "Get up! get up!"

Roberts pulled the trigger. The explosion frightened the horse, which jumped aside and threw both his riders; then the animal bounded away, back up the road. The men gathered themselves up out of the mud and limped away into a field, where they disappeared. Roberts waited a minute or so and then walked cautiously to the spot where the men had been tossed overboard.

There he found a hat, and in the hat a bullet-hole.

"By Jiminy!" ejaculated the lone sentinel; "maybe I hit one of 'em!"

Richard Roberts, confident that those two men would not reappear at that particular point, walked into the woods and awakened his derelict comrades. He told his tale and showed the hat.

"Huh! I guess maybe you imagine you've shot Jesse James," laughed one of the awakened.

"Well, maybe I have," admitted Richard Roberts.

And maybe he had. If he shot anybody that night, the chances are a thousand to one that he did shoot Jesse James, perhaps a glancing shot that did but little damage; for the probabilities are in just about that proportion that the men riding double were Jesse and Frank, Jesse forward and Frank aft. Frank James was believed to have been wounded in the right leg at Northfield, hence the bandage.

Nobody knows to this day, nor will anybody ever know absolutely, that those men were the Jameses. We must fall back upon the law of probabilities, which in this instance indicates most strongly that they were Jesse and Frank. Subsequent events bolster the belief.

When young Roberts reported the nocturnal incident to his commanding officer, and he in turn to other officers along the line, another picket squad had another important piece of news to tell. On the preceding night four men who were believed to belong to the bandit crew had walked across a railroad bridge spanning Blue Earth river, going westward.

"Well," said General Pope of Mankato, "I guess they're all through our lines again, and all we can do is to chase them. Those four perhaps have too much of a start by now, but surely we should be able to catch the pair young Roberts shot at."

General Pope reorganized the chase and took command. It was true that the six had split up after a week's sticking together, the two Jameses going out "on their own," and Sam Wells and the three Youngers remaining together.

For some years there was a tale to the effect that the Jameses had insisted that Jim Younger, who had suffered a terrible wound at Northfield and was so nearly helpless that he was impeding the flight of the party, be killed, so that the others might have a better chance to escape. The others, so runs the story, stood by Jim, there was a bitter quarrel, and the James boys cut loose from the crew. It was a tale that was told; its truth or its falsity is impossible of determination.

We shall follow now, even as did the forces under General Pope, the two Jameses, assuming—not under oath, mind you—that the men who had ridden double to the picket post of Richard Roberts were no others than they. After they crossed the field they took to the timber and had a run of luck which no doubt reminded them of their good old days back in Missouri.

Visiting by stealth a barnyard lot, they possessed themselves of two fine gray horses. They stayed not to search for saddles, but rode bareback. Due westward rode the James brothers, like the course of empire, and rapidly rode they. In two days and nights, urging their grays to the limit of speed endurance, they made eighty miles. Stonewall Jackson would have had those gray horses engraved on Stone Mountain, for their feat in pressing forward!

On Sunday, ten days after the flight from Northfield,

the Jameses left Minnesota behind them—and forever. Though the state's name began with a big M, it was by no means Missouri: it was considerably less hospitable, for one thing, to bandits in particular.

When they met persons on this ride they had a ready tale. They were officers chasing the James boys and the Younger brothers, or whoever it was that had raided the bank at Northfield. Their saddles had been stolen when they tied up to go into a restaurant and eat. Of course a civic-spirited citizen "loaned" them saddles, and other Minnesotans supplied them with food and refreshments.

By the time they reached the edge of Dakota Territory and were ready to turn southward and traverse a portion of what now is South Dakota, the riders' two grays were about worn out. That night, in the dark, the brothers found two black horses in a farmlot. They left the grays and rode away on the blacks. Perhaps just here we may be permitted to indulge the imagination as to what Jesse said to Frank when daylight came, and what Frank said to Jesse. The new horses had turned out to be stumblers. The riders alighted in the gray dawn and took a look at their steeds from the front.

"Gosh A'mighty, Frank—this beast is blind in the left eye!"

"Shucks, Jesse—that's nothing at all to kick about; this one is blind in both eyes!"

And is it not slightly probable that Frank James, devout student of Shakespeare as he was, exclaimed disgustedly:

"My kingdom for a horse with two good eyes!"

Anyhow, one of the trophies of the swap in the dark was one-eyed and the other was sightless altogether, as averred the farmer at whose home—when he wasn't looking—Frank and Jesse exchanged the blind blacks for a second pair of grays that could see far and travel fast.

Southward through Sioux Falls the riders passed, unchallenged. Still possessing plenty of cash from the Rocky Cut haul, they bought their meals en route. At Sioux City they visited a doctor, who dressed Frank's wound. The patient had been shot by accident, quite of course. Jesse, if it were he that lost the hat when Richard Roberts fired, had acquired a chapeau somewhere along the route; and at Sioux City both men donned new outfits of clothing. Their linen dusters, by the way, had been discarded shortly after they left Northfield.

From that point forward the retreat route of the Jameses pales to a dim trail. They are supposed to have ridden down through western Iowa a part of the way and down through eastern Nebraska for some distance. A cock-and-bull fabrication of the fictionists has it that they made their way down into Mexico and had startling adventures, romantic, gory, and movie-glorious. The strong probability is that they went, traveling by train from some point in Iowa or Nebraska and sleeping comfortably in Pullman berths, to Nashville, Tennessee, in or near which city the brothers had been living for many months under assumed names. The only son of Jesse James states that he was born at Nashville on Aug. 31, 1875.

It is not to be understood that the Minnesotans

pursued the Jameses beyond the state line. Picked men took up the chase of the pair from the point where Roberts challenged them. Scouting parties at points far ahead were on the watch. But the capture of the first span of grays gave the Clay County brothers a vast advantage. None of the possemen caught up with the fugitives, or if any of the pursuers encountered them at all they were misled by the Jameses' pretended rôle of being out chasing themselves, so to express it. Like Cole Younger, both were excellent actors. One of the divertisements most richly enjoyed by Jesse, throughout his career as a hunted outlaw, was that of pretending to be an officer on his own trail. This helped him to elude the real officers, and Jesse had the joy of the joke to boot.

Just a week after the chase was centered upon the Jameses, another big cartridge of news popped wide open in southern Minnesota. The other four had not escaped from the state, after all! They had been seen in the vicinity of the small village of Madelia in the northeast corner of Watonwan County. This place, the name of which has come down to history in tragic association with the well-known Missouri surname Younger, is about twenty-five miles southeast of Mankato.

Some days before the raid at Northfield, Cole Younger and Sam Wells had visited Madelia on a prospecting tour. They had stopped over Sunday at the Flanders House, kept by Col. Thomas L. Vought, a genial gentleman who made friends with his hotel guests. Younger, who registered as J. C. King, asked the landlord many questions concerning the neighborhood. Mr. King admired beautiful scenery. The adjacent lake region charmed him. He seemed to know quite a good deal about that general region, and Colonel Vought obligingly made him further acquainted with its topography and its geography. He impressed the colonel as a highly intelligent, affable, desirable citizen. Both Mr. King and his traveling companion, registered as Jack Ladd, rode fine horses and wore long linen dusters. Sam Wells, as we perceive, had assumed the farmhand name of the Pinkerton operative who worked for Farmer Daniel Askew during the months preceding the hand-grenade assault upon the mother of the Jameses and her children.

"Aha!" quoth Colonel Vought when he read about the Northfield affair; "my agreeable friend Mr. King and his friend Mr. Ladd are two of the linen-dustered gentry that did the bad business at Northfield. I can see now why Mr. King was so deeply interested in this section: he was figuring out a line of retreat."

Colonel Vought was wide awake. Also, he was a fighter. He had won his military title in the Civil War, and he was young enough to fight some more if necessary. He recalled that Mr. King had been especially interested in a highway which crossed a bridge between two lakes about eight miles from Madelia. With two other men the colonel went to this bridge and stood guard for a couple of nights. The bridge was an important station on the long picket line.

Both evenings when Vought and his companions were on guard at the bridge, a bright lad of seventeen named Oscar Suborn, whose name survives in outlaw history as the Paul Revere of the celebrated man-hunt, visited the picket station and sat chatting with the men.

Oscar lived with his father, a Norwegian farmer, not far from the bridge.

The colonel told Oscar how the two suspects he had entertained looked, and gave the boy further information calculated to aid in identifying members of the gang who might happen along that way.

"Gee!" remarked Oscar, "I'd love to take a shot at those fellows with Dad's old gun."

"You can help by keeping a sharp lookout," Colonel Vought told him. "If you see anybody you think might be the bandits, be sure to come into town and tell me at once."

Oscar promised. Early Thursday morning, Sept. 21, two men walked past the Suborn barnyard, where Oscar and his father were milking the cows. "Good morning," they said as they passed near Oscar.

"Say, Dad, there goes the robbers!" Oscar whispered.

"You're foolish, Oscar; go ahead with the milking."

"But that's them—I know it must be."

The excited youth quit his work and ran to the house. There he learned that four men, including the two who had greeted him, had stopped there a short time before. They had said they were on a fishing trip and wanted to buy some food. Four of them! Oscar told his father he had promised to report to Colonel Vought. The elder Suborn still was incredulous, but finally he consented for Oscar to take a horse and ride to Madelia.

The midmorn ride of Oscar Suborn still is remembered by oldtimers in that vicinity. Mounted upon an old farm plug, he used both switch and vocal persuasion, urging the animal to do his utmost. Shouting as he passed houses and people, "The robbers are near here!

Look out for the robbers!" he made the eight miles in marvelous time for such a sorry mount. When near Madelia the poor old horse stumbled and fell. Oscar pitched off into the soft and saving mud. Up again, on again, gone again!

Colonel Vought stood upon the front veranda of his hotel as Oscar drew rein. Both horse and rider were splashed with mud, both were panting.

"I saw 'em, Colonel! The robbers!"

Minnesota's Paul Revere was justified in his identification. After a brief talk with the lad, Colonel Vought picked up his rifle and rode swiftly to the Suborn farmhouse, accompanied by Sheriff James Glispin of Watonwan County, who happened to arrive during the conversation. S. J. Severson, W. J. Estes and Dr. Overholt, all of Madelia, also were of the party. Three other Madelians, Capt. W. W. Murphy, G. A. Bradford and C. A. Pomeroy, presently heard the startling news and made haste to get to Suborn's place. Already the boy's tidings were on the wires; and from the nearby town of St. James went B. M. Rice and G. S. Thompson to join the others near Suborn's farm.

Seven of the men just named became, that day, the captors of the three Youngers, after a last-stand battle.

CHAPTER XXII

THE THREE YOUNGERS SHOT DOWN AND CAPTURED

A T last this man-hunt of measurably Homeric proportions was at perihelion point. Fate fast was closing in upon the remaining half of the octet of rough riders from Missouri. Four stalwart men from Jackson County were about to be caught in the fell clutch of circumstance. Three of them, scions of a proud and once-prosperous family, whose deeds had made the Younger surname a symbol of terror throughout the nation, awaited but the ultimate assault upon their final and pitiful citadel of defense; and the fourth, Samuel Wells of Independence, who had ridden and robbed under the alias of Charlie Pitts, was under immediate compulsion to take his bitter medicine along with the others. In his case, however, the medicine was to be perhaps more merciful—a fatal dose of hot lead.

When the men from Madelia and St. James reached the vicinity of Suborn's farm they found many others gathering in the same general neighborhood. Parties of pursuers had heard the news of Oscar Suborn's report to Colonel Vought and had come riding in from various directions. The far-flung picket line was breaking up, its group units massing into an army of respectable size and converging upon the closing scene of violence.

The men from Madelia soon found the footsore fugitives. Vought and his friends saw them toiling painfully through a mucky morass known as Hanska Slough. The biggest of the bandits limped along, supporting himself with a stout stick cut from a sapling. All were unkempt and dirty. Their clothing was wet and tattered, and you may be sure that the conspicuous linen dusters had been discarded early in the flight.

"Halt!" shouted Sheriff Glispin.

The men kept going. The little posse fired a volley. The Missourians accelerated their progress, slightly, and took momentary refuge behind a knoll. Then, calculating their chances, they waded across a large and shallow body of water called Lake Hanska.

Unable to persuade their horses through the lake, the Madelians searched for fords above and below. Reaching the other side, Vought and Dr. Overholt glimpsed the robbers. Overholt fired at the big man. The bullet struck Cole Younger's walking-stick, knocking it from his grasp.

Richard the Third offered his kingdom for a horse. The four Democrats from Missouri probably approved the royal feeling at that moment, and if so they multiplied the number of mounts by four. A pastured herd of horses on a farm close by attracted their attention. They were making for the pasture when the Madelia men, with Sheriff Glispin and others who had come up, cut in between the bandits and the coveted beasts.

The Missourians fired a volley at the Minnesotans. The sheriff's horse was grazed by a leaden missile. Down the bank of the Watonwan river ran the desperate quartet, to a point opposite a farmhouse. They had observed a team of horses there. The farmer was outdoors. All pursuers at this moment were some distance away.

"Bring your horses over," called out one of the pursued. "We're after the bank robbers, and we want to borrow your horses."

It was too late in the game for that pretense to work. The farmer drove his team in the opposite direction. Finding a ford upstream, the four men waded across the river and approached two men from St. Paul, Horace Thompson and his son, at a hunting camp. The Thompsons had two teams which they had hired from a livery stable belonging to Colonel Vought. Four horses—four men! The four men made a dash for the four horses. But when they saw the Thompsons unloading their guns of small birdshot and reloading with big shot meant for wild geese—although of course the bandits could but surmise the exact nature of the ammunition exchange—they turned back and made for a brushy region in the river bottom.

This place was the seat of their final disaster.

A tangled growth of wild grapevines, willows, box-elders and wild plums covered most of a roughly triangular area of about five acres. Here and there were open spots. The ground was almost level. From one side arose a high bluff, along the other side ran the river. Curves of river and bluff almost enclosed the triangle. In this thicket the quarry was driven to bay.

Groups of exultant man-hunters gathered on both sides of the river. Those upon the bluff could look down into the thicket. Victor Hugo said that the French at Sedan were pounded to pieces in a mortar.

The last-stand fortress of the Missourians was something like a mortar, with the bluff curving like a bowl almost half-way around. The possemen on the crest probably could have wiped out the robbers by down-firing.

But it remained for a charge by seven gallant citizens, across the level ground of the triangle below, to achieve the victory. The sheriff and Colonel Vought posted guards on the bluff at a point where a possible escape might be effected through a ravine. Captain Murphy, a former Pennsylvanian who had been brevetted for gallantry on a Civil War battlefield in Virginia, placed strong guard lines on the other side of the river and then crossed over to the edge of the triangle.

"I propose," he said to the sheriff and others gathered near by, "that we go in now and rout them out of the brush."

Enough men to rout out a platoon of soldiers volunteered. However, most of these backtracked when Captain Murphy outlined his plan of battle. Six stalwarts stood firm. One of these was the sheriff, who yielded command to the courageous and capable captain. Here are the names of the seven who undertook and accomplished the final overthrow of the Youngers:

Capt. William W. Murphy, Sheriff James Glispin, Col. Thomas L. Vought, Benjamin M. Rice, George A. Bradford, Charles A. Pomeroy, S. J. Severson. These names make up Madelia's scroll of fame.

"Now, men," said Captain Murphy, "we are to form in line about eight feet apart, advance rapidly but hold the line formation, and the very instant that we glimpse the bandits we are to fire along the whole line."

The Missourians were invisible in the thick jungle, but their approximate location was known to the seven. Some of Captain Murphy's men had rifles, others carried sixshooters. They separated, four paces apart, and faced the thicket.

"Are you all ready?"

"Ready!"

"Forward!"

Forward, at quick trot, moved the stalwart seven. Having advanced about 200 feet, the ferrets saw their quarry crouched beneath shrubs and vines. One of the robbers fired a shot at a member of the advancing line. Instantly the seven drew beads and touched triggers. Their volley was returned by the four in the thicket. The Madelians kept rushing forward, firing as they ran. When the man at the center of the line was within 30 feet of the bandits the final volleys were exchanged.

Short and snappy was the engagement. Captain Murphy, seeing that all four of the enemy were prone, gave order to cease firing. Some of the stricken outlaws were writhing. One lay quite still, sprawled on the damp ground.

"Surrender, men!" called the commander of the line, wherein stood each man with weapon ready for further use.

Bob Younger arose slowly from the ground, sixshooter in left hand, bandaged right arm across his chest.

"I surrender," he said, weakly; "they're all down but me."

"Drop your weapon, then."

He dropped it.

Sharpshooters on the bluff, who had located the position of the enemy through the smoke from Missouri pistols, misinterpreted Younger's movements; some of them fired at him, inflicting a slight wound. Captain Murphy lifted a hand in protest. He lifted his voice, too:

"Cease firing! Stop it, up there, you men! It's all over!"

They stopped it.

And so, at last, 'twas all over.

Murphy and his men went forward into the jungle, scraping through the brush, fingers on triggers. Sam Wells lay dead, five bullets having marked him. Bob Younger had a wound in the breast, in addition to the one that had shattered his right elbow at Northfield. Jim Younger's wounds were five, including the one received at Northfield and a fresh one which crushed his upper jaw. Cole Younger was bleeding from no less than eleven wounds, most of which he got from the Murphy line.

Thomas Coleman Younger, who looked like a bishop and fought like a Bengal tiger, lay upon the ground soaked with rainfall and with his own blood—and smiled as he saw approaching him Colonel Vought of the Flanders House at Madelia, hot rifle in hand.

"How are you, Landlord?" was the feeble yet cheerful greeting from the colonel's recent guest.

"How are you, Mr. King?" was all the landlord could think to say—with the accent heavy on the you.

Sam Wells also might have recognized his recent landlord had the late Mr. "Jack Ladd" been still alive.

Sheriff Glispin formally placed the three survivors under arrest. Their arsenal of sidearms was transferred to official possession. The sixshooters, eight in number, including the dead man's pair, were in shipshape condition. Those fellows made pets of their metallic protectors. When the body of Wells was searched, the pistol he had snatched up in the Northfield bank, as Teller Bunker was reaching for it under the counter, was found in a pocket. That was "the little derringer" with which Bunker couldn't do any damage anyhow, as Sam Wells had told him at the time. Wells probably intended to take it back home as a souvenir.

Many members of the army of man-hunters made their way to the place of the overthrow and gazed curiously at the dead man and the wounded. Murphy and Glispin ordered them to stand back. A wagon was brought forward. The corpse and the three Youngers were lifted into the bed of the vehicle.

"Drive to Madelia," was the sheriff's instruction.

The victorious seven served as escort. Before the triumphant cavalcade reached town it was met by a large squad of men who had come to Madelia by special train to assist in the final assault. They turned about and accompanied the wagon to the Flanders House, where Cole Younger again became a guest of the landlord who had helped to capture him. The three brothers were put to bed and surgeons were called in to dress their many wounds. Their torn and bloodstained garments were ripped off, clean clothing was put on them. Food was given the wellnigh famished captives—their first adequate meal in a fortnight.

Despite their terrible suffering, the men seemed fairly cheerful. Each expressed deep gratitude for the kindnesses received, though Jim Younger could speak only in guttural whispers. They had expected nothing gentler than lynching, and they said so. Throngs of people came from various towns and from the outlying countryside to see the notorious prisoners. From the Twin Cities of Minnesota and from other large cities in the northern Mississippi Valley came newspaper photographers and reporters. Detectives, including a Pinkerton or two, visited Madelia to make sure that these were the Younger brothers.

When asked who they were, the three requested permission for a brief conference in private. This was granted. Then they told their names.

"And who's the dead man?" detectives inquired.

"We refuse to say, gentlemen," Cole Younger replied.

"The two members of your party killed at Northfield —who were they?"

"Again, we refuse to say."

"Well, then, tell us who the men are that got away— the other two, won't you?"

"We have agreed not to tell that, gentlemen."

"They are Frank and Jesse James, are they not?"

"They are not the Jameses," answered Cole Younger, "but further than that we shall say nothing."

Nor ever, to the days of their several deaths, did either of the Youngers give anybody the name of either of their five companions. But Chief of Police James McDonough of St. Louis and other police officials and detectives visited Northfield and Madelia, bringing means of definite identification of the three slain bandits —Stiles, Miller and Wells.

Two days after the capture Sheriff Barton of Rice County appeared in Madelia and took the prisoners to Faribault, his county seat, placed them in jail and put a strong guard in and around the building. This was done to discourage possible mobs.

At both Madelia and Faribault the Youngers talked freely about themselves. They expressed keen regret because the family name had been dishonored through their deeds; but they contended that they had become victims of circumstances and that their outlaw activities had been always in opposition to their own inclinations. They insisted that they never had been criminals at heart. They were in no sense boastful or scornful; to the contrary, they seemed contrite, and they requested that good people pray for them.

Within a few weeks the prisoners were able to walk about in their cells, though still suffering from their wounds. On the 9th of November they were shackled together, Cole between his younger brothers, and escorted under a strong guard to the county courthouse for trial.

Indictments by the grand jury charged all of them with being accessories to the murder of Acting Cashier Heywood; with attacking Teller Bunker with intent to do great bodily harm; and with robbing the First National Bank at Northfield. A fourth count in the bill of indictment charged Cole Younger as principal, and his two brothers as accessories, with the murder of Nicholas Gustavson, the Swede.

Judge Samuel Lord presided, Prosecutor G. N.

Baxter appearing for the state. In the courtroom, weeping, were Mrs. Fannie Twyman and Miss Retta Younger of Jackson County, Missouri, aunt and sister of the prisoners. They had reached Faribault the day before and had made a most favorable impression by their ladylike bearing and their evident refinement. Retta Younger, a beautiful girl of seventeen, sobbed piteously when she greeted her brothers. They were affected deeply.

Counsel for the accused requested that they be accorded two days in which to make decision as to their plea in answer to the indictment. This was granted. At the expiration of that period they pleaded guilty as charged. Conviction being a certainty, but for the plea of guilty they would have been sentenced to death. Under the Minnesota law of that time an alleged murderer who pleaded guilty could not be condemned to the gallows.

Judge Lord sentenced the three Youngers to imprisonment for life in the state prison at Stillwater. A few days later they entered the penitentiary. Robert Younger served out his time: he died in prison Sept. 16, 1889, nearly thirteen years later, from tuberculosis, his prison deportment being perfect. He was buried beside his mother in the family plot in the cemetery at Lee's Summit, Missouri, the old home town.

Coleman and James Younger—well, that's a different sort of story, and a most remarkable one, to be told later in this chronicle.

CHAPTER XXIII

THE CLEW OF THE RED BANDANNA IN NEBRASKA

ALMOST exactly a year after the Northfield raid and its tragic results, a group of men rode into the county-seat town of Ogallala, Keith County, Nebraska, far out on the plains. The horsemen were seven. They told citizens of Ogallala that they were stockmen who had ridden up from Texas, disposing of a bunch of cattle on the way. They might buy a new bunch of steers, they said. These men, all of whom were garbed in frontier cowboy fashion, made camp not far outide the town. Two or three of them visited the general store of F. M. Leech, in Ogallala.

"Why, hello, Jim!" Leech called out.

"Hello yourself; didn't know you were keeping this outfit."

"Yes, I'm the boss," replied Leech; "but I never expected to see Jim Berry out here. Where all you been, Jim, lately?"

"Oh, just cruising around. Been up to the Black Hills, for one place, and got me a nice little bunch o' gold dust. Think maybe I'll feel rich enough pretty soon now to take a trip back to old Callaway. Wife and children still there, on the old farm."

"What you doing now, Jim?"

"I'm in the cow game."

Merchant Leech was not particularly glad to see James Berry, whom he had known up at Plattsmouth as "Bad Jim." He had not known, until Berry mentioned it, that his visitor's old home was in Callaway County, Missouri. The "Kingdom of Callaway," far removed from the Jesse James country proper, was and remains one of the most progressive counties in northern Missouri. It is the original home and haunt of the far-famed Missouri mule. In Jim Berry's time and for many years thereafter the chief industry other than farming was the culture of the highbred jackass and his mating with mares no whit less patrician. His issue crossed the seven seas and brayed and balked, in peace and war, in every so-called civilized land. Callaway County mules became almost as widely known as did Clay County bandits.

Jim Berry had become, since he left his Missouri home, a somewhat boisterous Wild Westerner, but up to the time when he dropped into Leech's store he had not been known as a downright devil of a bold bad man. "Bad Jim" didn't signify so much as that.

Berry bought six big red bandanna handkerchiefs from Leech. It was a purchase common to the plains country, yet in that instance it was loaded with the dynamite of doom for several men. Moreover, the simple transaction was to prove to the world that a general merchant in a county town out on the Wild West prairies is excellent raw material for the making of a fairly shrewd private detective in the public interest.

Some miles west of Ogallala was a station called Big Springs, where Union Pacific railway trains in those days stopped for water. A couple of days after Leech and Berry renewed their acquaintance-ship, the east-bound Pacific express halted at the Big Springs tank. Dusk was settling down on the wide-spread prairies. Beyond the right-of-way the coyote was beginning to set up his dismal nocturnal howling. It was an eerie twilight scene.

Seven men arose from the sunburned grass, some on one side of the train, some on the other. All were masked with red bandannas. Each held a sixshooter in his right hand; several displayed a similar weapon in the left hand.

"Hands up, and step down, lively!" commanded one gruff voice.

The engineer and his fireman obeyed. For the time being four men stood by to guard the engine crew. A fifth uphanded the train conductor, who had stepped outside to learn what was up. The remaining two went through the day coaches and the Pullman sleepers, one of them carrying a wheat sack. Each held a weapon ready for wicked business.

"Hand over whatever you've got!"

Many of the passengers, men and women alike, gave up what they had. Some of them surrendered even bunches of keys. Whatever they contributed was tossed into the sack. In the meantime some of the other bandits entered the express car and ordered the Wells-Fargo messenger to open his safe. He complied. The contents that looked like money were dumped into another wheat sack. Much of this loot was in gold coin.

"Take it away now!" the leader of the freebooter band sang out to the engineer. "Good night, good luck!"

The engineer took it away at a speed exceeding schedule, making up most of the lost time before he shut throttle at Ogallala. There the news of the holdup was put on the wires. Towns east, west, north, south were warned to look out for seven suspicious strangers.

"We heard 'em," said the conductor to the telegraph operator, "loping away toward the south, but they may have turned tail and gone in any other direction."

"Must have been the James gang—what do you think?" suggested the operator.

"Who knows?" responded the conductor. "They've never operated this far west before, so far as I know, but that wheat-sack business makes it look like those Missouri fellows."

Ogallala was more than a trifle slow in starting pursuit. Nobody took the lead until early next morning, which was the 18th day of September, 1877.

"Them there cowboys camping out by the Platte ____"

"Sure! Let's take a look."

Three or four citizens rode out to the camp. They were all there, the seven stockmen, just beginning to fry bacon. They greeted their unexpected visitors with the common cordiality of the plainsman.

"Heard the news?" one of the Ogallalans asked.

"News? What news?"

It was Jim Berry speaking. The rest of the campers seemed to show a mild interest. Two or three edged closer to the men on horseback.

"Why, men, the U. P. express was held up and robbed at Big Springs last night, and ——" .

"The devil it was!" ejaculated Berry. "Who-all done it?"

"Who knows?"

The conductor's comment repeated! The James boys were mentioned by one of the Ogallala men as possible contenders for the doubtful honor.

"Oh, well, you can't never tell," Jim Berry said. "Started any chase yet?"

"Making ready to, right off."

"You'd better hurry," advised Jim Berry.

The citizens returned to town.

"Shucks!" they reported; "them cowboys didn't have nothing to do with it; they're too all-fired lazy and trifling."

At last a leader appeared. Leech the storekeeper evinced more activity, both mental and physical, than any other denizen of the somewhat somnolent place. By common consent he took things in hand. Shortly before the belated posse was organized, Jim Berry came lounging along the street. He said to Leech:

"I heard you was about to lead a chase after them train robbers. That right?"

"Sure is; and if I don't catch 'em it won't be my fault."

"Maybe you might like to have me come along and help?"

"First rate idea; come right along, Jim."

"Got to go back to camp first and let the boys know. Maybe some o' them'll join your posse, too."

Leech waited an hour or so and started forth without Berry.

"I told you so," said one of the men who had visited the camp that morning; "them fellers are too lazy to join any excitement."

Leech had a theory that the robbers had operated from Sidney, beyond Big Springs. A special train was provided for his posse. On the way to Sidney he stopped off at Big Springs to inspect the scene of the robbery. Leech had read about detectives searching anywhere and everywhere on premises where a crime had been committed. He bethought himself to emulate the professionals and look for clews. But he was about to reboard his special when the toe of his boot accidentally kicked up a small piece of red cotton rag. It fluttered for an instant in the breeze. Leech suddenly recalled his sale of six red bandannas to Jim Berry.

The posse chief stealthily stuck the red rag into a pocket and kept his mouth shut. The boys might laugh at him, call him a would-be detective, and Leech hated to be laughed at. Besides, that little old piece of cloth might mean nothing of importance in the case, after all. Ordering his train to Sidney, he got off and made inquiries. Nobody had seen any strangers about for a week.

"Not a soul that anybody might suspicion of doing such a job," said the town marshal, in plains parlance.

"Run back to Ogallala," Leech instructed his conductor.

"Not giving it up, Mr. Leech, are you?"

"Not exactly—wait and see."

Leech was not loquacious. Back in Ogallala he commandeered a saddled horse that was tied to a rack in front of the courthouse and rode swiftly to the camp of the seven cattlemen. He found the place abandoned. Lying about was a lot of refuse. Leech dismounted and poked about in this. A glimpse of red fascinated his gaze. He picked up a large piece of red cotton cloth, pulled the Big Springs rag from his pocket, smoothed out both on the ground.

The ragged edges fitted together neatly!

"One o' those fellows," mused Leech, "must have had a mighty small face, for he seems to have used only about two-fifths of this bandanna from my store to mask his features with."

Simultaneously Mr. Leech did some more musing, to the effect that M. F. Leech of Ogallala was more or less of a confounded jackass.

"Why in Sam Hill didn't I have sense enough to suspicion these men right in the first place? Seven masked men with red bandannas. Seven men in this cowboy camp. Six red bandannas sold to a member of this camp. But somehow I never felt that Bad Jim Berry had it in him to help rob a train. Well, I reckon I'm a rather rotten detective, but all the same I'm dead sure I'm on the right trail at last."

Even Sherlock Holmes, had he been operating in those troublous times and in western Nebraska, must have agreed with Mr. Leech as to his being on the right trail. The amateur sleuth warmed up to his task. The hoofmarks of the horses told the direction in which the seven had flown. All alone, Leech followed the trail, southwestwardly into Kansas. If they kept on in that direction the robbers would cross the Kansas Pacific tracks at Buffalo Station in Gove County, the third county south of the Nebraska line. The distance to that point was about one hundred miles. Leech wired his theory to Buffalo Station and kept on trailing the seven.

After a few hours' hard riding the Ogallala man found it wise to rein in his horse with a jerk. Not far in front was a group of horsemen, watering their mounts at a trickle of a creek. They rode on, hell-to-split, over the prairie. Why should honest men be in such a devil of a hurry? Leech rode on, keeping at a discreet distance. Once when the men in front turned out along a barb-wire fence he came perilously near to being seen by them. He was so close that he could count them—seven.

"They'd eat me alive," said Leech to himself.

Farther along the riders stopped in a ravine, the dry bed of a stream where water flowed in season. They dismounted. Leech alighted too, and peered over the back of his weary steed. He was near enough to discover, from certain gestures, that the seven were dividing their Big Springs loot. He saw what appeared to be a wheat sack—yes, two wheat sacks—being handled by the men. But why hadn't they split their booty last night in camp? Well, who knows?

Up and off went the seven riders. Up and after

them went the single horseman—keeping far back. In the ravine he looked for empty wheat sacks. Not a sack visible. The robbers had had sense enough not to leave such a clew. Leech presently lost the trail and returned home.

Leech's telegram to Buffalo Station proved fatal to a couple of men, supposed to be of the robber gang, who passed through that place. A local posse followed, there was a short, sharp battle between bandit pistols and citizen rifles, a few miles below. Both of the fugitives were killed. One was identified as Billy Heffridge, known as a bad man from Pennsylvania. The other was said to be one Jim Collins, antecedents not known definitely.

A second pair of the fugitives made their way into Texas, crossing the Kansas Pacific west of Buffalo Station. These men were Sam Bass and Jack Davis. More than a year later, Bass was slain by Texas Rangers who pursued him for alleged crimes committed in the northwestern part of the Lone Star state. Davis, who hailed from Fort Smith, Arkansas, disappeared into the unknown.

Of the remaining three, only one ever turned up for identification. That one was Jim Berry, who returned to his native Callaway County about two weeks after the Big Springs holdup. Amateur Detective Leech, remembering Berry's statement that he hoped soon to revisit the old home, had wired Callaway County officials to expect his arrival.

Berry first was seen at Mexico, Missouri, in the county adjoining Callaway on the north. Robert Arnold, cashier of a Mexico bank, was not aware that

Jim was wanted. The wanderer visited the bank and had Arnold accommodate him with some greenbacks in exchange for a considerable sum in gold. Berry already had told some Mexico acquaintances that he had made a big strike in the Black Hills. After getting the greenbacks he went along Saloon Row and indulged freely in whisky. Then he visited the town's leading tailor, leaving an order for a costly suit of clothes. Berry paid down a deposit.

Before completely sobering up, the returned native went to the farm in his own county where he had left his family. He told Mrs. Berry that he had struck it rich in the gold diggings and had so much money that all of them could afford to dress well. When fully sobered he repented of his start toward fashionable apparel in such an incautious manner. But he was determined to have that new suit. He wrote an order for the clothes and sent a friend named Bozeman Kazey to get them.

In the meantime Sheriff Glasscock of Audrain County, of which Mexico is the capital, had learned that Jim Berry was suspected of complicity in the Nebraska train robbery. He compared notes with the bank cashier, the tailor and others. Kazey was arrested when he called for Berry's new suit.

Sheriff Glasscock determined to go into Callaway and catch Berry, the Union Pacific Railroad Company having offered a handsome reward. He deputized three adventurous citizens and took Kazey along as guide. Kazey admitted that Berry was at the Kazey homestead waiting for his clothes. The party rode all night. About daybreak they came in sight of Kazey's house, tied the guide to a tree, and approached the place.

"Now if Jim Berry tries to escape," instructed the sheriff, "we are to order him to halt; if he won't halt, shoot him through the legs. Let's take him alive."

Off in the woods a horse neighed. Glasscock and one of his deputies went in the direction of the neighing. The horse snorted. The sheriff went down on hands and knees and crept cautiously through the underbrush. A man was trying to untie the animal. When the slip-noose was loosed, he began leading the horse directly toward Glasscock, who arose to his feet and ordered the man to halt. The latter dropped the bridle-reins and ran. The sheriff fired one shot wild. His second shot struck the fleeing man in the left leg. With seven buckshot in his leg, near the hip, the man fell prone. He drew his sixshooter and was on the point of firing when Glasscock and his deputy rushed up and disarmed him.

It was Jim Berry, of course. In a belt beneath his outer clothing the officers found $2,500, in his pocketbook $300. A costly gold watch and chain also were on his person. Berry was taken to Mexico, where he was placed in a room at the Ringo House, the pioneer hotel. Surgical attention relieved his sufferings to some extent, but three days later he died, partly from loss of blood and partly from acute alcoholism. Diligent questioning failed to wring from his lips a word concerning the Big Springs affair.

Third victim of the bandanna clew, fifth man in the Nebraska robbery accounted for: what of the two who got away?

"Why, Frank and Jesse James, of course," surmised and said citizens here, there and yonder. "Too cute for the posses, just as they were after the Northfield raid in Minnesota last year. Who else could they have been but Jesse and Frank?"

The story of the Union Pacific holdup is told here not because of any belief on the writer's part that the Jameses were at Big Springs, but merely to illustrate the graceful facility of the general public in attributing every crime of that character to Jesse and his brother.

Wherever a wheat sack was used in stowing the loot of a robbery, the public and the Pinkertons leaped at the conclusion that the James boys were on the job again. Border banditry began at Liberty, their home county seat, with a wheat sack as visible symbol. It is not to be disputed that wheat sacks appeared several times in later years in connection with robberies in which the Clay countians took part. Still, almost anybody might think up the idea of a wheat sack, particularly after somebody has used it first.

Reasoning from certain facts which would require too much space in the explaining, your outlaw historian is decidedly of the opinion that neither Frank nor Jesse had anything to do with the Big Springs affair. One who has studied the careers of the Jameses with more or less assiduity for some years cannot fail to have constructed a rather intangible tangle of evidence calculated to acquit these Missourians of complicity in an adventure such as the Union Pacific train holdup. Nevertheless, the record seems to belong to this narrative for the reasons stated.

CHAPTER XXIV

THAT fact is stranger than fiction every professional writer who is measurably honest will admit, at least to himself. By way of illustration it may be permissible to introduce here an incident in coincidence that bears important relation to the creation of this chapter, which has to do with the whereabouts of Jesse James in the long interval between the escape from Minnesota and the resumption of train-robbing in Missouri. More than three years elapsed before the king-bee bandit reappeared in any conspicuous outlaw activities.

Where was Jesse James during those three years, and where was Frank James?

Although this outlaw epic about Missourians is the work of a Missourian (anti-outlaw brand, if you please), up to this point it has been written in Far-South Florida, just across the drive from the Atlantic Ocean. The mellifluous rhythm of the tropical surf serves to soften somewhat the harsher sounds of cracking Winchesters and popping Colts which needs must punctuate the narrative in many places. It is not advisable, I may insinuate, for any historian of banditry to select for studio, let us say, a boiler factory: the task smacks of such violence in its very nature that some serene retreat is indicated.

History is not necessarily a thing dead and desiccated: at times it proves to be a breathing entity. Yet it is not often that a section of the living article stalks unexpectedly into the ken of the historian at the precise moment when he needs just that to fill a gap in his chronicle. Here, however, is a striking instance of that kind.

Immediately across the corridor in this apartment-house at Miami Beach sojourns for the time being a courtly Southerner of four score years. All the inches of a soldier appear unmistakably in his aspect. An old-school Southron and a gallant participant in battles long ago is Mr. James Koger of Paducah, Kentucky, formerly of Nashville, Tennessee, and now and then of St. Louis. Early in 1865, after four years of fighting with the Confederate army, he surrendered with the rest of Gen. Joseph E. Johnston's decimated forces. Beginning some years after the war closed, for two decades he was general manager and one of the owners of the St. Louis and Tennessee River Packet Company, which operates freight and passenger steamboats on the Mississippi and the Tennessee, with headquarters at St. Louis. Polite and polished, Mr. Koger impresses one as a natural-born gentleman, a citizen whose word is to be accepted at par.

For several weeks I had known Mr. Koger without suspecting that he was to have anything to do with this outlaw opus. Our pleasant conversations had been of a general nature—the romantic old days on the rivers, contemporary politics, Florida grapefruit and climate. Anent my present writing task I had told him nothing; nor had I mentioned in his presence the name of Jesse James or that of any other bold bad man. The housekeeper, however, had discovered the incriminating character of my employment. Rushing in one day, she cried:

"Why, Mr. Koger knew Jesse James—knew him well, for years—he saved a man's life once, a man Jesse James was about to kill!"

"And how did you learn all that?"

"Well, I—you see, I told him you were writing a life of Jesse James, or something of the sort, and then he told me about knowing that terrible man."

Forthwith to Mr. Koger posted your chronicler. The Paducan was positively the last living man anybody could suspect of having known Jesse James. Erect as a sycamore sapling, hale and hearty despite his years, mild-mannered as a high-born lady, courteous and kindly and charming, Mr. Koger became to me a distinct surprise, as well as an asset of some immediate value; for one of the most difficult tasks I have encountered in this work is that of filling in veraciously the so-called "missing years" in the career of Jesse James, and it turned out that those were the very years during which the now retired riverman knew the then retired—temporarily—bandit.

"Yes, I knew him—knew him rather well—for several years," said Mr. Koger, "beginning, if my memory be not at fault, in 1876. I made the acquaintance of Jesse James in Tennessee, when I was living at Nashville. I knew him in that city, and also in Humphreys

County, to the west, where he lived for a couple of years on a farm in the Big Bottom country.

"Of course, though, I did not know him as Jesse James. His name in Tennessee was Howard—J. D. Howard. I was connected with the grain and flour business of which the late Isaac T. Rhea was the head. It was an old establishment in Nashville.

"Mr. Howard was a young man, about thirty, I should say, with full-face whiskers of a dark brown color, worn rather short. He had snappy blue eyes. His face was of the roundish pattern, with a sort of stubby nose. He was not a large man, as I recall— medium height and weight. He dressed well and was a fairly good-looking fellow, and good natured enough except when he got excited. He seemed to have a very hot temper.

"One day another man I knew—he was living in a Nashville suburb—came into the office of Mr. Rhea when J. D. Howard was present. This man's name was Woodson—B. J. Woodson, if I recall his initials correctly. He was a tall man, apparently a few years older than Howard. Woodson also had blue eyes, but his face was of the angular type, and in build he was rather thin. He wore beard of the sideburn cut, with smooth chin. His sideburns and moustache were of a sandy color, as was his hair. There was absolutely no point of resemblance between Howard and Woodson.

"Both of those men had business dealings with the Rhea house. Howard bought a considerable lot of stuff, Woodson not so much. I believe Woodson was engaged in teaming, hauling sawlogs or something of that sort. Howard had a bunch of steers and several horses, and he bought a good deal of feed for them.

"When Woodson happened in that day, Mr. Rhea was talking with Howard. He called Woodson over to his desk and remarked:

"'I reckon you gentlemen are not acquainted. Mr. Woodson, this is Mr. Howard.'

"The two men shook hands, said they were glad to meet each other, and uttered further formal remarks common to such an occasion. One of them, as I seem to remember, remarked to the other that it looked like it might rain before night. The weather, as you know, is always a life-saver when strangers are introduced.

"Neither of the men gave the slightest indication of ever having seen or heard of the other. Woodson asked Howard what business he was in, and Howard replied that he was farming and raising cattle on a small scale. They stood chatting with Mr. Rhea for a time—talking crops, business, politics a little. Mr. Woodson and Mr. Howard proved to be strong Democrats.

"Ben Cornelius, the bookkeeper, told me shortly afterward what the two strangers thus casually introduced did immediately after they got through talking with Mr. Rhea.

"'It seemed odd to me,' said Cornelius, 'that those men, Howard and Woodson, went back of a high stack of sacked grain and talked together, in low tones, for pretty close to an hour, I should say. They'd never met before, you know, and I wonder what the dickens they had to talk about so long and so privately.'

"Well, after Jesse James was killed, some years later, we understood that incident considerably better. B. J. Woodson, it turned out, was Jesse's brother Frank.

"Woodson, as I knew him, was a quiet-spoken, modest sort of man, intelligent, interested in everyday affairs—just the average type of citizen one meets anywhere.

"Part of my business was to visit certain outlying towns for the firm. These duties took me frequently to Waverly and Humphreys counties, to the towns of Waverly and Box Station on the Nashville, Chattanooga & St. Louis Railroad. Box Station now is called Denver. It was a small village, and J. D. Howard lived for a time on a rented farm in the Big Bottom region close by. He got his mail at Box Station. I met him often there, and sometimes at Waverly, when I was out on my business trips. As he was a customer of our firm I cultivated his acquaintance to some extent.

"Howard had some racehorses on his farm, and he had fixed up a sort of temporary track on which races were run. He associated with some gamblers of notorious reputation, who also were interested in horseracing. I recall that one of them tried to cheat Howard out of a race in which the wager was $500. Howard got hopping mad. He rode up to the miscreant and plucked out a big pistol.

"'Hand over that money,' he demanded, 'or you'll be a dead man in two seconds!'

"The cheater handed over the cash, and Howard cooled down. Howard also played poker with the gamblers, and frequently with neighbors, but he nearly always lost. He was from Missouri, where draw poker is supposed to be the national game, but he couldn't win very often. The men he played with said he always played on the square, and if anybody tried to cheat, Mr. Howard got quite indignant.

"When I learned of Howard's intimacy with the crooked gambling fraternity I didn't approve of his cronies, and I told Mr. Rhea that I didn't think he ought to have much to do with that man Howard. A good while after I had warned Mr. Rhea not to trust him too much, the man from Big Bottom came to Nashville. He was leaving the farm, and as it turned out he was leaving Tennessee—for reasons known now to history but not suspected at the time. Mr. Rhea met him on the street.

"'Mr. Rhea,' said Howard, 'I owe you $265, and I'm a little hard up just now, but you're about the only man around here that has treated me like a gentleman, and I made up my mind some time ago that I'd pay you every cent I owe, even if I had to go out and work on the streets at a dollar a day.'

"Thereupon Mr. Howard pulled out his pocketbook, extracted $265, handed the money to Mr. Rhea, and walked away smiling."

Here now was an additional bit of evidence to bolster the present narrator's conviction that the late Jesse James was an honest man! Before you utter broadsides of raucous laughter and refuse to read the rest of this sincere effort at truth-telling, let certain qualifications and reservations be submitted.

We seem to have overwhelming evidence that Jesse

James, upon occasion, assisted his friends in robbing trains and banks; that he had a talent for helping himself to a horse when he needed a fresh mount in an emergency. Though there is testimony to prove that on a number of occasions he returned or paid for a horse thus commandeered, there is no evidence to indicate that he ever exerted himself in efforts toward returning money or jewelry which fell to his lot in the division of spoils following a raid.

But in the ordinary relations of life Jesse James actually was an honest man, whether you see fit to accept the statement or to reject it. And so I said to the gentleman from Paducah, when he had told me about Mr. Howard's voluntary settling-up with Mr. Rhea, when he easily could have beaten the Nashville merchant out of that $265:

"In some ways, Mr. Koger, Jesse James was a strictly honest man, as I have discovered, to my own surprise, in my investigations. You have supplied me with another item of proof. There were times when he went out of his way to discharge a debt which many a man in good social and civic standing would do his utmost to duck.

"I can give you another instance—out of many—bearing upon the same point. K. R. Ross, a farmer in Cass County, Missouri, was a family friend of the Jameses and the Youngers—related by marriage to the Younger family. From time to time the outlaws visited his home. He entertained them but had nothing to do with them as a freebooting gang. His friendship for the fellows made him unpopular with the police authorities, and so he notified 'the boys' that he'd much prefer they didn't come around his place any more.

"Well, the boys understood the situation and kept away from the Ross place. Ross made the statement that not long before Jesse James was killed a man called at his farm with a note addressed to him, signed 'David Howard.' Ross knew that 'David Howard' was Jesse James. The message carried a request that Ross go to a certain place in the woods, as the writer wished to see him. He went, and there he found Jesse James lying on the ground with his coat folded under his head and a pistol in each hand, his arms being crossed on his chest. He told Ross he had been down in the Mississippi river-bottom swamps and was suffering from malarial fever; and he looked it.

"'When I started back to Missouri,' said Jesse to Ross, 'I thought of everybody I might trust, and I figured I couldn't trust anybody but you. I have no money, and I'm very sick.'

"James then opened his shirt and showed Ross where, in the spring of 1865, a Federal bullet had entered the right side of his chest; the place of the wound was 'all inflamed,' as Ross described it.

"'I need a horse, too,' said Jesse.

"Ross provided him with a horse, saddled and bridled, and with $40. Jesse mounted the animal, with assistance, and rode away. In less than a month, so Ross declared, he returned horse, saddle and bridle and repaid the money."

"Well, anyhow," said Mr. Koger, gazing meditatively at a cocoanut-palm tree symbolizing tropical peace and plenty, "Jesse James was honest about what he owed Mr. Rhea; but I understood that he left the Big Bottom neighborhood without settling up for a herd of stock he had bought and sold."

Mr. Koger testified also to one of Mr. Howard's favorite forms of recreation, that of sounding people as to what they thought of the James boys of Missouri.

"He asked me that question," said Mr. Koger. "I told him I didn't uphold the Jameses at all in their outlawry.

"'Well,' said Howard, 'don't you think those men have been driven into outlawry, persecuted and hounded, chiefly because they belonged to Quantrill's guerrillas in the war? I was one of the guerrillas myself, Mr. Koger, when I was a youngster, and I happen to know a good deal about what happened to a Quantrill man after the war closed.'

"'Well, Mr. Howard,' I said to him, 'I fought in the war myself, on the Southern side, for four years, and I wasn't always treated the best ever; but that didn't drive me to robbing banks and trains.'

"Howard smiled, and turned the subject of conversation to something else. He seemed to be always looking for sympathy for the James boys from old Confederate soldiers. He told me at one time that he knew Jesse and Frank in the war, and they weren't such bad sorts as people had painted them."

Finally the interview got around to the man whose life Mr. Koger was supposed to have saved from the wrath of Jesse James. He described that episode thus:

"The postmaster at Box Station was a storekeeper named Jackson. One day when I was in the village this man Howard came along. He was looking visibly angry; his eyes snapped; he could hardly control himself. I inquired what was wrong.

"'I'm going right over and kill that damn postmaster, Mr. Koger—that's just what I'm going to do!' announced Howard. 'Look here—see this envelope?'

"From his coat pocket he drew an opened letter. He had slit the envelope very carefully, at the top, lengthwise. Turning down the severed top of the fold-over flap, he said to me:

"'Now do you see those marks—pencil marks—inside the flap?'

"I saw them, and I said so.

"'Well,' snapped Howard, 'I've been suspecting for some time that Jackson has been tampering with my mail—opening my letters, I reckon, for curiosity. He's certainly opened this one, and I'm going right over to the postoffice now and kill the damn skunk!'

"Howard started toward Jackson's store in a great fury. I had noticed that the letter was from Isaac T. Rhea—the envelope had our firm name on the outside, and I knew Mr. Rhea's handwriting. Suddenly it occurred to me that I could prevent a tragedy—if Howard really meant to kill Jackson; and I have no doubt now that he did mean to. I recollected that Mr. Rhea sometimes opened a letter he had written, after sealing the envelope, to make some alteration or addition to the contents. He always used a lead-pencil in doing the unsealing, a round instrument being required for that work.

"I called Howard back to me, and he returned with reluctance.

"'Here, Mr. Howard,' I said, 'I think I can explain this matter so that you'll see Mr. Jackson hasn't tampered with your letter at all.'

"Then I explained Mr. Rhea's habit of opening his outgoing letters with a lead-pencil now and then. Howard calmed down, slowly, and at last he went away smiling. So Postmaster Jackson's life was saved, and Mr. Howard was saved from having to disappear suddenly from Tennessee to keep from being arrested and identified. No doubt he suspected that Jackson was in league with the Pinkertons and was trying to learn from his correspondence that Citizen Howard was in reality Jesse James."

Let us give Mr. Koger full credit for saving that life. Those who knew Jesse James will not be inclined to doubt for an instant that he would have shot Jackson "on suspicion."

Self-preservation was the pre-primary law of Jesse's life. All other laws faded and fell before that one. Jesse James was the most dangerous of all the border outlaws because he was the most desperately determined of them all to retain his life, which involved, in his case, retention of his liberty—such as that was. A sorry thing, yet precious!

Mr. Koger told me of an incident which, he thought, would serve to show "what a brave and fearless man" was Jesse James. "I think it was in the fall of 1878," said he, "when the State Fair was being held at Nashville. A handsome cash prize was offered in a competition to determine the most graceful horseback rider. It was the gentlemen riders' event. I recall that there were about thirty entries. I sat in the grandstand with thousands of others as the riders passed in front.

"Mr. Howard, mounted on his favorite horse, was one of the contestants, and he rode well up toward the front. Knowing him to be a most skillful rider, I took particular interest in watching him. The riders passed in review two or three times. When the event was over I encountered Howard and asked him why he hadn't won the prize.

"'Oh, I can beat any of these men riding,' he replied, 'but the judges had to give the money to one of these dudes.'

"Right under the eyes of the Nashville police and Pinkerton detectives who were looking for Jesse James, to get the high reward offered! I think that was a rather remarkable exhibition of courage."

There can be no doubt that the adventure required a certain sort of courage. Jesse James frequently rode as his own jockey in horse-races at county and neighborhood fairs, and sometimes he took the money. But in those instances, as at Nashville, a shrewd common sense is to be credited even more than the quality of courage. The outlaw knew that if he acted exactly like any ordinary citizen he would be safer than if he acted otherwise. He knew that the detectives had no pictures of him and that none of them knew how he looked. None of them would suspect that the notorious bandit would have the nerve to appear thus at a public event. For that matter, throughout his career this man mingled with the general populace, wherever he happened to be, going and coming as other men go and come. In his way, Jesse was a wise man.

One morning in April, 1882, when aboard one of his steamboats of romantic memory, Mr. Koger picked up a daily newspaper. He read about the assassination of Jesse James in St. Joseph, Missouri. The fact was stated that the victim of Robert Ford's bullet had been living in St. Joseph as Thomas Howard and that he had lived for some years in and near Nashville as J. D. Howard. Further details of identification caused Mr. Koger to exclaim to the captain of his vessel:

"Aha! that's the very fellow who was going to kill the postmaster at Box Station! Well, well, now! I certainly never suspected he was anybody other than J. D. Howard. And he asked me what I thought of Jesse James! And I told him, frankly!"

CHAPTER XXV

THE HAPPY MARRIED LIVES OF FRANK AND JESSE

IT is an amazing fact that both of the Jameses married, and married well, in the very midst of their careers of outlawry. Each became the husband of a handsome young woman of irreproachable moral character. Nor in either case was there the slightest effort at deception upon the part of the wooing bandit. Both girls walked gladly, if not indeed gaily, into marital union with men who for a considerable period, as the blushing brides were fully aware, had been dodging sheriff and marshal, police and Pinkerton, in a dozen states.

The further astonishing fact survives for record here that both of these were highly successful marriages, as judged from conventional standards. This is not to aver that the two couples "lived happily ever afterward," although in the romantic meaning of the phrase they appear to have done so. Each of the hymeneal pairs lived and loved and struggled and endured together, husband and wife devoted and faithful, until death did them part. Philandering was not in the code of either Frank or Jesse. Morally speaking—and in this instance sexual morality is meant—these outlaws must be credited with having been thoroughly circumspect, in the absence of all evidence to the contrary. The fact is that there is no record of even a suspicion against them in this respect.

Fiction hardly could invent alliances more strange. Considering all of the exceptional circumstances, if any marriages in the history of what the late Bert Leston Taylor termed "the so-called human race" have presented to the student of sociology an aspect more remarkable in any respect, your present commentator must confess total ignorance thereof.

If either Mrs. Jesse Woodson James or Mrs. Alexander Franklin James had possessed the talent for writing and had chosen to write the true story of her life as the wife of a hunted outlaw, what an extraordinarily interesting human document that book would have been! This may be looked upon as an idle "if," yet it holds deep fascination for at least one writing man who knew personally, in their home life, one of these wedded pairs. That, to be sure, was long after Mr. and Mrs. Frank James had begun enjoying the happy privilege of living at peace with all the world and were safe in issuing visiting cards in their own name.

Mrs. James, then in middle life, was a woman of charming personality. Poise and dignity were hers. She was of the home-loving and home-making type. She retained much of the facial beauty which had distinguished her as an unusually pretty girl when, in 1874, as seventeen-year-old Miss Annie Ralston of Jackson County, Missouri, she eloped with the slim and sinewy outlaw after a courtship necessarily clandestine. She was the daughter of a prosperous farmer.

The Ralstons were highly respected by their neighbors.

Samuel Ralston was both amazed and enraged when he learned that his beautiful daughter had run off with Frank James, a dozen years her senior and indubitably more sophisticated than the little country girl, and that the pair had been joined in the holy bonds of matrimony by a Baptist minister. It was not the difference in years—it was the difference in station, so to speak—that offended the highly respectable farmer. Forthwith the bride's father went to Kansas City and called upon Col. Morrison Munford, a personal friend who was editor of the Kansas City *Times*. There was a private conference in the old wedge-shaped temple of journalism at the "Junction," and next morning the *Times* published a letter, signed by Mr. Ralston, in which the farmer virtually disowned his daughter.

The whereabouts of the happy couple, it should be unnecessary to point out, were not known to the public. Bride and groom were not interviewed as to their plans, which undoubtedly were more hazy than are those of the average newlyweds. Somewhere, somehow, they honeymooned under protection of an assumed name, with the bridegroom's brace of Remington forty-fours in close touch as emergency protectors.

For several years Mr. Ralston was more or less obdurate, but ultimately he relented to the extent of welcoming his daughter back to the old home when she desired to visit the folks. She carried thither such favorable reports of her husband insofar as his treatment of herself was concerned that the family came to feel more kindly disposed toward the relative-in-law who was living, perforce, outside the law's protecting pale. But it was more than eight years before the couple were safe in calling themselves Mr. and Mrs. Frank James. In the meantime they went under various surnames, that of Woodson being their favorite. It was a family name in the James connection, being borne by an uncle, by Jesse as middle name, and by a Kentucky cousin who was to become a member of the outlaw band and to die miserably at the hands of another member.

Robert, the only child of this union, namesake of the Rev. Robert James, never knew his real surname until his father unstrapped the faithful Remingtons and handed them over to the governor of Missouri late in 1882. Those years "on the dodge" were passed in several states, including Missouri, Texas, Kentucky, Tennessee and Maryland. In each of these and in other states where they sojourned from time to time Frank James engaged in legitimate business or employment, working hard, when he found it practicable and possible. Fear of discovery and capture, or of being killed in a running fight for his life, was the hypothetical wolf that howled always at his door.

But Frank James possessed, in degree approaching the superlative, the presence of mind which was his temporal salvation. My old and esteemed friend "the gentleman detective," Mr. Samuel E. Allender of St. Louis, now chief special agent for the St. Louis-San Francisco Railway Company and formerly chief of detectives in the St. Louis police department, told me some years ago, at his desk at police headquarters, this story in illustration of the point mentioned:

"No doubt you recall that some time after Frank James surrendered to Governor Crittenden in 1882 and stood trial and was acquitted by a jury of Missourians, he came to St. Louis and was employed by the late Col. Ed Butler, owner of the Standard Theater, as doorkeeper at that celebrated home of variety. When he was so employed I was a young city detective, and I became well acquainted with the ex-outlaw. The neighborhood of the theater, as you know, was fertile for detective work.

"One night when the show was on I stood outside the door of the theater, chatting with Frank James. The curtain went down for an intermission, and the major part of the male crowd filed out to patronize the bar. In the crowd I espied a police character, some petty thief or pickpocket. I stepped aside, led him away, called the patrol wagon and sent him in. A few minutes later the audience returned, the curtain went up and the door was closed. As I stood there again with James he remarked that he had seen me do an unwise thing when arresting the suspect. 'Why didn't you cover the fellow with your gun?' he asked me. I explained that such a procedure was not practicable in a city like this, where forty thousand arrests were made annually; if every officer whipped out a gun whenever he made an arrest he would be considered a nut, and in fact he wouldn't remain very long on the job.

"'That's all right,' Frank James said, 'but the officer always gets it when he least expects it.'

"He then illustrated the point by relating a little experience he had had at a time when, as he put it, 'they thought they wanted me.' He said he was stopping in Baltimore, had a room in a house built in a solid block of dwellings with no space between. One night he wanted something to eat, so he picked up a basket and went to an all-night market close by. On his way back to his lodgings with the laden basket on his left arm, his coat collar turned up and his hat brim turned down, he noticed a number of policemen walking up and down in front of his house, as it appeared from a short distance.

"'I could think of nothing else,' said James, 'than that the officers had been tipped off to my rooming there, and that probably some of them had been searching the house and they were waiting for me to return. I was too close to them to turn back without arousing their suspicion. Directly across the street from the policemen I noticed a white horse hitched to a buggy; the street was lighted by gas-lamps and the horse showed up quite visibly in the mellow gleam. I decided quickly upon my plan of action. Probably the officers, I thought, had the block surrounded. My plan was to walk straight on past them if they didn't interfere with me; I would not go into my room at all. If they attempted to capture me I would try to reach the horse and buggy by shooting it out with the officers, and then drive away as fast as the horse could travel.'

"James said he walked along with his right hand on his sixshooter, which was harnessed under his left arm. His right hand thus was concealed under his coat and under the arm on which the basket hung. Approaching the bunch of officers, he edged out toward the curbing, intending to walk around them as though he had not noticed them specially. When he was opposite the officers, one of them reached out a hand to stop him. James sprang backward into the street, off the sidewalk, toward the horse and buggy, pulling his pistol from its place but not quite getting it out—not so that it was visible to the policemen.

"'Well, sir, what is it?—What is it?' James asked the officer who had tried to stop him. 'Don't be so scary,' said one of the other policemen, with an oath; 'we're not going to hurt you.' James again said, 'What is it?' expecting every second to find it necessary to open fire and 'get' as many of them as he could, when another officer, in a rather gentle tone, said, 'Say, don't be afraid of us; we're not going to harm you, man; we simply want to get men enough to serve as a jury in a coroner's case where a man in the house next door to my own house has died without medical attention, by natural cause or otherwise.'

"James then saw, he stated, that the policemen were in front of the house adjoining the one where he roomed, instead of immediately in front of that house. That seemed to end his story," continued Detective Allender, "but my curiosity prompted me to ask how he got along on the jury.

"'I simply told them,' said James, 'that I was not a citizen of Maryland, that I lived in Washington, D. C., and I walked on into my house. That was the end of it so far as I was concerned.' Frank James told his story to illustrate the narrow escape those

Baltimore policemen had. I was struck by his great presence of mind as indicated by his rapidity in planning his escape, but more especially by his explanation that he was not qualified by residence to serve as a juror."

Jesse James was in his twenty-seventh year when he married Miss Zerelda Mimms, his first cousin, who was of about even age. The courtship was unusually long, almost nine years, and was carried on under difficulties sufficiently obvious. When the wounded young guerrilla was brought home from Nebraska, early in August, 1865, he was carried on a stretcher from a Missouri river steamboat to the home of John Mimms, at Harlem, now North Kansas City. Mimms had married a sister of the Rev. Robert James. The elder daughter of the Mimmses was the wife of Charles McBride, a well-to-do builder of houses in Kansas City. The younger daughter, Zerelda, named for the mother of Jesse James, helped to nurse the suffering boy back toward health. It was late in October before the patient was able to be taken, by wagon, from Harlem to the old homestead near Kearney. Relatives have stated that Jesse and Zerelda, before he left the Mimms home, entered into a compact to be married if Jesse ever got well of his wound. Many months afterward, when at last he was able to get around outside the house, Jesse said to Mrs. Samuel:

"Ma, Zee and I are going to be married."

But the wedding was deferred from year to year. Miss Mimms, her mother having died, went to live with the McBrides. She attended school at Liberty.

In Kansas City she became popular with the younger set in the social circle of which she was a member. There were suitors for the hand of the handsome blonde, young men who knew not that the fair Zerelda was waiting for Cousin Jesse. The latter was waiting for such time as he might be able to settle down and begin married life without imperiling the happiness of his bride. That time, as we know, never came. So the cousins determined to take each other for woe or weal, love laughing at gunsmiths; and on the 24th of April, 1874, they were married at the home of a friendly neighbor near Kearney. The officiating clergyman was a paternal relative of the Jameses. That family, it seems, ran considerably to preachers.

Old inhabitants recall that Jesse, dressed spick and span, mounted upon a handsome horse and carrying a Winchester rifle across his saddlehorn, rode through Kearney's principal street on his way to his wedding. Beneath his coat undoubtedly were at least two concealed weapons, a Colt and a Smith & Wesson. Jesse never traveled without this pair of companions. He fancied each make with equal fervor as an engine of aggression, but in all probability the Colt held first place in his heart because of its old-time guerrilla associations.

To right and left as his steed trotted through town the bandit bowed to old acquaintances, smiling affably. He looked unusually happy, as was but meet.

"Congratulations, Jess," called out one who was on the friendship list. "Long life and prosperity!"

"Thank you, Sam," replied the hopeful bridegroom. "Come and see us—after we get settled down."

Both Sam and Jesse smiled still more broadly at the latter's grim little joke.

As in the case of the Frank Jameses, the Jesse Jameses necessarily concealed their identities. Howard was the favorite surname under which they lived in more than one state; but there were other aliases, chosen to fit the changing environments. Two children came, Jesse Edwards and Mary. The boy's middle name was in honor of Maj. John N. Edwards, the gallant Confederate veteran and famous Missouri editor who befriended Jesse James to the death, and beyond. But young Jesse never knew his own name —first, middle or last—until he was nearly seven years of age and the fatal bullet made him fatherless and relieved the little family of further necessity for concealment of identity. His father always called him Tim; to his mother he was Eddie.

Jesse James, such was the exigency of his situation, never had the blessed privilege of alluding to his wife in presence of outsiders as Zee, the abbreviation he used in private. Other Christian names were invented for Mrs. James, to go with such other selected surnames as the family employed from time to time. Jesse himself was Thomas, or David, or some other name as different from Jesse as could be found. One might fancy that there were many occasions when a slip of the tongue would have proved perilous.

The home life of the Jesse James family, discreetly aliased always, was in many respects of the great American average, in spite of everything. We have the testimony of neighbors in Nashville, in the Big Bottom country west of Nashville, in Kansas City and in St. Joseph, to the effect that "the Howards" were by no means undesirable neighbors. They were hospitable people, particularly when they lived in Tennessee. On the Big Bottom farm there was much entertaining of neighborhood folk. Mrs. Howard was a skillful cook; she and her husband liked to invite the neighbors in to dinner. Aged persons still living in that section recall with pleasure, not unmixed with a certain quality of awe, the delightful social affairs in which they participated at the Howard farmhouse.

One thing noticed by the neighbors was the chivalrous attitude of Mr. Howard toward women and children. Upon occasion, when a member of a stag party, he would utter a mild oath; but when women or children were present his language was as circumspect as that of a Sunday-school superintendent in active service. Somewhere in this chronicle—and here it seems to fit in—must be told the harrowing tale of the eleven ladies that were not scalped by Jesse James. The affirmative version is found in one of the old blood-and-thunder books, probably having taken root from the wartime story to the effect that after Jesse's guerrilla chieftain, Bill Anderson, was slain in a skirmish in northern Missouri, the scalps of two women were found dangling from the headstall of his horse's bridle.

According to the imaginative romancer, Jesse James was a lady-killer in both the actual and the slang senses. In the autumn of 1864 the blue-eyed guerrilla boy of seventeen was with Anderson's command at Fayette, capital of Howard County, Missouri. During a lull in the general slaughtering, there was a dance in which the belles of Fayette tripped it lightly with the young guerrilla gallants. Certain of the over-shirted Othellos awed the girls with tales of their prowess as man-killers. Jesse felt that he was losing favor: he too must show 'em that he was from Missouri.

Quitting the hall of gaiety, he ran outside, where his warhorse was hitched to the yard fence. Stripping from the beast's equipment a string of human scalps —the long and flowing tresses of no less than eleven deceased ladies—he rushed back and waved these grisly trophies in the faces of Fayette's fair. The girls were impressed. As spokeswoman for all her sex in Howard County, one of them is represented as saying, in a horrified tone:

"Mr. James, if you don't take those horrid things away this very moment we'll never have anything more to do with you! Take 'em away—ugh!"

The discomfited lad took 'em away, and thereafter Jesse James never scalped another lady! This is perhaps the most ghastly of all the many lies invented with the object of showing up the outlaw emperor as an inhuman monster. By way of offset we may relate a well-authenticated incident that took place aboard a railway train in Minnesota, shortly before the Northfield bank raid. A masher was annoying a young woman in a day coach. His antics had attracted the attention of several men, some of whom grinned, none of whom went to the girl's aid until a quiet-looking stranger arose from a seat several rows back and approached the miscreant.

"You dirty loafer," he remarked, "get out of this

coach, or I'll kick you out, right through this window!"

The dirty loafer got out. The indignant stranger returned to his seat. In the old family Bible back home the stranger's name was written thus, "James, Jesse Woodson, born Sept. 5, 1847."

In some respects this outlawed Missourian, under stress of compelling circumstances, was bad enough to suit the most exacting tastes in specific iniquities, but there is no authentic record that he ever harmed or insulted a woman.

CHAPTER XXVI

"THE PERFECT CRIME"—JESSE'S MASTERPIECE

ONE of the most widely current stories about the James brothers, told and retold in various and varying versions, supplies weighty evidence that a woman's tears could not fail to evoke the underlying chivalry of Jesse James, even when the outlaw was in the midst of a get-away from the scene of a successful raid against bank or train. This is the incident of Jesse's paying off the weeping widow's mortgage. The fact that upon the edge of the instant he conceived a plan whereby he could—and did— recover the cash in toto without embarrassing the grateful widow or reviving the canceled mortgage, indicates that Jesse was a rapid thinker as well as a quick actor.

Somehow this episode, in the authenticity of which I believe most implicitly, has appealed to me for many years as the premier pleasantry in the long and complex annals of outlawry the wide world over. I offer no apology when I aver that the eminently successful execution of Jesse James' most glorious joke gives me a delight such as I am wont to derive now and then from the reading or the rereading of a splendid sonnet, or from the viewing of a noble statue or a master-piece in oils.

There was high art in Jesse's jesting here. Moralize as you may, I for one shall continue to applaud his achievement in this outstanding instance of inspiration. There was pathos in it, there was chivalric sentiment, there was simple human tenderness—despite the drawing of the conquering Colt in the climax; and there was humor such as I am sure must have appealed strongly to that other eminent Missourian, Mark Twain, who undoubtedly heard the happy tale. There was present conspicuously the unstrained quality of mercy and justice which the just and merciful Mark Twain could not have failed to approve.

> Gargantuan laughter leaps to lips of gods
> On high Olympus, so say I, whenas
> They think upon this joke of Jesse James;
> And Jove himself guffaws in thunderbolts
> That shake the topless towers of the skies. . . .

And if I were sufficiently a poet I should like to write this portion of the record in Marlowe's mighty line. However, this opus of outlawry being but a plain prose epic, I shall endeavor to tell the weeping widow's tale without further wingbeats in possible poetics.

For years I was unable to verify the story, to give it even an approximate localization. Nearly everybody with whom I talked about Jesse James volunteered a version. It seemed to hop about from state to state even as did the outlaws. Now it alighted somewhere in Kentucky or in Tennessee, to reappear in the hillbilly regions of Arkansas, and then to fix itself upon some indefinite acre of Missouri. Now, happily, I am able to place it permanently upon Missouri soil, although "somewhere in northern Missouri" must remain for all time its not altogether satisfactory locale.

Again do we call upon our accommodating detective friend, Mr. Samuel E. Allender of St. Louis, who but recently has volunteered the version which he got directly from the lips of Frank James after Jesse's elder and sometimes abler brother had become unbandited for good and all. You may be sure that Frank never told Sam Allender or anybody else the exact locality or date or circumstantial setting of the mortgage-lifting masterpiece of Jesse's generous jesting. Frank James never told anybody anything which could be calculated to pin a public label upon the front of any offending charged against him and his friends. He was of the close-lipped corporation of the Jameses and the Youngers, each of whom died with lips sealed against revelation of all past misdeeds. Some bandits have bleated and boasted, but never one of these.

Sam Allender possesses a pigeon-hole memory. I believe that he could sit down and dictate to his stenographer, if he had the time and the inclination, plus the endurance, a million-word chronicle of his recollections as a public and private detective through a long period of years, without making more than one-half of one per cent of errors. This compliment I hand him by way of laying a foundation of verisimilitude for his remembered version of the tale which is to follow just as soon as we shall have laid down some further base of preliminaries, chiefly conjectural.

We are to assume that the Jesse James gang had but recently robbed a train or a bank in the northern part of Missouri. We know, in a general way, about the robberies in that near-half of the one-time Robber State which fact and fiction have charged up against the gang. But we do not know, and unless one of the presumably late widow's children or grandchildren shall come forth and supply complete verification as to date and place we never can know, just what enterprise in freebootery preceded the immortal episode. Possibly—just possibly, mind you—Jim Cummins might know the intimate details; but Jim, being of the brotherhood, would remain silent like the others.

The fact that the outlaws were flush with funds leads to the conclusion that they had made a handsome haul. The further fact that they forsook the main-traveled road for a sequestered farmhouse upon a byway when they found it desirable to stop somewhere for an impromptu dinner, indicates that they were fearful lest some posse of pursuers might overtake them and give battle.

The fleet horses of the Missouri rough riders could negotiate dim trails which balk nowadays even the modern flivver that has earned the reputation of being able to climb a tree. They were pathfinders, these highwaymen who took to byways when highways became roads of too-perilous adventuring. Many a time and oft did they forsake even the byways, finding invisible trails which they left invisible. We are to fancy them, then, as seeking the widow's house not because it looked like a square-meal prospect, since it didn't, but for the more intimate reason that the open roads were peopled, actually or potentially, with mounted and armed sheriffs, deputies, citizens, Pinkertons perhaps, all bent upon running down the robbers and running up scores in the nature of claims for large monetary rewards.

We are to visualize Jesse James and his brother Frank, with their unidentified companions of the raid and the retreat, one of the group toting the inevitable wheat sack crammed with golden loot, all hungry for a meal and willing to accept any substitute for the square article and pay the market price—and no questions asked or answered. Jesse, for this occasion, is captain of the crew; for we find him custodian of the sack and apparently official spokesman when the lone and lorn widow sheds the tears that touch his heart.

Perhaps McClellan Miller of Clay, if the occasion antedated the Northfield bank raid and the tragic end of Clell, rode alongside Jesse. They had been neighbors in their native county, and they met in their outlaw days only at long intervals. When they did meet, as a rule, something happened—something similar to the professional enterprise which had engaged their combined talents almost immediately preceding this occasion. Clell Miller was a resourceful bandit, and one to be depended upon in almost any emergency. Jesse was fond of Clell, even though he did kill Clell's brother Ed in a quarrel some years after the former had taken violent exit.

Or it may be that Jim Cummins, if Jim was amongst

those present—and nobody, mind you now, is insinuating that he was—it may be that Jim, who grew up with Jesse and who still reveres his memory despite the fact that Jesse once made specific threats against the life of Jim—yes, possibly Jim Cummins was riding side by side with Jesse James when the gang galloped off the main road and made for the lowly cottage of the woman they did not then know as a widow with several small children and one large mortgage on her farm.

Assuredly Jim was not riding as side-partner to Frank James, for Jim and Frank somehow never seemed to get along well together. Several of these bandits dearly disloved certain others of the outfit, the feeling being mutual, as you are to discover farther along. In the inner circles of outlawry, as elsewhere, familiarity breeds contempt.

We must assume that Cole Younger and Frank James were galloping in close comradeship. They always liked each other. They had much in common: close contact in the old times of guerrilla warfare; ambitions of a semi-literary sort—for reading, not for writing, though Cole did write letters and articles of meritorious composition, and Frank collaborated with the present chronicler in writing a serial account of the career of Harry Tracy, the Northwestern outlaw who came to his violent end by way of a self-sent bullet in 1902, when cornered in a Washington wheatfield; and in many ways Frank and Cole were the most intelligent, not to say intellectual, of all the outlaw company.

Unfortunately we do not know the number of men

in the group that dropped in thus unexpectedly as guests of the widow. Did we but know that, we should have ground for deciding between a bank raid and a train robbery as the activity just preceding the occasion now under study. If they were but five—and we have named three possibilities in addition to Frank and Jesse, the only known and acknowledged members of the party—if but a quintet of the oldtime Quantrillian quickshots rode up the grass-grown trail to the abode of the widow, then most likely it was a bank raid. But if they were seven, if Jim Younger and his younger brother Bob, let us surmise, were of the group, then the wheat sack concealed under Jesse's coat— along with a crowded belt of cartridges and a couple of Colts, or perhaps a Smith & Wesson and a Colt— probably had been crammed with coin and currency acquired from the train-traveling safe of an express company.

For that matter, who really cares, now or ever henceforward, where and how they got the money? They had it, and presently a dignified amount of it was to be diverted—briefly, to be sure—from the plebeian bag of banditry to a nobler usage. That sum was to pass from the hands of Jesse James into those of a widow who was worthy and into those of a grasping skinflint of a man who was merely wealthy, before sundown of that dateless day in the romantic history of Missouri; and whilst yet the light of that day shone upon sinner and saint with equal blessing, the self-same money was to repass into the hands of Jesse James and by those hands—slim and smallish they were, and always well-kept, and nearly always neatly gloved for a certain important reason (a missing finger-tip which might have helped to identify Jesse to the sleuths)—by those hands with the nimble trigger-digits the roving cash was to be crammed back into the sack, where it was to companion the rest of the loot, which had no share in that day's deathless glory, until such time as pursuit waned sufficiently to permit the victors to divide the spoils.

We approach now the perfect outlaw episode, the one sole holdup in the whole category which beings normally human may approve without stretching conscience until it creaks. Even as our outlaw outfit reaches the widow's home, and as unexpected help for the widow's sons and daughters hovers closer and closer, so do we arrive at last where the real story starts. Sam Allender, living, and Frank James, dead, say on!

"One day," says Sam Allender, "Frank James told me that on a certain occasion he and his pals were traveling on horseback somewhere in northern Missouri. It being about noon, they were hungry. They pulled off the main road and found a lone woman in charge of a small farmhouse. They asked her if she could supply them with something to eat.

"At first the woman hesitated. The men displayed money and assured her they would be glad to pay for what they ate. She then proceeded to prepare such scant food as she had on hand. As she was making coffee and cooking eggs, the James crowd sat around the room. They noticed that she was weeping; tears were rolling down her cheeks, sobs were heaving her bosom.

"'Jesse,' said Frank in telling me the story, 'was always tenderhearted—couldn't stand a woman's tears. He asked her why she was crying. She tried to smile it off, and said that seeing us men around the house reminded her of the happy time when her husband was living and had other men now and then helping him do the farm work; she was just thinking how sadly things had changed since his death, and that was what made her cry, so she said.

"'Jesse kept on asking questions. The woman said she had several children at school, some miles down the road; there was a mortgage on her farm, she went on to say, for $1,400; it was overdue, and this was the last day of grace.

"'"Aha!" said Jesse, "and so that's really what's making you cry—you're afraid you're going to lose your home. I see."

"'Yes, that was it, she admitted. That very afternoon, said the weeping widow, the man who held the mortgage was coming out from town to demand his money. He was a hardhearted old miser, she stated, and she didn't have a dollar to apply on the debt. The man would be sure to foreclose and turn her and her helpless little ones out.

"'"Huh!" said Jesse, "that so?" his eyes blinking fast and furiously. "Well, now ma'am, I don't know about that; I—well, now, I think maybe you won't lose your farm after all."

"'The widow looked rather puzzled. She put the food on the table and all of us sat down and turned to. After we finished eating, Jesse produced a sack and counted out on the table $1,400.

""""Here, lady," said Jesse, "you take this money and pay off your mortgage."

"'The lady was amazed. "I can't ever pay you back," she said, "and so I won't borrow it."

""""But it's no loan," said Jesse; "it's a gift."

"'The widow said she couldn't believe it was anything but a dream—things never happened that way—but Jesse assured her it was no dream; the money was good money and it was for her use. Jesse then sat down and wrote out a form of receipt, which he had the woman copy in her own handwriting. He put the original into his pocket, so that his handwriting wouldn't get into other hands. Jesse instructed the woman to pay the mortgage-holder the $1,400 and have him sign the receipt—in ink. He then handed her a handful of cash for her immediate needs.

"'Jesse asked the grateful widow to describe the man who held the mortgage. She did so, telling the kind of rig he drove and about what hour she expected him, and the road by which he would come out from town. We then bade her good day and mounted our horses. The widow was still weeping, but weeping for joy.

"'We rode some distance from the house and hid in the bushes beside the rocky road along which the mortgage man was to come in his buggy. Presently we saw him driving toward the widow's house, and pretty soon driving back, looking prosperous. He was humming "Old Dan Tucker was a fine old feller" as he came opposite. We stepped out into the road, held him up and recovered the $1,400.'

"I asked Frank James," said Sam Allender, "if

they had any more difficulty in getting the money on that occasion than they had had on the occasion when they first acquired it; and he replied, with a laugh:

"'Now, Sam, I'm not being sweated.'"

CHAPTER XXVII

THE APOTHEOSIS OF JESSE JAMES

BORDER outlawry's historian would be remiss in duty did he fail to make of 1877 a red-letter year in the record. There was no bloodshed in that year, unless we are to include the Nebraska affair of very doubtful Jamesian origin, but the shedding of ink provided a substitute almost as sensational. Early in 1877, not many months after the Northfield disaster and its resultant publicity for the ex-guerrillas intimately engaged therein, the apotheosis of Jesse James as a hero took place. High priest in that ceremony was Maj. John N. Edwards. This Virginia-born Missourian was the most outspoken of the many apologists of the James brothers. With the exception of Gen. Jo Shelby, his old commander and lifelong friend, Edwards was the most conspicuous of those who defended the outlaws on the assumption that they did what they did because they could not do otherwise.

Printer and poet, soldier and journalist, John Edwards was a man of gentle habits and violent convictions. Deeply beloved by those who knew him best, he reciprocated the affections of all. For many years a student of literatures ancient and modern, his penchant for heroics had developed into a ruling passion. There were no comparatives in the opinions of John Edwards: superlatives held the field alone. What he believed he expressed, sans qualification or equivocation.

Those who read the scintillant editorials by this man, in the newspapers of several Missouri cities for a score of years altogether, knew always exactly where he stood: they could not fail to hear his boots hit the planks whenever he made a stand. When, for instance, Major Edwards wrote in the Kansas City *Times* that he hoped to see the day when whisky should be free, running knee-deep all over Missouri, with a pint tin-cup suspended invitingly from every twig in the wild-woods, his readers knew that he was not and never could be a prohibitionist. They knew also that John Edwards really did not mean for anybody to take him literally. In writing that sentiment he had but exercised his characteristic method of driving home a point with one decisive swat of the hammer. He had fought that way for the Confederacy; and now he was fighting similarly in behalf of a square deal, as he conceived it, for Jesse W. James.

Major Edwards, notwithstanding his predilection for the shrill tone in editorializing, was a man of extraordinary modesty and of unusually tender human feelings. Others have said of him that in battle he gave his horse to a wounded infantryman and remained in a perilous position to fight on foot; that he took off his only shirt and tore it up for bandages at a field hospital, going shirtless for days thereafter; that he gave away his coat more than once to shivering private soldiers and in his plucked aspect offended the hifalutin attitude of certain brother-officers in Shelby's Iron Brigade, of which he was adjutant and chief understudy to the general in command. One who knew John Edwards intimately in war and in peace has written:

"In battle he was a very Mars; in camp he was as gentle as a woman. The men loved him, and little wonder. He could never do enough for them. Brave men all of them, they recognized him as the bravest and the brainiest . . . He was the bravest man in war and the gentlest man in peace that I ever saw. He was the soul of honor. He was one man in a million. He was the Chevalier Bayard of Missouri."

It was in a book by Major Edwards, published in 1877, that the semi-deification of Jesse James was set forth. In *Noted Guerrillas* the Clay County outlaw may not have been erected into a veritable god, but he was placed upon the battlements where the half-gods rattle their mail and flash their steel. In that tremendous tome the wartime prowess of many guerrillas of the border country is delineated with superlative strokes of hero-worshipment. These characterizations include Coleman and James Younger, Frank James, Allen Parmer, Dick Maddox, George and Oliver Shepherd, Jim Cummins, Arch Clements, Bill Gregg, Peyton Long, Fletch Taylor, John Jarrette and many others who rode conspicuously with Quantrill, Anderson and Todd; but to Jesse James, youngest and possibly fiercest of them all, is reserved premier place in the Edwardsian expressions of sympathy and defense.

The reason why Jesse could not settle down permanently is indicated in a picturesque passage from the book mentioned. The introductory part, not quoted here, tells of the young guerrilla's return from Nebraska to his mother's home, still suffering from the last wound he received in the Civil War; and the story goes that the boy who had fought under the black flag was shot down when carrying a white flag of truce. Thus wrote John Edwards of Jesse James:

"In the spring of 1866 he was barely able to mount a horse and ride a little; and he did ride, but he rode armed, watched, vigilant, haunted. He might be killed, waylaid, ambuscaded, assassinated; but he would be killed with his eyes open and his pistols about him.

"The hunt for this maimed and emaciated guerrilla culminated on the night of Feb. 18, 1867. On this night an effort was made to kill him. Jesse James had to flee. In those evil days bad men in bands were doing things continually in the name of law, order and vigilance committees.

"He had been a desperate guerrilla; he had fought under a black flag; he had made a name of terrible prowess along the border; he had survived terrible wounds; it was known that he would fight at any hour or in any way; he could not be frightened out of his native state; he could be neither intimidated nor robbed; and hence the wanton war waged upon Jesse James, and hence the reason why today he is an outlaw, and hence the reason also that—outlaw as he is and proscribed in county or state or territory—he has more friends than the officers who hunt him, and more defenders than the armed men who seek to secure his body, dead or alive.

"Since 1865 it has been pretty much one eternal ambush for this man—one unbroken and eternal hunt twelve years long. He has been followed, trailed, surrounded, shot at, wounded, ambushed, surprised, watched, betrayed, proscribed, outlawed, driven from state to state, made the objective point of infallible detectives, and he has triumphed.

"By some intelligent people he is regarded as a myth, by others as in league with the devil. He is neither, but he is an uncommon man. He does not touch whisky or tobacco in any form. He never travels twice the same road. He never tells the direction from which he came nor the direction in which he means to go. There is a design in this—the calm, cool, deadly design of a man who recognizes the perils which beset him, and who is not afraid to die.

"He trusts very few people, two probably out of every 10,000. He comes and goes as silently as the leaves fall. He never boasts. He has many names and many disguises. He speaks low, is polite, deferential and accommodating. He does not kill save in stubborn self-defense. He has nothing in common with a murderer. He hates the highwayman and the coward.

"He is an outlaw, but he is not a criminal, no matter what prejudiced public opinion may declare or malignant partisan dislike make noisy with reiteration.

"The war made him a desperate guerrilla; and the harpies of the war—the robbers who came in the wake of it, and the cutthroats who came to the surface as the honorable combatants settled back again into civilized life—proscribed him and drove him into resistance.

"He was a man who could not be bullied, who was too intrepid to be tyrannized over, who would fight a regiment just as quickly as he would fight an individual, who owned property and meant to keep it, who was born in Clay county and did not mean to be driven out of Clay county, and who surrendered in good faith, but who, because of it, did not intend any the less to have his rights and receive the treatment the balance of the Southern soldiers received.

"This is the summing up of the whole history of this man since the war. He was hunted, and he was human. He replied to proscription by defiance, ambushment by ambushment, musket shot by pistol shot, night attack by counter-attack, charge by counter-charge; and so he will do, desperately and with splendid heroism, until the end."

And that end was inevitably violent, as Major Edwards intimated here and as Jesse James himself never doubted; but the end was not yet. For five years more the proscription, the hunting, the desperate resistance to the inevitable were to continue. The impassioned defense of Jesse in the Edwards book, which had a wide circulation throughout the Jesse James country, made many converts to the theory that the outlaw had not received a square deal in the shuffle of human events. But it did not serve to stay the chase after the two who got away from Minnesota and returned to their accommodating Nowhere. The avid sleuths of a dozen states remained on the outlook. To catch Frank and Jesse meant a handsome sum of money for the catchers, plus a degree of prestige not to be despised. Both glory and gain thus figured in the man-hunt.

Copies of *Noted Guerrillas*—and author's autographed copies, at that—reached two humble homes in Tennessee and were read with especial interest by the recipients. Needless to say, their names were not on the flyleaf along with that of Major Edwards; nor, for that matter, were their assumed names there. The devoted major was not giving any possible clews to the whereabouts of the James boys, nor to the identities of the quiet and industrious residents of Nashville who were known as the Messrs. Howard and Woodson, each in his separate sphere.

For more than two years longer they remained industrious and quiet. Up in old Missouri the James-Younger gang became but a memory; a vivid memory, to be sure, yet none the less beginning to fade from the general public canvas. There were vague rumors that Jesse had been killed, that Frank had died of tuberculosis. Their friends, laughing far upsleeve, helped to spread these aidful rumors. Since the Northfield debacle they had subsided into quiescence; and if still alive, why hadn't they been heard from again? Since the middle of September, 1876, neither Frank nor Jesse had rearisen from the smoking pyre of Northfield and the misty reek of the memorable get-away. Yes, truly, they must have gone the way of all flesh.

The Jesse James country was becoming indifferent about the boys. A feeling of comfortable languidity almost overcame the officials of Jackson and Clay

Counties whose business was supposed to be that of running down the Jameses. They were glad to get a little rest, after so many years of labor—sincere or otherwise—in trying to justify public confidence.

But down in Tennessee the Messrs. Howard and Woodson had no such blissful rest after arduous labors as comes from a sense of security. They carried their cognitoes and their Colts by no means lightly. The one might be knocked off as a chip from the shoulder of either man any day or night; the other might be whipped out necessarily at any moment, in defense of self which meant offense to society. These two and their wives, and a few time-trusted friends, knew that Jesse and Frank James were not dead, and the Messrs. Howard and Woodson learned at last that the poet's counsel to "let the dead past bury its dead" was not applicable to their own outlaw past, which refused to stay dead because the public refused it decent burial.

And so, with the Jesse James country drowsy under the drug of an imaginary Nepenthe, suddenly out of his Nowhere popped again the palpable presence of Jesse James himself—no apparition save in the suddenness of his coming and going. A train robbery in the oldtime style took place in Missouri—and right in Jackson County, too, almost under the nose of Kansas City. It was the first of a series of three, the second being committed in Daviess County, the third in Jackson.

Jesse James had resurrected himself and reorganized his band.

The hand of Jesse showed unmistakably in each of these robberies. First came the affair at Glendale, a small station in Jackson County on the Chicago & Alton railroad, Oct. 7, 1879. The six men who robbed the express train there were Jesse James, Edward Miller, Robert Woodson Hite, William Ryan, James Andrew Liddil and Daniel Tucker Bassham. Ed Miller came from Clay County, being a brother of Clell, killed at Northfield. Hite, familiarly known as Wood Hite, was from Logan County, Kentucky, and was a first cousin of the James brothers. Bill Ryan belonged in Jackson County. Liddil, known to outlaw history as Dick Liddil, also was a native of Jackson. Bassham, whose name survives in tragedy and comedy as Tucker Bassham, was a simple-minded farmer in Jackson County, living near Independence. The Old Dan Tucker of the oldtime song may have been "a fine old feller," but his Missouri namesake was a naturalborn human jackass.

Much new blood, as we perceive, was introduced at Glendale. Frank James had no part in that train holdup; he was at his Tennessee home, plugging away at a hard-work job in support of his wife and child. There is a considerable volume of rather hazy evidence to the effect that Frank tried hard to persuade Jesse not to return to Missouri—or to the active practice of outlawry. The probability is that Frank made the effort. He was some years older than Jesse, as we know, and he was wiser in the first place.

But in the next train robbery, which resulted in two murders, Frank James was believed to have been of the company present. This is known as the Winston holdup. At the town of that name in Daviess County, July 15, 1881, a passenger train on the Chicago, Rock

Island & Pacific Railroad was robbed. William West-
fall, train conductor, and Frank McMillan, an elderly
workman employed by the railway company, were shot
to death. The other outlaws at Winston were Jesse
James, Wood Hite, the latter's younger brother Clarence Browler Hite, and Dick Liddil.

Third and last of this series and the final act committed against the law by the Jesse James band was
the Blue Cut affair in Jackson County, Sept. 7, 1881,
exactly five years after Northfield. The men who held
up and robbed the Chicago & Alton express train in
this instance were Frank James, Jesse James, Wood
Hite, Clarence Hite, Dick Liddil and Charles Ford.
The latter was from Ray county, next to Clay. About
six months later he became one of the conspirators in
planning and carrying out the assassination of Jesse
James.

These three crimes aroused the Jesse James country and regions far beyond. The ultimate one, following the penultimate one after less than two months,
was more than sixteen years from the close of the
Civil War and more than fifteen years from the initial
ex-guerrilla raid at Liberty, a few miles to the north.
Major Edwards' heroizing volume was four years old
and its influence was fading fast.

The Jesse James country had a deal of new blood
on the opposition side, and things had become different in many ways. Shortly after Blue Cut, Annihila-
tion came riding, spurred and booted, into the camp
of the border bandits.

CHAPTER XXVIII

IMMEDIATELY following the name of the Hon. William H. Wallace of Kansas City the word Crusader would not be misplaced. This venerable gentleman is the man who broke up the "James Boys' Band" of outlaws. He it was who, conceiving a public office as a public trust several years before Grover Cleveland set that conception into an imperishable sentence, leaped headlong into the hustings and defied the devils of disorder to do their worst against him. If ever any man in public office or campaigning for election "took his life into his hands," that man was "Will" Wallace, who served two terms as prosecuting attorney of Jackson County, Missouri.

His friends in those early days called him Will; his enemies called him Bill, and by various other names and titles by no means complimentary. Almighty God, so Will Wallace devoutly believed, had called him to a career of righteousness as he conceived righteousness.

Like Frank James, whom he tried hard to hoist to the gallows as a convicted murderer, Wallace was a preacher's son. His father was the Rev. Joseph William Wallace, a pioneer Presbyterian minister in

Kentucky and Missouri. A grandfather of the Crusader was a Kentucky colonel of militia long before the Civil War. A great-grandfather was a Virginian captain under George Washington throughout the Revolutionary War.

Let it be made known with all possible emphasis that the doughty prosecutor whose personal and official nerve—and it required just exactly what all of us understand as nerve—put the swift-sliding toboggan underneath the bandit crew and gave it the energetic shove which landed the outfit in the ditch, was a Southerner of Southern forbears. In politics he was, of course, a Democrat. We employ past tenses here, although Mr. Wallace, at 78 in 1926, is alive and active in crusading of a kind quite different from that which prompted him to prosecute the Missouri outlaws at imminent risk of his own life.

So important to the purposes of this narrative are the name and fame of Mr. Wallace that a skeletonized biography of the man belongs here. He was born on a farm in Clark County, Ky. When he was only eight years old the family removed by steamboat to western Missouri, settling on a Jackson County farm between the sites of the present towns of Lee's Summit and Blue Springs—right in the heart of the Cole Younger country. That was in 1857, the year Quantrill went to Kansas from Ohio, and one of the bloody years of the Missouri-Kansas warfare over the slavery problem. Thus the little lad from the Dark and Bloody Ground was thrust forthwith into a settlement which was a part of a darker and a bloodier ground, from that time until nearly a quarter of a century later, when he himself turned on the light and wiped up the gore, than any section of the Bluegrass State ever was.

Will Wallace was too young to comprehend the situation then. But it was inevitable as he grew from a small boy to a big boy, through the rest of the pre-war troubles and through the four years of the Civil War, that he absorbed certain indelible impressions. The blood and the darkness of those years became a part of the boy's stock of mental and spiritual experiences. It is to be conceived that the lad had shuddery nights and shadowy days, when the moonlight lacked for him the romance ascribed to it by poets, and the sunshine was beclouded with the lurid reek of burning houses and the smoke of battle. For battle, be it known to you, raged all around the preacher's farmhouse on the open prairie, and upon many a day and far into many a night the sound of the guns—cannon and musket, rifle and pistol—roared and crackled from many a modest battlefield in Jackson County.

Both the father and the stepmother of Will Wallace owned slaves. "My parents," he says, "treated their negroes just as they did their own children, except that the blacks lived in their own quarters. They never separated husband and wife."

When little Will was nine years old he began plowing with a yoke of oxen. Later he did all sorts of work on the farm. Side by side with the negroes he plowed and hoed, harvested and hauled. Like the Baptist father of Frank and Jesse James, a few miles across the Big Muddy river to the north, the Presbyterian father of Will Wallace worked on the farm during the week and preached on Sundays.

"My father, though a preacher, was well-to-do," says Mr. Wallace. "He had about twenty horses, most of them good ones, brought from Kentucky. The farm was well stocked with cattle, hogs and sheep. Ours was a happy home."

That reminiscent paragraph is pathetic in its significance. The happy home was destined presently to be broken up, the beautiful farm laid waste, the livestock and much of the inanimate property stolen, and the family itself finally driven out of the county. The experiences of the Wallaces were of cut and kind with those of thousands of other families in the border counties of Missouri. War, in that section, was hell on earth.

A band of Federal soldiers belonging to the command of the notorious Kansas cutthroat, Col. Charles R. Jennison, rode up to the preacher's farm. They took Negro Alf away with them, and five of the best horses. The night preceding that raid two of the Jennison soldiers spent at the Rev. Mr. Wallace's as self-invited guests. The preacher never missed having family prayers at bedtime and before breakfast. That night he read a chapter from the Bible, then said "Let us pray." One of the soldiers knelt with the family. The other squirmed and hesitated.

"But finally," says Crusader Wallace, "he came down on his knees, his sabre ringing on the floor as he did so. Those two men took none of our property, and they tried to dissuade the others from doing so when the larger band arrived next day.

"Another circumstance of that eventful day is branded forever in my memory. My father was sitting on the front porch. A soldier cocked his pistol and gave him three minutes to get a gold watch which he had been told my mother had in bed with her, for she was sick. I felt sure he would shoot. My father, without so much as rising from his seat, said without a tremor in his voice, 'You can shoot on. The watch is my wife's, and I will never ask her to give it up.'

"I saw him afterward when his life was threatened and actual violence resorted to, and he was just as cool. I do not believe that during his pilgrimage of eighty-three years he ever was frightened. But 'he feared God and kept His commandments.'"

Safely are we to infer that the Crusader came of stern stuff!

It hardly is possible to refrain from quoting here an eloquent autobiographical passage from the pen of the Crusader, since his words supply so vivid a picture of those mad, sad, bad events and days:

"The border warfare now was fully on, and for two long years the land was ablaze with horrors. No pen can depict it, no picture fully portray it. Bands of soldiers were ever shooting across the prairies, their guns and sabres glistening in the sunlight. Solitary horsemen were ever dashing from this scene or that. Little battles were being fought on all sides.

"I can see myself now, sitting on a rail fence, listening to the roar of the cannon at Lone Jack—said to be the bloodiest battle of the war in proportion to the number of men engaged in it.

"The tragic story of one scene was hardly told until

another was going the rounds. Citizens were arrested and lodged in jail, and women and children were left alone and defenseless. The day of vengeance came. Men were hanged to trees or in their barns, or were called from their homes in the night-time and shot.

"Meantime the torch was vying with the sword. A burning house could be seen across the prairies in the night-time at a distance of at least twenty-five miles. One night I looked out of a second-story window and counted twenty-two houses on fire.

"The prairies were fired frequently. One day when the wind was very high I saw a band of soldiers on a high ridge some three miles away. Two in the rear seemed to stop. A blaze arose. The flames came leaping toward where I was, and I believe that in less than ten minutes they had covered the three miles. The whole sky was black with smoke. Some neighbors fought the fire and escaped injury to their farms. Others did not."

Those others, very likely, asked themselves "What's the use?" They were in the maelstrom; they knew they were to be caught up by it, sooner or later, and swept away. Hell had blown off its lid long before, and the sulphurous flames and fumes thereof were sweeping forward and spreading outward like the prairie fire the soldiers had set. Those who permitted the flames to despoil their farms had become numbed by misery and trepidation. There were very many such in Jackson County, the one restricted area in all the Union to which the war came home and raged and harried with the most superlatively demoniac fury. Jackson County was the reddest spot on the map of the United States. This writer defies any student of American history to attempt disproof of that concrete statement's accuracy.

Will Wallace was not quite fifteen years old when the Federal commander at Kansas City, Gen. Thomas Ewing, issued his celebrated Order No. 11. This order required everybody in rural Jackson County and other territory adjacent to emigrate within fifteen days. The Wallaces were a trifling fraction of the tremendous exodus. As the family outfit crept slowly toward its destination in far-off Callaway County, Preacher Wallace drove the leading wagon, drawn by a yoke of oxen—he who had owned but lately twenty fine horses from Kentucky.

Will Wallace and a small stepbrother remained behind until the last day of grace, "a dangerous experiment caused by hauling for neighbors." They were one night overtime in leaving the old homestead. Marshall, a faithful negro, was with the two boys. That night they lay down to sleep atop the loaded wagon which the oxen, lying silent in the barnlot, were to pull forward in the morning.

"We had no cover for the wagon, and I gazed at the stars as they came out," remembers the Crusader. "Though I knew I could see them when I reached my destination, it seemed that I was telling my boyhood stars goodby forever. It was August, and the balmy air was not stirring a leaf; the hush was intense. After a while the silence was broken. A dog left behind at a neighboring house began to howl piteously. The dogs throughout the neighborhood took it up. Their howls rang out upon the stilly air, some of them seeming miles away. They missed their masters and the children with whom they had played, and their doleful voices continued throughout the night. Thus was the awful reign of 'Order No. 11' howled in."

The family reached Fulton, county seat of Callaway, after days of toilful journeying. Westminster College, a Presbyterian institution then stricken with poverty, gave the Rev. Mr. Wallace a professorship at a pittance of a salary. He rented a farm near town. That winter the family came perilously near to starvation. Sub-zero weather was suffered during a considerable part of the season. Will Wallace had no overcoat. Relatives of his stepmother had bought him a thin fall suit as the sorry caravan passed through Columbia, "the Athens of Missouri," on the way to Fulton. Thus the Crusader:

"I had nothing to wear except that fall suit and a cotton shirt under it. I said to my mother one day that I got a little cold while milking, feeding the stock and getting up wood. She made me a flannel shirt. My! what a comfort I got from it! Some church in St. Louis, hearing of our condition, sent us a big goodsbox full of old second-hand clothes. My mother said we had some pride still left, and that we would shiver in the winter's blast rather than wear them. The box and contents were returned. Our food that winter was about as scanty as our clothing. When people get poorer, Heaven pity them!"

Preacher Wallace returned to his Jackson County home at the close of the war and found the farm laid waste. Will Wallace remained in Fulton and attended Westminster College for more than seven years, working his way. Returning to his old home, he helped his father on the farm, taught country schools, studied law, was admitted to the bar, and became a practicing attorney at Independence, the county seat. In 1880 he removed to Kansas City. That autumn, at the age of thirty-two, he was elected prosecuting attorney.

The business of running for prosecutor in Jackson County had not been, up to that year, anything at all of a ticklish proposition. The man who got the Democratic nomination also won the election. All he had to do with regard to the border bandits was to keep his mouth shut down perfectly tight. So far as any candidate for that office was concerned, banded outlaws and their outlawry simply weren't. No aspirant ever had mentioned the "James Boys' Band," either by name or by inference, in public utterance. It was not considered exactly good—or one might insinuate safe—form so to do.

But in the campaign of 1880 appeared a most sensational candidate. Will Wallace, that preacher's son who grew up, mostly, right in the midst of the James boys' favorite raiding and robbing territory, had the nerve to announce himself for prosecuting attorney and to declare that if elected he would do his level best to put those illustrious fellow-citizens upon the scaffold at Independence or into prison cells at Jefferson City.

Why, Will Wallace had grown up with some of those outlaws, and knew them intimately, as one might express it! He knew their folks, their friends, their neighbors who stood pro or con as the case might be. Moreover, he knew just how the old guerrillas felt with regard to Frank and Jesse and the rest of the appearing and disappearing outlaws; they felt so kindly toward their old comrades under Quantrill or Anderson that they would stand by them and for them, if need be, to the death. And then the new generation that had grown up since the war—it contained a great many young fellows who had come to look upon the bandits as heroes of a sort. The nerve of a man running for prosecutor on a law-enforcement platform involving prosecution of the James outfit! And a Southern man, too, who himself as a boy had been driven out of the county by the infamous Order No. 11!

Those Jackson County people imagined that they had known Will Wallace, but that notion was purely imaginary. They had known a small boy and a youth and a young man named Will Wallace. What of that? Assuredly they had not known that underneath the calm exterior of the Kansas City lawyer seethed the pent Utica of a modern Crusader.

Gen. James A. Garfield and Gen. Winfield S. Hancock were running for the presidency of the United States that fall, but Jackson County hardly knew it. Jackson County concentered its interest upon the race of the young lawyer whose platform was built directly over a dynamite cache. Old-timers still talk about it, now and then, and some of them wonder if Will Wallace was a brave man or just a natural-born fool who happened to be in luck. Opinion drifts far in the direction of the brave-man theory.

As we have seen, Wallace was nurtured in the old-fashioned religion. He was a church-going Presbyterian when he secreted a sixshooter somewhere near his anatomy and took to the political warpath in 1880, and he sticks steadfastly today to the creed of his fathers. His armor buckled on, he was of a Cromwellian cast and character when he saddled his horse and set forth, alone, to "'lectioneer" amongst the friends and apologists of Jesse James et al. Into the Crackerneck neighborhood he rode, through the Six-Mile section, into and through the throbbing heart of the region where the bandits never failed to find seclusion and succor. He spoke in churches, school-houses, outdoors, usually at night. And Wallace the Crusader spoke in forthright fashion.

"I charged specifically and by name that Jesse James, Frank James, Ed Miller, Dick Liddil, William Ryan and another man, whose name I did not know, were the men who were committing the train robberies, bank robberies and murders throughout the state," says Mr. Wallace. "I had been raised in Jackson County, had practiced law for five years at Independence, and I was sure of the accuracy of my declarations.

"My foolhardiness—for such, indeed, it was—occasioned astonishment and intense excitement. Some of the friends of the outlaws knew that my list was correct. Others honestly believed I was charging innocent men with crime, and the feeling for and against me was at fever heat.

"Word was sent me that I would not be permitted to speak at some of the places advertised, but I went and spoke, and repeated my charge. I remember that a man who said he had killed two men and whose name I need not give—he is dead—accosted me on the streets of Independence in a towering rage because I had charged publicly and by name that his nephew was a member of the James band and a train robber. In less than a year afterward his nephew gave himself up to the officers and confessed his guilt."

Dick Liddil was the nephew mentioned. Who the uncle was doesn't matter. Time and tide have discounted his unrighteous indignation

CHAPTER XXIX

APPARENTLY Jesse James was getting careless, or was it that first-class raw material for the making of train robbers had become scarce in Jackson County? Jesse seems to have liked even numbers. He figured that six was the proper size of a gang organized to hold up a railroad train. When he came up from Tennessee he had already enlisted with him four followers he felt he could trust. According to his mathematics another was needed. Some one of his gang suggested a young farmer, Tucker Bassham, who lived in the Crackerneck neighborhood near Independence.

Jesse never had met Bassham and knew very little about him. It appears that Ed Miller arranged an interview between the leader and the rustic.

Bassham balked at first, but after Jesse had assured him that the gang might have the joy of dividing as much as $100,000 and that there really was little or no danger, Tucker capitulated to the temptation and agreed to help arrange the preliminaries and take part in the big show.

The holdup was an easy one, the train being detained but a few minutes. The illustrious Missouri wheat sack reappeared in a modified form, and the division of spoils took place about half a mile from the scene of the robbery, in an abandoned log schoolhouse to which the rough riders galloped at top speed. Tucker Bassham's part was something less than $900, but even that comparative pittance looked like a fortune to him. He could not refrain from flashing his funds in public. Nor could he keep his loose mouth from boasting that he had been chosen by the great and glorious Jesse James as equal partner with the others in a train holdup.

Col. Maurice Langhorne and Maj. Whig Keshlaer of the county marshal's office picked up Tucker Bassham and brought him into Independence, where he made a confession which he repudiated later; but Tucker went to Jefferson City with a sentence of ten years in the penitentiary, just about the time Will Wallace was being elected prosecuting attorney. Wallace went into office in January, 1881. The anti-outlaw voters who had elected him hoped he possibly might show some actual backbone, though many of them really didn't expect him to do so. Those who had opposed him because he had announced his determination to run down the James band felt that he was just bluffing. An ex-guerrilla of Crackerneck locale remarked at a crossroads country store:

"The young buck has got nerve—you can't say he ain't and git away with it; but I'm bettin' my new forty-five agin a toy pistol that he hain't got enough nerve to go out after the weakest sister in the James bunch if he gits a clew that a baby could foller; and I'll bet my farm, hosses and wagons throwed in, that

Bill Wallace won't stand up in no court and prosecute if one o' the boys gits ketched—so help me!"

"Amen!" aspirated a couple of the old guerrilla's cronies. "You said it!"

Slantwise, perhaps, the eyes of the nation rested for a brief spell upon the nervy young buck who had set out to exterminate the free-bootery brotherhood which for fourteen years had had pretty much its own way with Jackson County, not to speak of a vast outside area. Then the name of William H. Wallace faded from public print, to reappear only when the new prosecutor had opportunity to prove that he meant what he had said in his campaign. Such opportunity was presented less than three months after he took office.

In a rural village a few miles out of Nashville, Tennessee, on the 26th of March, 1881, a warlike male individual mounted upon a splendid horse and garbed in fashionable tailormade clothes dismounted in front of a general store and liquid-refreshments place. He hitched his horse to the rack and went inside, walking somewhat unsteadily. The stranger ordered raw oysters served with raw whisky, both of which he gulped greedily.

Much more whisky than oysters descended his gullet. In about thirty minutes the fresh customer was more than visibly intoxicated; he was, to be literal, howling drunk. The owner of the establishment felt peeved when this liberal spender began to create a disturbance, but he was discreet enough to call in some citizens who happened to be near at hand. One of these was W. L. Earthman of Nashville, collector of back taxes. Having been a detective, Earthman had had experience also in collecting bad men in arrears to society.

"Stand back! Stand back!" yelled the drunken man when the newcomers approached. "Everybody stand back, now, or somebody'll get shot! I'm a desperado and an outlaw, and my name's Tom Hill!"

Tom Hill at the same time reached both hands to his rear, beneath his new coat, and was in the act of pulling forth two big revolvers when Earthman, darting behind, pinioned the arms of the desperado and outlaw close to his body by clasping him around the waist. Others disarmed the disturber, who was taken to Nashville and placed in jail.

It was discovered that next to his body Tom Hill wore a buckskin vest in which was $1,300 in gold coin. This caused the police to opine that Mr. Hill had some reason for not depositing his money in banks and, on the other hand, that just possibly he might be a man who would take other folks' cash from a bank if he could do so without being caught in the act or afterward. As to his identity they had no clew.

The chief of police telegraphed a detailed description of Tom Hill to the police in all the large cities of the United States. Chief Speers of Kansas City showed the telegram he received to Whig Keshlaer, who remarked:

"Looks to me, Chief, like it might be a description of Bill Ryan."

"I don't think so," said Speers. "I've seen Bill a few times, and it doesn't seem to me that this fits him."

Keshlaer felt that the new prosecutor ought to see the dispatch, anyhow, so he notified Wallace, who proceeded to police headquarters at once. Wallace had been well acquainted with Ryan at Independence, before the latter entered outlawry. He was convinced that the Nashville chief had described his old acquaintance, and he wired that official to that effect.

"Hold your man; photograph coming," was the substance of a telegram that followed shortly.

"The prisoner is Bill Ryan," wired the Nashville chief immediately after he received the photograph of Bill.

Requisitional courtesies having been exchanged between Missouri and Tennessee governors, Whig Keshlaer went to Nashville and got the "desperado and outlaw" whose name, in Tennessee, was Tom Hill. Ryan had been living there as a guest of Jesse James. He was exceedingly sober and despondent when he arrived back at his old home town and was locked up to await trial. His recent host at Nashville was deeply disgusted with Bill. Jesse, who didn't drink whisky, couldn't understand how a load of liquor could so befuddle a man's brains as to cause him thus to give himself away and incidentally to endanger the safety of his friends.

Will Wallace now had his chance to make good. He had also upon his official hands a task of a nature exceedingly ticklish. It was to be his business to stand up in a crowded courtroom, turning his back to an audience composed largely of armed friends of the outlaws, and try to send a conspicuous member of the James Boys' Band to the penitentiary. The grand jury had indicted Ryan as an alleged participant in the Chicago & Alton train robbery at Glendale.

The chief witness against Ryan was Dan Tucker Bassham. Prosecutor Wallace needed Bassham's testimony, but at that period the word of a convict was not acceptable as evidence in a Missouri court. Bassham must be a free man, and one officially purged of the taint of felony. Will Wallace, knowing the fellow as a raw recruit who had been pressed into the James gang service for that one robbery only, argued successfully with his Presbyterian conscience that Jackson County, the state of Missouri, the United States of America and the world in general would be considerably safer with Bill Ryan inside the prison and Tucker Bassham outside than the other way about. He knew Ryan as "a regular member of the band—next in boldness to Jesse James."

Gov. Thomas T. Crittenden, to whom the prosecutor applied, coincided with this view. The governor issued a pardon for Bassham, but not to him, as we are to see. Mr. Wallace was too keenly shrewd to play his trump card first. An official wearing nobly enough the interesting name of Amazon Hays—incidentally he was a great-grandson of Daniel Boone—went to Jefferson City and returned to Independence with young Bassham, who had served but a few months in prison.

"I was compelled to have Hays guard Bassham throughout the trial," recalls Mr. Wallace. "He slept in an adjoining room to Bassham at night, in order to protect him from the rage of the friends of the outlaws. When they heard he would testify, they set fire to his house in the Crackerneck neighborhood, and his wife and children fled to Independence for safety. The old oak floor of the house would not burn, and his household goods were piled up in the yard, set fire to and burned.

"Just before Bassham was sworn, I handed him the pardon of the governor in the presence of the jury, telling them that it had been issued upon the express promise of Bassham to become a witness in the case and tell the whole truth, and, as was usual in such cases, he was to go free."

The former prosecutor is convinced that the Ryan trial was the most exciting one that ever took place in a criminal court in the Middle West. According to him, it was far more thrilling than was the trial of Frank James in another Missouri county two years later, at which again Will Wallace appeared as chief prosecutor.

The Ryan trial was a test case between law and order on one side, anarchy and disorder on the other. Many of Wallace's close friends counseled him to dismiss the case and let Ryan go free. They argued that it was worth a man's life to conduct the prosecution, and that in any event Ryan would be acquitted. No Jackson County jury, they declared, would convict a member of the James band; no jury would dare do it, even if so inclined by personal feeling against outlawry, in addition to convincing evidence of the defendant's guilt.

"But it seemed to me that I would rather be shot than to show the white feather then," says Wallace the Crusader.

He had prepared thoroughly the state's case. First

he visited the Crackerneck neighborhood on the hunt for evidence. Then he went to Nashville and interviewed Earthman and other Tennessee witnesses.

And just here do we arrive at a fact which indicates, perhaps more strongly than any other circumstance, the absolute terror in which the James Boys' Band as an organization for outlawry was held by railroad officials and employes. Mr. Wallace requested the Chicago & Alton railroad officials to have the members of the train crew at the time of the Glendale robbery present to testify.

"But, to my astonishment," he states, "such was the terror in which the outlaws were held that the managers of the road refused. They said it was of no use; that no man could convict one of the James boys in Missouri, and that if they tried to help me it would simply make the outlaws mad, and they would rob the company's trains more than ever, and probably would shoot down the conductors and the engineers. The railroad officials finally, upon my insistence, agreed to send the trainmen, but when they came and saw the jam of the friends of the outlaws at Independence they all backed out, saying they could identify nobody, and I did not place any of them upon the witness stand."

In his autobiography, published in 1914, William H. Wallace tells this astounding story:

"Memory calls up now a circumstance which shows the lengths to which men sometimes will go under excitement. Two train robberies, the one at Blue Cut and the one at Winston in which two men were killed, had been committed in the summer of 1881 while

Ryan was in jail. It looked as though the bandits were defying the law as never before because the law was daring to imprison one of their number.

"Just after the Ryan trial a man who formerly had been a deputy sheriff in Jackson County came to me and said that he had been sent to me by some good citizens to get a list of men in Jackson County who harbored the James boys. I asked him what they wanted with it. He said they wanted it 'for a certain purpose,' but would not tell me exactly what. He said those who sent him said I was the only man who could give a list they would feel sure was accurate. I suspected something, and refused to give the list.

"A few days afterward a prominent railroad employe came up from St. Louis to see me. He asked if the man above referred to had asked for the list. I told him he had. He then asked me for the list himself, and I declined to give it. He said he might as well tell me why they wanted the list. He said they had determined to put an everlasting end to train robbery in Missouri by making it impossible in the future for the James boys to find any one who would be willing to harbor them.

"He said the plan was to make up a train of box-cars in St. Louis, place in it men and guns and horses and saddles and bridles. He said the train would stop at Little Blue in Jackson County, on the Missouri Pacific, just after dark. Then the men were to unload the horses and mount them and go in squads and put to death every man whose name appeared on my list.

"I told him I certainly disapproved of any such plan, and refused to furnish the list. The plan was abandoned. If carried out it would have been as bad as Order No. 11, and based upon the same merciless logic."

Before reknitting the thread of Bill Ryan's trial we should insert another little story, our valuable friend Detective Sam Allender being the narrator. Mr. Allender supplies it specifically for this chapter:

"When Missouri was celebrating in 1921 the one-hundredth anniversary of admission to statehood, at a meeting of the St. Louis Railway Club at the Hotel Statler in that city one night, a gentleman was speaking on 'History of Railroads in Missouri.' After he was through there was a kind of experience meeting, a number of railroad people telling stories. One gentleman told of his many years with the Burlington railroad and explained that during the Jesse James rule of railroads in Missouri the Burlington was one road never disturbed by the James crowd or by any other people who followed the policy of taking what they wanted.

"The explanation of it was that during all of the time of the reign of the James gang the Burlington always fixed up the mother of Frank and Jesse, Mrs. Zerelda Samuel, with an annual pass good over the entire system of the Burlington line. This, as you know, was in the days when passes were allowed to anybody the railroads cared to give them to."

We are to assume, beyond peradventure, that it was not the Chicago, Burlington & Quincy Railroad that sent its emissaries to Prosecutor Wallace with the amazing proposition which he described.

Mr. Wallace recalls that the engineer of the train

held up at Glendale, a fine looking man of middle age, begged almost piteously to be excused from testifying at the Bill Ryan trial.

"And please, Mr. Wallace, don't talk so loud, right here in the courthouse yard. We're both liable to be shot at any moment. I can't identify anybody, anyhow."

"When I told him to go," relates the Crusader, "he actually went off in a trot."

The Tennessee witnesses told of the capture of Ryan, of the gold coin found on his person, and of his Tom Hill alias. A young Jackson County farmer testified that he recognized the voice of Ryan, whom he had known since boyhood, when a group of men rode past his farm from the direction of Glendale, the night the robbery took place. The express messenger testified that "a large man" struck him over the head with a revolver and that as he lay unconscious from the blow, $9,400 disappeared from the safe. It was in evidence also that the pistol firing and the oldtime Rebel guerrilla yelling so terrified the mother of the station agent, who lived in the upper story of the railroad depot, that she went instantly insane and had to be placed in an asylum without hope of recovery.

There appears to have been solid cause for the trepidation of the locomotive engineer. When the case was called, friends of the Jameses and their gang members crowded the courtroom. Many of them were known to be armed, and probably most of them were. Numbers of them slept at night on the grass in the courthouse yard, pickets being posted. But for the fact that the sixshooters were concealed, it was almost a replica of the regulations in a wartime camp of Quantrill's guerrillas.

"Many law-abiding citizens could not get into the courtroom," the venerable prosecutor avers. "Jesse James and his men were close by during the trial, and it was rumored that plans were being considered for the rescue of Ryan. Every night skyrockets were sent up, out in the woods near Independence, said to be signals to Ryan that his comrades were not far away.

"Dick Liddil, who was then with the outlaws, told me after he gave himself up that they were secreted near Independence and that a rescue of Ryan was discussed, but it was abandoned when they heard that Capt. Maurice M. Langhorne, an ex-Confederate— said to have been one of the coolest, gamest men in Shelby's brigade—had charge of Ryan's safekeeping not only in the courtroom but was conducting him personally from the jail to the courthouse."

Ryan had men of more than local eminence for counsel. One was R. L. Yeager, who had served as prosecuting attorney and had bestirred himself not at all in the direction of running down the robbers. Another was Blake L. Woodson, a criminal lawyer of wide practice. A third was B. J. Franklin, formerly a member of Congress. Associated with Prosecutor Wallace was Col. John N. Southern, who had suffered a broken thigh in Civil War days when a Federal bullet struck him. When the trial was in progress, Wallace and Southern received a letter warning them to desist from prosecuting the accused, telling them plainly that their lives would be in danger if they kept on. They kept on. Wallace opened and closed the case,

Colonel Southern made a brilliant argument in between. Says Crusader Wallace:

"I put my whole soul into an effort in the closing
argument to inspire the jury with courage to convict,
for I was afraid that some of them, knowing the danger
of a vote to convict, might falter. I have always regarded this as the supreme hour of my practice as a
lawyer."

And—the jury convicted! Astounding fact! Prose-
cuted by two Southerners, one of them actually named
Southern and a gallant ex-Confederate colonel, a
member of the James Boys' Band was found guilty
by a Jackson County jury of complicity in a Jackson
County train robbery—and a majority of the jurors
themselves were Southern men!

Twenty-five years in state prison was the sentence.
Ryan's counsel moved for a new trial, setting forth
that whilst the case was before the court Governor
Crittenden had shipped to Independence two large
boxes of rifles, and that this act "overawed the jury."
The governor actually shipped the arms, which never
were unpacked. Each of the jurors told the prosecutor,
later, that they never heard about the arms shipment
until they had rendered verdict and been discharged.

Ryan got no new trial. He was pardoned out of
the penitentiary after serving seven years by Gov.
A. P. Morehouse, a St. Louisan, on the plea that he
was suffering from tuberculosis.

"The air was full of threats of assassination," the
Crusader recalls, "especially against the witness Bassham and myself. Bassham said he had been assured
that he and I were on the death list, and he pleaded

for me to leave the country with him, but I declined."

Fancy, if you can, Wallace the Crusader and Bassham the Bandit (if, forsooth, one train robbery can make a man a bandit)—fancy the college-bred lawyer and the illiterate rustic, the astute prosecutor and the stupid moronic misfit, the Cromwellian Presbyterian and the churchless peacher on his pals, leaving the country together and beginning life anew, somewhere in Mexico perhaps, or upon a lone sea isle, in fear and trembling! Jesse James himself surely must have laughed loose a front tooth if he ever heard about Tattling Tucker's naïve suggestion. But that was exactly like Dan Tucker Bassham—he was the one big joke of the whole bandit outfit's sixteen-years' career; and yet what an immensely important man he was, nevertheless—for the state!

"He took to his heels, and I have never heard of him since," says the Crusader.

Bassham returned to Jackson County some years later, died a natural death, and was buried in his native soil.

CHAPTER XXX

DICK LIDDIL KILLS WOOD HITE AND "COMES IN"

IT is not to be doubted that Jesse James became increasingly irritable as the years heaped upon him their accumulative agonies of mind and spirit. For full three lustrums the man had faced a hostile world. At no time, day or night, had he dared turn his back upon any part of that hostility. Eternal vigilance was the price of his pitiful liberty.

Year by year, month by month, day by day, his situation had become more precarious. Friends were decreasing, foes increasing in numbers. Places of security in earlier years had become places of peril. Protection was yielding to detection. His incognito, amazingly effective as it was, could not fend him forever against revealment of identity, well did he know. It was but a question of time when the veil must be pierced and Jesse W. James himself emerge from the shadow and stand forth unmasked, visible and inviting fodder for fatal bullets.

Has there been in all the world, at any period or in any country, another instance of such hunting and eluding? Has any other man in all the annals of time confronted such a host of enemies and stood them off for so many years? Can you wrest from fact or from fiction any tale of pursuit and escape that parallels the experience of Jesse James? If so, you should tell it to the world, providing thus a story of superior thrills. In whatever other way his name goes down to history, the name of this outlawed Missourian must be preserved as that of the man who made the most desperate fight for life and liberty, and for the pursuit of such happiness as might be possible under the circumstances, written thus far into human records. In that respect, at any rate, Jesse James has won supremacy.

This being granted, we may forgive Jesse much of the madness of his later years. As Major Edwards wrote of him in 1877, "He was hunted, and he was human." Madness is the word we mean just here. Tormented with a thousand terrors, the man had come at last to be at least a half-madman. He loved his wife, his little children and his maimed old mother. The love of life, the urge to be, the will to survive, were strong within him. He believed himself an immortal being and he was not afraid to die, but he shared in the general human inclination to maintain the mundane sphere of existence as long as that existence seems desirable; and I, for one, do not believe that Jesse James ever entertained the slightest thought of suicide. Quitting was not in his code.

Fate had woven about him a net of hideous mesh. We are not concerned here with the proportional part his own deeds had contributed to the weaving of the mesh. We write not for morons, but for minds capable of calm analysis. Motives and emotions alike may be left to moralists who carp and cavil, to those whose lines are cast in pleasant places and who would cut all men by a common pattern. The point to be made is that Jesse James, being human and not superhuman, began to crack under the strain.

Always of a nervous temperament, constitutionally disposed to act first and think afterward, Jesse acquired in time a case of nerves. His environment being such that he could not afford to indulge for a moment in the comfort of giving way to an attack of nervous prostration and letting things slide, he fought off the devils of neurasthenia as he had fought off for fifteen years the innumerable foes who could fire bullets at a breathing target—given the target.

The upshot was that Jesse James became a case of walking and watchful nervous prostration unprostrated, so that his moral responsibility, whatever may have been the degree thereof which he possessed at any time, was weakened to the point that it made him more desperate than ever. If, as Major Edwards estimated in 1877, he trusted only about two persons in every 10,000, it may be assumed that by 1880 he had come to trust only one in that number, and mistrusted even that one at times. There were tales to the effect that, in his semi-madness, he fancied that his own brother had turned against him.

Jim Cummins relates that some time after the train holdup at Glendale he was at the home of Frank James, on the High Ferry pike three miles from Nashville, and that Jesse "did all he could that day to get Frank to say something to get up a row with him, but failed in this, and Jesse got up a row with Dick Liddil and drew his pistol on Dick."

"I stepped between them to keep Jesse from killing Dick," says Cummins, "and I told Jesse that if that was the way he was going to conduct himself I wouldn't stay with any of them."

Jim recalls that he told the Jameses that he was not going to board or sojourn anywhere with Bill Ryan, who was getting drunk all the time; and that Frank James had said to Jesse, Dick Liddil and himself, when they went down from Missouri with Ryan:

"Are you fellows going to bring that damned Irishman down here to give us all away?"

"Frank also said to me," recalls Cummins, "'Jim, you are welcome at my house any time, but won't you be so kind as to go over to Nashville and tell Dingus (meaning Jesse) not to bring that damned Irishman to my house?' I did so. Jesse raved and swore and said he believed Frank would like to see him dead and see his family suffer."

As we have observed, "that damned Irishman" got on one drunk too many and did give them all away; for it was Bill Ryan's arrest and identification that broke up their happy homes.

Ed Miller was missing mysteriously, and Jim Cummins asked Jesse several times, he states, what had become of Ed. Jesse replied that Ed was in Eastern Tennessee, was sick, and he didn't believe Ed ever would recover.

Some time later Jim Cummins discovered that he himself was dead and buried. It appears that Jim had given Ed Miller a brown horse. One Sam Burton, living near Norborne, in Carroll County, Missouri, was gathering blackberries when he saw two men riding past. Burton recognized one of them as Jesse James, whom he had known for some time. The one who rode the brown horse he mistook for Jim Cummins, having seen Jim aboard that animal several times. It may be wise to explain for certain citified readers that all horses don't look alike to farmers; they can recognize a noble beast as easily as they can recognize a man. Sam Burton was right in his identification of the horse.

"Burton went home," according to Cummins, "and said he'd seen Jesse James and Jim Cummins riding by the blackberry patch. Later he heard of a man having been killed near his place. He went and helped bury the remains. The body was badly decayed and the features unrecognizable. Burton thought he was burying me, and he believed for years that I was the corpse, and plenty of other folks believed it, but I didn't. It was Ed Miller that he helped bury. Jesse James had shot Miller. He soon showed up at Charlie Ford's hangout, in Ray County, leading the brown horse. Charlie asked Jesse where Ed was, and Jesse said Ed was seriously ill and had had to go to Hot Springs, and he didn't believe Ed would live long."

There is a tale to the effect that Jesse and Ed had a quarrel, followed by a pistol duel, and that Jesse's bullet beat Ed's to the mark. Jesse, as we know, was tremendously agile with the trigger. Before the date of Miller's sudden demise Jesse had begun to suspect that both Miller and Dick Liddil were getting shaky in their fidelity to him.

The chief outstanding fact is that Edward Miller of Clay was buried in Carroll as James Cummins of Clay.

Some months before Miller met his fate he was cast in a minor rôle for an earlier act in the comedy of errors preceding the grand tragedy. This was the killing of Jesse James by George Shepherd, which didn't happen save in Shepherd's vivid imagination. If Shepherd had been a writer instead of a fighter he could have done a blood-and-thunder business with the best-worst of them.

Shortly after the Glendale robbery Marshal James Liggett of Kansas City, one of the most persistent pursuers of the Missouri outlaws, determined upon an audacious plan for the elimination of Jesse. He enlisted the services of Shepherd as a detective. After his release from the Kentucky penitentiary, where he did time for his part in the bank robbery at Russellville, Shepherd had returned to Kansas City. He was working in a dry-goods store when Jesse came out of his Tennessee retirement and engineered the Glendale job.

Marshal Liggett proposed to Shepherd that the former guerrilla and reformed outlaw pretend that he was under accusation in the Glendale affair and get into the confidence of Jesse James. A piece of job work that counterfeited a newspaper clipping was done by a clever printer. Shepherd mounted a horse and rode to the Samuel farm. He showed the ostensible clipping, in which he was accused as one of the Glendale robbers, to Dr. and Mrs. Samuel. Having been Jesse's guerrilla leader at the end of the war, and having suffered for the Kentucky bank robbery, Shepherd was not suspected of insincerity.

The amateur detective was conducted at night, blindfolded, according to his story, to the camp of Jesse

James, Jim Cummins, Ed Miller and another man unknown to him. Shepherd was received as an old friend. He showed Jesse the faked clipping and pretended to be eager to join the James Boys' Band. A plan was laid for the robbing of a bank at Empire City, Jasper County, far to the south. Shepherd, armed with three big Smith & Wesson revolvers and mounted upon a good horse, rode down with the others. There was no bank robbery, but some days later Shepherd turned up with a wound in one leg.

"I've killed Jesse James," he told Marshal Liggett, "and wounded Jim Cummins, and either Jim or Ed Miller shot me in the leg. I was riding along with Jesse, drew back a bit, and fired one shot through his head. He tumbled off his horse, and I watched him for fully a minute; he didn't move. Jesse's dead and done for. The other fellows attacked me, and they got away after a running fight."

Neither Jesse nor Jim turned up dead or wounded—although both were reported missing; and George Shepherd's leg wound remains as much of a mystery to this day as does the bullet hole in the hat of a celebrated mayor of Kansas City, in later years, who showed the injured chapeau as a mute testimonial to his bravery in a political fracas.

There was neither fake nor jest in the fate that overtook Robert Woodson Hite, cousin of Jesse Woodson James. Wood Hite had taken part in the train robberies at Glendale, Winston and Blue Cut. He was about thirty years old and of appearance far from prepossessing—a gangling, awkward, untidy person.

After the Blue Cut holdup Wood Hite had returned

to his home in Logan County, Kentucky, on a farm. There he killed a negro who, he averred, had insulted him. The victim was sitting on a fence. Hite's bullet toppled him off. The body remained unburied for several days, until hogs began eating the festering flesh. Hite had fled, returning to Missouri, and he found refuge with Mrs. Martha Bolton, a young widow, sister to Charles and Robert Ford, on a farm near Richmond, Ray County. This house was a place of frequent resort for members of the James Boys' Band. "Cap" Ford, an elder brother of the outlaws, was there much of the time.

The Jackson County farmhand known to outlawry as Dick Liddil, who had surrendered to Sheriff James R. Timberlake of Clay County on the night of Jan. 24, 1882, signed and swore to a long confession in the presence of Police Commissioner Henry H. Craig of Kansas City on March 29. Toward the end of his confession Liddil stated that he arrived at Mrs. Bolton's Saturday night, Dec. 3, 1881.

"Next morning," continues the Liddil confession, "I came down to breakfast, and Wood Hite, who had come from Kentucky three or four days before, was there, and Bob Ford came down a few minutes afterward. When Wood Hite first came in he spoke to me, and I told him I did not want him to speak to me, as he had accused me of stealing $100 at the divide in the Blue Cut robbery. I told him he lied; he said he could prove it (his accusation) by Mrs. Bolton, and I wanted him to prove it. He then denied ever saying anything of the kind. I told him he did say it, and we both commenced drawing our pistols.

"We fired about the same time.   He shot me through the right leg between the knee and the hip, and I shot him through the right arm.   He fired four times at me and I five times at him, and then I snapped another barrel at him.   I drew my other pistol when he commenced falling.

"Bob Ford fired one shot at him.   I did not know this until afterward, when he (Bob) exhibited the empty chamber.   The wound that killed Hite was through the head.   It struck him about two inches above the right eye and came out in front of and a little above the left ear.

"Bob claimed that his shot was the fatal one.   Hite lived 15 or 20 minutes, but did not speak.   We carried him upstairs, and that night of Dec. 4, Cap and Bob dug a grave in the woods about half a mile from the house and buried him.   My leg was too sore to help. We did not use a coffin."

What they did use instead of a coffin, as disinterment some weeks later proved, was a filthy old horse blanket.   Unwashed, clad in his bloodstained clothing and wrapped in the stinking stable rag, the corpse of the Kentucky white man who had shot the negro and left his body to be eaten by the hogs was thrust into a shallow hole scooped out in a patch of weeds, without benefit of clergy.

Clarence Hite, Wood's brother, a consumptive youth of 21, who had taken part in the Winston and Blue Cut train robberies, was arrested at his home near Adairsville, Kentucky, by Police Commissioner Craig, who brought him back to Missouri.   He made a confession, implicating the other members of the gang and corresponding in chief essentials with the revelations of Liddil. He was sentenced to the Missouri penitentiary for 25 years, served a short time and was pardoned because he was near death. Clarence was taken to his old Kentucky home, where he died a few weeks later.

Dick Liddil's capitulation was the result of a prolonged process of persuasion on the part of the authorities, headed by Governor Crittenden, plus fear of death at the hands of Jesse James. Early in January Commissioner Craig and Sheriff Timberlake, both of whom were persistent in efforts to induce some member of the gang to purchase immunity by turning traitor to the outlaw cause, made a raid on the home of Mrs. Bolton. The raid was the last straw in the breaking down of Liddil's failing nerve. A straw of most considerable weight in the piled-up burden may be found fluttering in this paragraph from Dick's confession:

"On the night of Thursday, the 29th of December, Jesse and Charlie Ford came down to Mrs. Bolton's where I had been since being wounded, and tried to get me to go with them. They claimed to have come from Nebraska. I declined to go. I mistrusted Jesse wanted to kill me, and so left. This was on Saturday night, Dec. 31, 1881. Jesse and Charlie left the next night for the old lady's, I was told. This was the last time I ever saw him, and I have not seen Charlie Ford since."

Dick Liddil's confession bears date just five days prior to the death of Jesse James. It is easy to find elderly citizens of Clay and Jackson Counties today who will tell you, without coaxing, that if Jesse James had lived five weeks instead of only five days the funeral of Dick Liddil would have taken place several years before it did and that his death would have been from unnatural causes.   They knew Jesse!

CHAPTER XXXI

"AND THEY LAID JESSE JAMES IN HIS GRAVE"

NEWSPAPERS had not developed, as early as 1882, what is known in journalistic terminology as the scare-head. Undoubtedly that accounts for the fact that the St. Joseph *Gazette* of the morning of April 4, that year, carried but a single-column heading above the biggest news story that ever "broke," before or since, in that sprightly metropolis of northwest Missouri. To be sure, the top line was set in the boldest-faced type that would fit between the column rules, no room being left for the exclamation point which the phraseology demanded. The line ran, leapingly, with truly Jesse Jamesish alliterative lilt:

JESSE, BY JEHOVAH

Following this shriek of apparent exultation were five three-line decks, and surely the occasion justified the headliner's prodigality. We run the decks together here:

"Jesse James, the Notorious Outlaw, Instantly Killed by Robert Ford—His Adventurous Career Brought to an Abrupt Close on the Eve of Another Crime—Ford Gets into His Confidence and Shoots

Him from Behind While His Back is Turned—Jesse a Resident of St. Joseph Since the Eighth of November Last—An Interview with Mrs. James and the Testimony Developed Before a Jury."

The *Gazette's* seven-column account of the assassination and the subsequent proceedings began:

"Between eight and nine o'clock yesterday morning Jesse James, the Missouri outlaw, before whom the deeds of Fra Diavolo, Dick Turpin and Schinderhannes dwindled into insignificance, was instantly killed by a boy twenty years old, named Robert Ford, at his temporary residence on the corner of Thirteenth and Lafayette streets, in this city.

"In the light of all moral reasoning the shooting was unjustifiable; but the law is vindicated, and the $10,000 reward offered by the state for the body of the brigand will doubtless go to the man who had the courage to draw a revolver on the notorious outlaw even when his back was turned, as in this case."

The St. Joseph *Evening News* of April 3, of course, had first whack at the huge tale, its headlines being:

"JUDGMENT FOR JESSE.—The Notorious Bandit at Last Meets His Fate and Dies with His Boots On."

The Kansas City *Journal* had room for the exclamation point in its top line: "GOOD-BYE, JESSE!" Much of the *Gazette* story was wired verbatim to the *Journal*, from the files of which newspaper these passages are copied, the date line being St. Joseph, Mo., April 3:

"There is little doubt that the killing was the result of a premeditated plan formed by Robert and Charles

Ford several months ago. Charles had been an accomplice of Jesse James since the 3d of last November, and entirely possessed his confidence. Robert Ford, his brother, joined Jesse near Mrs. Samuel's (the mother of the James boys) last Friday a week ago, and accompanied Jesse and Charles to this city Sunday, March 23.

"Jesse, his wife and two children, removed from Kansas City—where they had lived several months, until they feared their whereabouts would be suspected—to this city, arriving here Nov. 8, 1881, coming in a wagon and accompanied by Charles Ford. They rented a house on the corner of Lafayette and Twenty-first streets, where they stayed two months, when they secured the house No. 1381 on Lafayette street, formerly the property of Councilman Aylesbury, paying $14 a month for it, and giving the name of Thomas Howard.

"The house is a one-story cottage, painted white, with green shutters, and is romantically situated on the brow of a lofty eminence east of the city, commanding a fine view of the principal portion of the city, river and railroads, and adapted by nature for the perilous and desperate calling of Jesse James. Just east of the house is a deep, gulchlike ravine, and beyond that a broad expanse of open country backed by a belt of timber. The house, except from the west side, can be seen for several miles. There is a large yard attached to the cottage, and a stable where Jesse had been keeping two horses, which were found there this morning.

"Charles and Robert Ford have been occupying one

of the rooms in the rear of the dwelling, and have secretly had an understanding to kill Jesse ever since last fall. Ever since the boys have been with Jesse they have watched for an opportunity to shoot him, but he was always so heavily armed that it was impossible to draw a weapon without James seeing it. They declared that they had no idea of taking him alive, considering the undertaking suicidal.

"The opportunity they had long wished for came this morning. Breakfast was over. Charlie Ford and Jesse James had been in the stable currying the horses preparatory to their night ride. On returning to the room where Robert Ford was, Jesse said:

"'It's an awfully hot day.'

"He pulled off his coat and vest and tossed them on the bed. Then he said:

"'I guess I'll take off my pistols, for fear somebody will see them if I walk in the yard.'

"He unbuckled the belt in which he carried two 45-calibre revolvers, one a Smith & Wesson and the other a Colt, and laid them on the bed with his coat and vest. He then picked up a dusting brush with the intention of dusting some pictures which hung on the wall. To do this he got on a chair. His back was now turned to the brothers, who silently stepped between Jesse and his revolvers.

"At a motion from Charlie both drew their guns. Robert was the quicker of the two, and in one motion he had the long weapon to a level with his eye, and with the muzzle not more than four feet from the back of the outlaw's head.

"Even in that motion, quick as thought, there was

something which did not escape the acute ears of the hunted man. He made a motion as if to turn his head to ascertain the cause of that suspicious sound, but too late. A nervous pressure on the trigger, a quick flash, a sharp report, and the well-directed ball crashed through the outlaw's skull.

"There was no outcry—just a swaying of the body and it fell heavily backward upon the carpet of the floor. The shot had been fatal, and all the bullets in the chambers of Charlie's revolver, still directed at Jesse's head, could not more effectually have decided the fate of the greatest bandit and freebooter that ever figured in the pages of a country's history.

"The ball had entered the base of the skull and made its way out through the forehead, over the left eye. It had been fired out of a Colt's .45, improved pattern, silver-mounted and pearl-handled pistol, presented by the dead man to his slayer only a few days ago.

"Mrs. James was in the kitchen when the shooting was done, separated from the room in which the bloody tragedy occurred by the dining room. She heard the shot, and dropping her household duties ran into the front room. She saw her husband lying extended on his back, his slayers, each holding his revolver in his hand, making for the fence in the rear of the house. Robert had reached the enclosure and was in the act of scaling it when she stepped to the door and called to him:

"'Robert, you have done this! Come back!'

"Robert answered, 'I swear to God I didn't!'

"They then returned to where she stood. Mrs. James ran to the side of her husband and lifted up his head. Life was not yet extinct, and when she asked him if he was hurt, it seemed to her that he wanted to say something but could not. She tried to wash the blood away that was coursing over his face from the hole in his forehead, but it seemed to her that the blood would come faster than she could wipe it away, and in her hands Jesse James died.

"Charlie Ford explained to Mrs. James that 'a pistol had accidentally gone off.' 'Yes,' said Mrs. James, 'I guess it went off on purpose.' Meanwhile Charlie had gone back in the house and brought out two hats, and the two boys left the house. They went to the telegraph office, sent a message to Sheriff Timberlake of Clay County, to Police Commissioner Craig of Kansas City, to Governor Crittenden and other officers, and then surrendered themselves to Marshal Craig" (Enos Craig of St. Joseph).

"When the Ford boys appeared at the police station they were told by an officer that Marshal Craig and a posse of officers had gone in the direction of the James residence, and they started after them and surrendered themselves. They accompanied the officers to the house and returned in custody of the police to the marshal's headquarters, where they were furnished with dinner, and about 3 p.m. were removed to the old circuit courtroom, where the inquest was held in the presence of an immense crowd."

The body was removed to an undertaking establishment two hours after the tragedy, Mrs. James accompanying it. She left her children, Jesse and Mary, 6½ and 3 years old, with the woman who lived next door and who had known "the Howards" as "very quiet people." Mrs. James, the newspaper account continues, "was greatly affected by the tragedy, and her heartrending moans and expressions of grief were sorrowful evidence of the love she bore for the dead desperado."

Throughout St. Joseph "the news spread like wildfire," as the reporter described the spreading. Hardly anybody credited it. Nearly everybody "laughed at the idea that Jesse James was really the dead man." A man had been killed, that was evident; but it was quite too much to expect anybody to swallow the silly tale that the corpse was that of the unkillable Jesse. Besides, hadn't the *Gazette* carried that very morning a dispatch from Texas to the effect that the James gang had robbed a bank in that state the day before? How could Jesse James be in Texas and in Missouri at one and the same time?

Not until the *Gazette's* "Jesse, by Jehovah" confirmation appeared next morning did the general populace of St. Joseph accept the fact. That day, April 4, was city election day. The hottest mayoralty campaign in local history, the Posegate-Piner contest, had closed. Of Mr. Posegate, the Republican candidate, the *Gazette* said that morning: "This man has no character. His tongue is forked. You cannot trust him and you cannot believe him." Who cared? In the clutch of the new excitement many citizens failed to reach the polls. Mr. Posegate even neglected to take a shot at the *Gazette* editor.

The press report included this interesting description of the body after it had been laid upon a table at the undertaker's: "The features appeared natural, but were discolored by the bloody hole over the left eye. The body was neatly and cleanly dressed; in fact, nothing in the appearance of the remains indicated the desperate career of the man or the many bloody scenes of which he had been the hero. The large, cavernous eyes were closed as in a calm slumber. Only the lower part of the face, the stout, prominent chin covered with a soft, sandy beard, and the thin, firmly closed lips, in a measure betrayed the determined will and iron courage of the dead man. A further inspection of the body revealed two large bullet wounds on the right side of the breast, within three inches of the nipple, a bullet wound in the leg and the absence of the tip of the middle finger of the left hand."

It should be explained that all these were but the marks of old wounds, the two in the breast having been made by Federal bullets in the Civil War. The missing finger-tip explains why Jesse James habitually wore gloves when in public: some of Mr. Pinkerton's men, you know, might have learned somehow that he had lost that particular finger-tip. Jesse took no chances that he could avoid.

The Kansas City *Journal's* local columns stated that the news from St. Joseph created such an excitement on the streets of Kansas City as had not existed since the assassination of President Garfield by Charles J. Guiteau, nine months earlier. "People would not believe it, and it is probable that when the patrons of the *Journal* read the account of it this morning many of them will be unable to realize that the famous bandit, whose name is better known in Missouri than that of any statesman in America, has ended his eventful career. . . . Occasionally a man is seen who denounces the deed as cowardly, and the wish was heard expressed that the man who did the killing might hang. . . . Mayor Frink and a crowd of the clerks and city officials were engaged in an animated discussion of the affair. Said the mayor, 'I fully believe that he is dead this time.'"

In the Kansas City *Times* appeared this paragraph about the bereaved family: "The widow of Jesse James is a neat and rather prepossessing lady, and bears the stamp of having been well brought up and surrounded by influences of a better and holier character than the reader would at first suppose. She is rather slender, fair of face, light hair, blue eyes, with high forehead and marks of intelligence very strikingly apparent. The two children, a little boy and girl, were neat and intelligent, and seemed to grieve much over the deed which had in one short moment deprived them of a father's love and protection."

Of the victim of Bob Ford's bullet the *Times* printed this informative description: "Jesse James was about five feet eleven inches in height, of a rather solid, firm and compact build, yet rather of the slender type. His hair was black, not overly long; blue eyes, well shaded with dark lashes, and the entire lower portion of his face was covered by a full growth of dark-brown or sun-browned whiskers, which are not long and shaggy but are trimmed and bear evidence of careful attention. His complexion was fair, and he was not sunburnt to any considerable extent, as the reader is generally led to suppose. He was neatly clad in a business suit of cassimere, of dark brown substance, which fit him very neatly. He wore a shirt of spotless whiteness, with collar and cravat, and looked more the picture of a staid and substantial business man than the outlaw and desperado that he was."

At the inquest the chief business was the formal identification of the corpse. Jesse's mother arrived from home late in the evening of April 3. She and her daughter-in-law spent the night in the house where her son was slain. When instructed by the coroner to raise her right hand to be sworn, Mrs. Samuel lifted the stump of the forearm that had been blown off by the Pinkertonian bomb in 1875. Virtually everybody present knew the tale of that tragic midwinter night. There was absolute silence in the chamber for a moment; then somebody, overcome by the compelling pathos of the incident, caught breath sobbing-wise. The coroner's voice was husky as he proceeded:

"Mrs. Samuel, are you the mother of Jesse James?"

"I am—oh, my God!" she sobbed.

Her age, she said, was fifty-seven. Her son Jesse was midway in his thirty-fifth year. The corpse she just had viewed, she said, was that of her son.

The widow of Jesse James testified that she was born in Kentucky, that she had been the wife of Jesse James for nearly eight years, and that her age was thirty-five.

"We came here," she said, "to live as other people do. They tell some hard things on my husband, but a better man never lived."

"Was Jesse a drinking man?" she was asked.

"No, sir. He never drank, smoked nor chewed. He

never liked whisky. He never swore in my presen ce and he wouldn't allow others to do so."

Mrs. James stated that the family had lived at Nashville and elsewhere in Tennessee, in recent years, and for a time in Baltimore, Maryland, and for some months in Kansas City just before removing to St. Joseph.

Another woman who identified the remains was Mattie Collins, common-law wife of Dick Liddil. This woman had visited Governor Crittenden, at Jefferson City, as a veiled go-between in the preliminaries leading to Liddil's giving himself up and turning state's evidence against Jesse and the rest of the outlaws. Remember Mattie Collins until you read, in the next chapter, the final paragraph of the editorial which Maj. John N. Edwards wrote when he received the news that Jesse James had been killed.

Dick Liddil himself, fresh from confession, identified the body. When Mrs. Samuel espied Liddil, she lifted high her one arm and denounced him as a traitor. Capt. Harrison Trow, one of Quantrill's men, was another identifier. Sheriff Timberlake of Clay County testified that he had known Jesse James from 1864 to 1870, had not seen him since the latter date, but recognized the corpse.

The two Fords testified, Robert admitting proudly that he had killed the outlaw and Charles stating that he had stood ready with pistol cocked to shoot but had withheld his fire when he saw that his brother's bullet was fatal. Mrs. James, before she left the courtroom, cried, alluding to the Fords:

"There is no justice if they are not punished! They

ought to be punished as severely as Guiteau, and more, because they are traitors."

The coroner's jury found that the deceased was Jesse W. James and that he came to his death through a pistol shot fired by Robert Ford. The Ford boys posed as heroes. They were indignant when locked up on charges of murder in the first degree. John McCullough was playing "Virginius" at Tootle's Opera House in town, and the Fords insisted that they should be permitted to see the play. They didn't see it.

Robert Ford, aged twenty, and Charles Ford, twenty-four, were found guilty of the murder of Jesse W. James and were sentenced to be hanged. Two hours after the court pronounced sentence, the wires carried news of the issuance of a pardon to each from the governor of Missouri.

Contrary to popular tradition since 1882, Governor Crittenden had not offered a reward of $10,000 for Jesse James "dead or alive." The official files at the state capital show that the reward proclaimed by the governor was $5,000 for the apprehension of the outlaw and $5,000 for his conviction in any court. The executive, therefore, did not "conspire" with the Ford boys for the assassination of Jesse James. But did the assassins get the $10,000? They did not. They got but a small part of it. To set forth in detail what disposition was made of the balance, the major portion, is not of the "now-it-may-be-told" variety of state secret. There's a reason, and for the present we leave the mystery veiled.

CHAPTER XXXII

"TEAR the two bears from the flag of Missouri! Put thereon, in place of them, as more appropriate, a thief blowing out the brains of an unarmed victim, and a brazen harlot, naked to the waist and splashed to the brows in blood!"

Our old-time and eloquent friend Maj. John N. Edwards, "the Chevalier Bayard of Missouri," foremost lifelong friend and chief public defender of Jesse James, should have put that pulsating paragraph first instead of last in his Sedalia *Democrat* editorial leader the day after Jesse was murdered. But the gallant and generous major was a poet, and so he needs must open his obituary editorial with a quotation from a poem of dubious application here, it seems:

> " Let not Cæsar's servile minions
> Mock the lion thus laid low!
> 'Twas no foeman's hand that slew him,
> 'Twas his own that struck the blow.

"No one among all the hired cowards," proceeds Major Edwards, "hard on the hunt for blood-money, dared face this wonderful outlaw, one even against twenty, until he had disarmed himself and turned his back to his assassins, the first and only time in a career which has passed from the realm of an almost fabulous romance into that of history.

"We called him outlaw, and he was, but Fate made him so. When the war came he was just turned of fifteen. The border was all aflame with steel, and fire, and ambuscade, and slaughter. He flung himself into a band which had a black flag for a banner and devils for riders. What he did he did, and it was fearful. But it was war. It was Missouri against Kansas. It was Jim Lane and Jennison against Quantrill, Anderson and Todd.

"When the war closed Jesse James had no home. Proscribed, hunted, shot, driven away from among his people, a price put upon his head—what else could the man do, with such a nature, except what he did do? He had to live. It was his country. The graves of his kindred were there. He refused to be banished from his birthright, and when he was hunted he turned savagely about and hunted his hunters. Would to God he were alive today to make a righteous butchery of a few more of them!

"There never was a more cowardly and unnecessary murder committed in all America than this murder of Jesse James. It was done for money. It was done that a few might get all the money. He had been living in St. Joseph for months. The Fords were with him. He was in the toils, for they meant to betray him. He was in the heart of a large city. One word would have summoned five hundred armed men for his capture or extermination. Not a single member of the attacking party need have been hurt.

"If, when his house had been surrounded, he had refused to surrender, he could have been killed on the inside of it and at long range. The chances for him to escape were as one to ten thousand, and not even that; but it was never intended that he should be captured. It was his blood the bloody wretches were after—blood that would bring money in the official market of Missouri.

"And this great commonwealth leagued with a lot of self-confessed robbers, highwaymen and prostitutes to have one of its citizens assassinated, before it was positively known he had ever committed a single crime worthy of death.

"Of course everything that can be said about the dead man to justify the manner of his killing will be said; but who is saying it? Those with the blood of Jesse James on their guilty souls. Those who conspired to murder him. Those who wanted the reward, and would invent any lie or concoct any diabolical story to get it. They have succeeded, but such a cry of horror and indignation at the infernal deed is even now thundering over the land that if a single one of the miserable assassins had either manhood, conscience or courage, he would go, as another Judas, and hang himself.

"But so sure as God reigns, there never was a dollar of blood-money obtained yet which did not bring with it perdition. Sooner or later there comes a day of vengeance. Some among the murderers are mere beasts of prey. These, of course, can only suffer through cold, or hunger, or thirst; but whatever they dread most, that thing will happen. Others again among the murderers are sanctimonious devils who plead the honor of the state, the value of law and order, the splendid courage required to shoot an unarmed man in the back of the head; and these will be stripped to their skin of all their pretensions, and made to shiver and freeze, splotched as they are and spotted and piebald with blood, in the pitiless storm of public contempt and condemnation. This, to the leaders, will be worse than death.

"Nor is the end yet. If Jesse James had been hunted down as any other criminal, and killed while trying to escape or in resisting arrest, not a word would have been said to the contrary. He had sinned and he had suffered. In his death the majesty of the law would have been vindicated, but here the law itself becomes a murderer. It leagues with murderers. It hires murderers. It borrows money to pay and reward murderers. It promises immunity and protection to murderers. It is itself a murderer—the most abject, the most infamous, and the most cowardly ever known to history. Therefore this so-called law is an outrage, and these so-called executors of the law are outlaws. Therefore let Jesse James' comrades— and he has a few remaining worth all the Fords. and Liddils that could be packed together between St. Louis and St. Joe—do unto them as they did unto him.

"Yes, the end is not yet, nor should it be. The man had no trial. What right had any officer of this state to put a price upon his head and hire a band of cutthroats and highwaymen to murder him for money?

"Anything can be told of man. The whole land

is filled with liars and robbers, and assassins. Murder is easy for a hundred dollars. Nothing is safe that is pure and unsuspecting, or just; but it is not to be supposed that the law will become an ally and a co-worker in this sort of a civilization.

"Jesse James has been murdered, first, because an immense price has been set upon his head and there isn't a low-lived scoundrel today in Missouri who wouldn't kill his own father for money; and, second, because he was made the scapegoat for every train robber, footpad and highwayman between Iowa and Texas. Worse men a thousand times than the dead man have been hired to do this thing. The very character of the instruments chosen shows the infamous nature of the work required.

"The hand that slew him had to be a traitor's! Into all the warp and woof of the devil's work there were threads woven by the fingers of a harlot. What a spectacle! Missouri, with splendid companies and regiments of militia. Missouri, with a hundred and seventeen sheriffs, as brave and as efficient on the average as any men on earth. Missouri, with a watchful and vigilant marshal in every one of her principal towns and cities. Missouri, with every screw and cog and crank and lever and wheel of her administrative machinery in perfect working order. Missouri, with all her order, progress and development, had yet to surrender all these in the face of a single man—a hunted, lied-upon, proscribed and outlawed man, trapped and located in the midst of thirty-five thousand people—and ally with some five or six cutthroats and prostitutes that the majesty of the law might be vindicated, and the good name of the state saved from all further reproach!

"Saved? Why, the whole state reeks today with a double orgy—that of lust and that of murder. What the men failed to do, the women accomplished.

"Tear the two bears from the flag of Missouri! Put thereon, in place of them, as more appropriate, a thief blowing out the brains of an unarmed victim, and a brazen harlot, naked to the waist and splashed to the brows in blood!"

Newspapers throughout the country made editorial comment on the passing of Jesse. The Cincinnati *Times-Star* said: "If Governor Crittenden of Missouri reads the newspapers extensively, he has discovered that public opinion severely condemns assassination by law, even in the case of a notorious desperado and outlaw. Not a single reputable paper in the land justifies the part he plays in the conspiracy to murder James."

Comments in the St. Louis *Post-Dispatch* and the St. Joseph *Herald* caused the Kansas City *Times* to remark: "Frank James might find a safe asylum either in the *Herald* office at St. Joseph or the *Post-Dispatch* office at St. Louis. These papers mourn the loss of his brother Jesse as they have never mourned the loss of any of Missouri's great men."

"It becomes our solemn duty," the *Post-Dispatch* replied to the *Times*, "to inform you that you utter a malicious and vicious and utterly indefensible lie when you say that this paper has mourned the loss of Jesse James. We have never failed to express satisfaction with his death, and we congratulate the state now that he is no longer alive. We have severely criticized our asinine governor for the lawless and uncivilized way in which he compassed the bandit's murder, and in this we have the indorsement of such journals as the New York *Sun*, *World*, *Telegraph*, *Graphic*, and *Tribune*, Chicago *Inter Ocean and News*, Cincinnati *Enquirer*, Louisville *Courier-Journal*, and a host of other intelligent and influential representatives of public opinion. We do not see how our Kansas City contemporary hopes to help itself by lying about our position on this question."

The correspondent of the St. Louis *Globe-Democrat* at Jefferson City interviewed many members of the legislature on the subject of Jesse's removal. "The result," he wrote, "is the stereotyped answer to the effect that the member is glad for the sake of Missouri that the bandit is dead, but he would have preferred that the killing had been done in some other manner."

"That, we may remark, is the platform of the *Post-Dispatch*," commented that paper. "We have never ceased to believe that Crittenden inflicted more disgrace on the state by the manner in which he brought about the murder of James than the bandit could if he had been left to continue his career. His death was a blessing, but the manner of his taking off was a reproach upon our civilization."

"Let anyone read the account of the circumstances under which Robert Ford killed Jesse James," suggested the New York *Sun* (was it Dana's hand that wrote the editorial?), "and then consider how enjoyable Mr. Ford's society would be, and how much safety could be insured to a train carrying treasure through any district which he may happen to haunt hereafter. To make a new murderer in the process of getting rid of an old one, is a practice which cannot be justified.

"The governor feels 'confident that it will meet with the sanction of law-abiding citizens, not only of this state but throughout the United States.' Time will show, he adds, that the end justifies the means. The end was doubtless important. The destruction of the notorious outlaw will naturally and properly give satisfaction everywhere. But the manner in which it was brought about can only excite regret among right-minded men. The crime of murder is detestable irrespective of the victim; and those who condemn it when committed by Jesse James should not be heard to defend it when committed by Robert Ford. We share with the people of Missouri their contentment at the termination of so dangerous a life; but we dissent emphatically from their governor's approval of the means by which that life was taken away."

An editorial in the New York *Evening Post*, assumed to have been written by Carl Schurz, dignified the death of Jesse by use of learned historical allusions: "All the great robbers of old times, and of other countries, lived in caves, or in mountain fastnesses, to which it was difficult for troops to pursue them, or kept the sea in long, low, rakish black schooners. James, however, lived in a comfortable house, surrounded by a loving family, and went off on his expeditions apparently as a business man goes off to collect debts or to solicit orders. Moreover, although the state of Missouri had for long years been trying to arrest him it never was able to do so, and in order to compass his death the governor had to resort to the means by which the Venetian Council of Ten and other medieval powers occasionally tried to get rid of the obnoxious foreign sovereigns. He hired an assassin to go and kill him unawares, so that James really died what may be called a royal death. He fell as Henry IV and William the Silent and Admiral Coligny fell, the victim of the hostility of a great community, who were unable to get the better of him in open fight but felt that his taking off was necessary to their safety and prosperity. The governor, in fact, justifies his own course in language which might have been used by Elizabeth after the defeat of the Armada. He describes the assassination of James as the relief of the state from a great hindrance to its prosperity, and as likely to give an important stimulus to real estate speculation, to railroad enterprise and to foreign immigration."

The Fords failed to achieve the popularity they craved. They seem to have expected that the whole world would applaud them loudly. Such of the world as came in casual contact with them looked upon the conspirators as curiosities, when not regarding them with contempt. Everybody refused utterly to heroize the fellows who shot their trusting friend in the back of the head—it was simply something that wasn't done, you know.

Robert and Charles went on the stage in a blood-and-thunder melodrama called "The Outlaws of Missouri," but their career before the footlights was brief: the public demanded real heroes. The boys tried themselves out as dime-museum freaks. Even that was a failure: people preferred the bearded lady or the ossified man, or even "the skeleton of Charles J. Guiteau when he was a boy"—a successful museum exhibit of those times! The boyhood bones of President Garfield's assassin fooled more of the public than did the adult living entities of the assassins of Jesse James.

About three years after Jesse's assassination Mrs. Zerelda Samuel and little Jesse Edwards James were walking along a street in Kansas City when they encountered Charlie Ford. Mrs. Samuel upbraided him for conspiring to murder her son. He told her he had been stricken with remorse ever since, and begged her forgiveness.

"If God can forgive you, I can," said the Spartan mother.

Ford also told Mrs. Samuel that he and his brother got only a few hundred dollars of the $10,000 reward. The rest appears to have been divided between some of the officials who connived the conspiracy. Less than a year after that street encounter Charlie Ford shot himself to death in a weed patch near Richmond, Missouri.

Bob Ford survived the killing of Jesse James for more than ten years. After various wanderings he settled in the tough new mining town of Creede, Colorado, where he opened a low bar and gambling den. With him was one Nellie Watterson, who had played in "The Outlaws of Missouri" some years earlier. She passed as his wife. A deputy sheriff named Ed Kelly led a raid on Ford's place in February, 1892. Ford was wounded, and for a time he retired from business. Shortly after he reopened the place he was standing behind his bar one day when the Watterson woman warned him that Kelly, who was no longer a deputy, was entering the door armed with a double-barrel shotgun.

Ford's revolver was on a shelf behind him. He reached for it, but Kelly turned loose both barrels of his gun. Buckshot severed the jugular vein, and Bob Ford died suddenly with his boots on.

Kelly served a term in the Colorado penitentiary for this crime, which he committed because he coveted the favor of Ford's mistress. Some years after his release he was killed in a sidewalk fight with a town marshal in Texas. He was a native of Missouri.

CHAPTER XXXIII

THE LITTLE WHITE HOUSE WITH THE GREEN SHUTTERS

JESSE JAMES had two burials but only one funeral. I witnessed the second burial, which took place twenty years after the first. On that occasion I made up my mind to tell the world, so far as might lie within my ability, the truth about Jesse James. This narrative, written more than twenty-three years later, is the outcome of that purpose.

Although familiar for many years with the birthplace and the two burial places of the most widely known of the Missouri outlaws, it was not until a pleasant afternoon in the March of 1925 that I visited the house where he was killed. It no longer is "the little white house with the green shutters." The white paint has been supplanted by a coat of fading brown. The shutters have disappeared. The stable in the rear, where the distinguished tenant kept his two horses ready for fast flight, also has disappeared. The street in front has been cut down about eight feet to grade, leaving a ragged bank a rod from the house. Tacked on the outer wall just to the right of the front door—through which the Fords ran out after the assassination—I found a small board bearing the words "Jessie James House—Admission 15 Cents."

When Mrs. Mary Dycus, widow of Francis Marion

Dycus and for twenty-one years tenant of the historic cottage, admitted me to the front chamber in which the outlaw was slain, I handed her thirty cents, and she looked behind me for the other visitor. I was alone. Mrs. Dycus was grateful. I called her attention to the feminine misspelling of Jesse's Christian name on the placard. The widow smiled.

"That's the Missouri of it," she explained; "I didn't make that sign myself."

Mrs. Dycus is not a native. Since her husband with the Revolutionary fighter's name died a few years ago she has lived alone in the house of the tragedy.

"Don't you get a bit scary here?" I inquired.

"Scary—what at?"

"Why, at—well, at Jesse James' ghost, for instance."

"Huh! the only ghosts I ever see are live ones. And I wouldn't be scared of Jesse James if he came back here, anyhow. He'd never harm a woman, I'm certain. There's lots of worse men than he was. These bandits we've got today are a whole lot worse; they are so awful mean and cruel."

"Mrs. Dycus," I said, "I fully agree with you; the facts prove you perfectly correct."

In my coat pocket I carried a copy of the St. Joseph *News-Press* of that very day. On the front page was a dispatch from New York City under these headlines: "BEATEN BY BANDITS, ROBBED OF $50,000— Three Masked Men Chop Way into New York Woman's Apartment—Bite Rings from Fingers—Mrs. Fay Perkins Tortured Until She Reveals Jewelry— Burglars Believed Gangsters That Murdered Two Victims."

Mrs. Dycus has a picture on the wall at the spot where hung the one that Jesse James was dusting when he was shot. She said that the one Jesse was dusting was a likeness of "Skyrocket," his favorite horse. Jesse dearly loved horses. The Ford boys said shortly after they killed him that he was "the most expert horsethief in the Middle West," but they added that he never took horses for gain but merely for use in emergencies, and that he always returned them or paid for them later when he could do so without peril. This I know, from more reliable evidence, to have been a fact. An outlaw of strange parts, that Jesse James!

Mrs. Dycus said that many persons visit the old house, women seeming to be particularly curious about the bandit. She showed me through the four rooms of the cottage. There was a kitchen at the rear, in the Jesse James days; it has disappeared, and the James dining room is the Dycus kitchen. The house belongs now to the city, having been taken over because of unpaid taxes.

"It's nice and quiet up here on this hill," remarked Mrs. Dycus; "I like it here—right nice place to live at."

Jesse James liked it. He could see about him in all directions and take note of any suspicious-looking person approaching. But he liked life on a farm still better: it was safer, for one thing. There is good reason for the belief that in his last days he was hoping he might be able to buy a farm in Nebraska and settle down to make a living by agriculture. The Fords said he had not "done any job" since the Blue Cut train robbery of the preceding September. He was laying plans, they declared, to rob a bank at Platte City, Missouri, and they had agreed to assist. He had only about $700 or $800 on hand. Three weeks before his death he had visited Pawnee, Nebraska, registering at the local hotel as Tom Howard of St. Joseph. He wished to rent a house there, he stated, and he looked at outlying farms with a view to purchase.

In the days following the assassination, St. Joseph was rife with stories of rich local color anent the slain bandit. Mr. Howard, the preceding winter, had entertained the Ferrell girls at 1320 Lafayette Street, adjoining his home, by playing with them at snowballing. He was an expert marksman with a snowball, and when one of the girls hit him with a snowy missile he took it with great good nature. "He laughed like a schoolboy," the girls recalled.

Mr. Howard was a regular customer of August Brokaw, a druggist on lower Sixth Street. He became a warm favorite there. He bought cigars to give to his friends—including the Fords. Nearly every day he would sit in the drug store and tell stories—clean ones, stories with points. He told Brokaw he was a railroad man out of a job. The druggist promised to get him a railroad job! Undoubtedly Mr. Howard laughed, upsleeve, at this. After all, and after a fashion, Jesse enjoyed life. Major Edwards wrote, comparing the two brothers: "Jesse laughed at many things, Frank laughed not at all. Jesse was lighthearted, reckless, devil-may-care; Frank was sober, sedate, a splendid man always for ambush or scouting parties. Both were undaunted."

Mr. Howard liked to play billiards. Late one night,

after a game in a St. Joseph billiard hall, another player remarked to him that he was afraid to go home alone—he might be held up and robbed. Mr. Howard volunteered to escort the fearsome citizen home. At the man's door he called out a cheery good night.

Under caption of "Worthy of Notice," the *Gazette* said on April 6, 1882: "It is positively known that Jesse James attended the Sunday services at the Presbyterian church, opposite the World's Hotel, repeatedly. Last Sunday he was seen with his entire family at the Union Depot, viewing the improvements."

The same newspaper stated that rain fell ceaselessly as Mrs. Jesse James and Mrs. Zerelda Samuel were removing the effects from the house, after the inquest. Some of the effects had been removed by the officials. These included a shotgun, two revolvers, two watches, two watch-chains, a diamond ring, a gold ring, a breastpin, shirt buttons, a pair of cuff buttons with coral setting, a pin with the initials "J. W. J." on it—and one of Mrs. James' earrings. The property was returned to the family.

Another article observed in the house was a well-worn Bible. Mrs. James, when asked by a newspaper reporter if her husband ever read it, replied:

"Yes, he read it very often."

Now, by this roundabout route, we approach the funeral and first burial of Jesse James. A St. Joseph dispatch of April 5 to the Kansas City *Times* said:

"Craig and Timberlake, the principal men who engineered Jesse's capture [*sic*], have been delayed and obstructed all day by the St. Joseph officials, through jealousy. The special train has been waiting since 10 A.M. to take the body, but the city marshal would not give it up. The body was not secured until 6 P.M. and taken quietly to the depot, where Sheriff Timberlake's party prepared to go out on the regular train to Cameron. From there they go by a special to Kearney. Jesse's widow, children and mother accompany the remains. They are very nervous. The body is in a $500 coffin furnished by Craig and Timberlake. The funeral will take place tomorrow."

The *Times* correspondent wrote that "a perfect mob was at the depot to see the party off." Mrs. Samuel insisted that she be taken to the baggage car to see the body put on the train. Timberlake and his party sat in the baggage car as guards.

"Mrs. James was accompanied by Luther James, a cousin of Jesse's, from Kansas City. While in the depot at St. Joseph a short, thickset man tried to pull a pistol on Mrs. Samuel but was promptly thrown out of the door and landed in the street. He was shot at, but not hit.

"At all stations along the road crowds gathered, anxious to see the body, the family, the officers, or anything, and great excitement prevailed. We arrived at Cameron at 9.11 P.M. and were met by an immense crowd. The ladies were taken to a private room at the depot while waiting for the train, and the body was taken from the baggage car, followed by a mob who stood around the windows, eager to catch a glimpse of the pine box that enveloped the coffin. Mrs. Samuel and Mrs. James are very much worn out. A dispatch received here by Mrs. Samuel says her youngest son is dying at home."

There was delay in getting the special train, but at last the special came, and the party departed at midnight for Kearney. The train was furnished by officials of the Rock Island railroad. It will be remembered that it was a train of the Rock Island system that suffered in the first train robbery, nearly nine years earlier. It is surmisable that the officials of that line were glad to extend this final courtesy.

The train reached Kearney at 2.45 A.M. The baggage car that carried the corpse was sidetracked. The rest of the rolling stock pulled out to continue traffic on the esteemed Rock Island. Mrs. Samuel, wearied and worried, hastened out to the farmhouse to reach the bedside of John T. Samuel, her son, a youth of twenty who had been shot in a scrimmage at a neighborhood "party" a few nights earlier. He was believed to be dying, but he recovered. At this writing Mr. Samuel is living at Long Beach, Calif.

The casket was placed upon two chairs in the office of the Kearney House, the small local hotel. After daylight the lid was removed. Throughout the forenoon the body of Jesse James "lay in state" in his old home town. Many persons passed by to view the dead face and folded hands. Old acquaintances said the corpse "looked natural." Hundreds of oldtime residents saw Jesse for the first time. Some Kearneyites said they had seen him before but had been unaware of his interesting identity.

Funeral services were held in the afternoon at the Kearney Baptist church of which Jesse had been a member. The pallbearers were five local men and a mysterious stranger. Nobody seemed to know this man, who appeared to be somewhat in authority.

"It's Frank James!" whispered a spectator, hoarsely.

But it was a stout man, and Frank James was slender. Two clergymen took part in the services, which opened with the singing of "What a Friend We Have in Jesus," a hymn sung frequently by Jesse in boyhood and when he was a church member—and probably after he was "excluded." The Rev. R. H. Jones of Lathrop, Missouri, read the passage from the book of Job beginning "Man that is born of woman is of few days and full of trouble." He read also two verses from the Thirty-ninth Psalm, beginning "Lord, make me to know mine end."

After a fervent prayer by the Rev. Mr. Jones, the funeral sermon was preached by the Rev. J. M. P. Martin, pastor of the church. His text was Matthew 24:44, "Therefore be ye ready, for in such an hour as ye think not the Son of Man cometh." He said, by way of introduction, "It would be useless for me to bring any new information before this congregation respecting the life and character of the deceased." That was his sole allusion to the dead man. The sermon was an appeal to all present to bear in mind the transitory nature of the earthly pilgrimage and to be ready for the ultimate and inevitable transition.

In closing, Pastor Martin stated that Mrs. Samuel wished him to request that those present refrain from going out to the farm, where interment was to take place. John Samuel, he said, was lying very low, and as the grave was quite near the house it was feared that the gathering of a crowd might affect the patient seriously. "It is therefore requested that none but friends and relatives go to the grave."

When the cortège reached the Samuel farmhouse a considerable number of country folk had gathered there. All were quiet and respectful, as befitted the solemn occasion. Jesse James was buried in a corner of the yard, on the premises where he was born, where his mother could look from her windows upon the mound at the foot of a big coffee-bean tree. Mrs. Samuel planted flowers upon the grave, and for twenty years she tended them with affectionate care. A tall white marble monument was erected there, on which the mother had this inscription carved:

In Loving Remembrance of My Beloved Son
JESSE W. JAMES
Died April 3, 1882
Aged 34 Years, 6 Months, 28 Days
Murdered by a Traitor and Coward Whose
Name Is Not Worthy to Appear Here

And so at last the world's most hunted man—and according to his friends the most hounded—after nearly twenty years of warring and worrying, came home to rest undisturbed for another score of years.

CHAPTER XXXIV

THE HISTORIAN AT JESSE'S SECOND BURIAL

IN newspaper parlance a "pick-up" is something a writer doesn't have to write. Just here the writer finds a pick-up of chapter length ready to hand, in the files of the St. Louis *Post-Dispatch*. He wrote it himself, as the top signature indicates, as a piece of staff correspondence from Kearney, Missouri, and wired it to his newspaper on Sunday night, June 29, 1902, which date the reader is to bear in mind:

> Jesse James had a wife;
> She's a mourner all her life;
> His children, they were brave.
> Oh, the dirty little coward that shot Mr. Howard!
> And they laid Jesse James in his grave.
>
> *—From the Old Song.*

"And they laid Jesse James in his grave," for the second and, doubtless, the last time.

Not as a bandit, but as a brother in arms, as a soldier, as a guerrilla rough rider of the border warfare, as a fighter in the lost cause, a squad of Quantrill's men who rode and shot with the boy Jesse James in the last two years of the Civil War, bore his bones this Sunday afternoon to his new grave between those of his wife and his little half-brother.

"Not a sound was heard, not a funeral note," not a word was spoken at the grave during the twenty minutes required for carrying the coffin from the hearse, lowering it into the earth, shoveling in the clay and rounding off the mound.

Yes, there was one sound—just for a moment or two—the sobbing of Jesse's mother.

It was a burial in silence. A preacher, in white necktie, stood in the crowd, but merely as a spectator. There was no religious ceremony, either at the farmhouse or at the cemetery.

Frank James, who had stood uncovered at the head of the grave beside his aged mother, Mrs. Zerelda Samuel, and young Jesse James, his nephew, turned away as the last spadeful of sod was tossed upon the mound, saying:

"Well, boys, that's all we can do."

Then some flowers, brought from the yard of the old home, were planted on the mound by the comrades who bore the pall—and it was all over.

Disinterment of the remains this morning revealed the fact that somebody—either the great state of Missouri or an undertaker—had deceived the James family at the first burial twenty years ago. It was represented at that time that the coffin in which the body was shipped from St. Joseph was an enduring metallic casket, costing $500, and that the body had been embalmed. When the old coffin was lifted out of the grave it fell apart, and there was nothing inside but the skeleton in clothing.

This was indeed a dreary day for a disinterment and reburial. From early morning until noon the rain poured. As a consequence the crowd in attendance was small, many who had intended to come apparently believing that the burial would be postponed.

But there was no thought of postponement. Jesse James, the bandit's son, came out last night from Kansas City and found his uncle, Frank James, sick in bed, suffering from an attack of grip. There was a quiet talk between the two, and very early this morning young Jesse went to the home of John T. Samuel here in town, a half-brother of the James boys, and the two men drove through the rain out to the Samuel farm, three and a half miles northeast of the little town. With them went Zach Laffoon, the old grave-digger of Kearney, and his nephew and assistant, Zip Pollock. A handsome new coffin, covered in black, with a silver plate bearing the name "Jesse James," was taken out with the little party.

The men reached the farmhouse shortly after five o'clock, and the two grave-diggers set to work at once, in the heavy rain, to open the grave. In a corner of the yard, toward the rear, under a gigantic coffee-bean tree, were the grave and the monument—a white marble shaft erected by the devoted mother of the dead man.

Laffoon and Pollock, with pick and spade, dug away the hard earth whilst Jesse James and John Samuel stood by, partly sheltered from the rain by the spreading branches of the tree, and watched the work.

The ground was very hard and dry beneath the first few inches. Every spadeful of earth turned to mud before it struck the ground. It was a job of digging that brought out the perspiration on the men, already drenched. Old Zach Laffoon said it was about the hardest job of the kind he ever attempted.

Jesse James was buried deep. His mother, apprehensive lest the body might be stolen, had had the grave dug seven feet deep. Zip Pollock is a tall man, but when he stood in the bottom of the grave his head was a foot below the surface of the ground.

Nearly four hours' work was required to reach the coffin. All this time the rain beat upon the men and into the grave. At last the pick struck against metal, boring through rotten plank, and the rusted top of the coffin was revealed. The men dug aside the earth near the foot and passed a plank underneath, raising the coffin slightly. Then they lifted that end of the coffin— and a startling thing happened.

The top and sides of the metal casket came up, leaving the bottom to fall back into the grave, with the remains of Jesse James lying thereon. The men stepped down into the grave and lifted the bottom of the casket to the top. The foot came up first, and from the other end the skull rolled off into the grave. Zach Laffoon picked up the skull and replaced it.

As the coffin bottom was being turned around above ground, the skull again fell off and dropped to the bottom of the grave. Zip Pollock jumped down and picked it up, placing it once more upon the old coffin bottom. At this juncture John Samuel picked up the skull and began to turn it over in his hands, closely examining it.

"What are you looking for, John?" asked old Zach Laffoon.

"Bob Ford's bullet hole," replied the bandit's half-brother; "and here it is."

There it was, a little more than an inch behind the left ear, and as large as a quarter. A small piece of the skull above it had broken in; otherwise the hole would have been round.

Young Jesse James looked curiously at his father's skull, glad to find the bullet hole and the gold-filled teeth, for those marks proved to him that the body of Jesse James never had been stolen; and he could go back to his grandmother and allay her fears that, possibly, in spite of her twenty years' vigil, her son's grave had been violated.

But there are said to be persons in Clay County who still refuse to believe that the real Jesse James is dead. To such doubters as these a postal card received this morning by the city marshal of Kearney—the town has 700 people and a city marshal—furnished new proof, but to the rest it is a ghastly joke. It was mailed in a Kansas town and signed "Original Jesse James." The writer said:

"I will not be buried in Carny next Sunday. I am not dead. I was not shot by Bobie Ford. Tom Howard was shot by Bobie Ford, but I wasn't there, so you can't bury me."

Laffoon and Pollock lifted the coffin bottom and carried it to the side of the new casket. They scraped the skeleton into the coffin. The hands were folded over the breast, just as they had been placed twenty years ago.

The new coffin was closed and placed in the little parlor room of the house, to await the coming of the pallbearers later in the day, and James and Samuel returned to the town.

Mrs. Samuel did not know that the body had been disinterred until young Jesse returned to the Burlington Hotel. She was there awaiting him, in the little parlor. She inquired immediately as to the condition of the body and appeared relieved when she learned that it undoubtedly was Jesse's.

Meanwhile Frank James, in his bed upstairs, was receiving old comrades. Seven Quantrill troopers came in on the morning train from Kansas City. They went at once to Mr. James' room. The men are William H. Gregg of Kansas City, who was a captain under Quantrill; his brother, Attorney J. Frank Gregg of Grain Valley, Missouri, a lieutenant in the same command; James Sim Whitsett, Lee's Summit, Missouri; Hiram J. George, Oak Grove, Missouri, who was a captain; Benjamin H. Morrow, Lake City, Missouri; Warren W. Welch, Independence, Missouri, and J. C. Ervin, Marshall, Missouri. The first six served as pallbearers and Mr. Ervin followed to assist.

Captain George brought his wife along. The captain is called Hi by his comrades. In fact, all of these old men call each other by the names known to them when they were young fellows with Quantrill. Captain Gregg is Bill and Mr. Whitsett is Sim.

The veterans gathered around the bed and told stories of the war days, in which Frank James joined with zest. Bill Gregg sat on the edge of the bed and remarked:

"Did I ever tell you, Frank, about the time I and some more of the boys caused our wives to eat dog? No? Well, our wives happened to be along with us that time, and we had been killing Indians all day."

Possibly Captain Bill meant palefaces instead of Indians, but that doesn't matter; he was talking of war.

"We had killed forty or fifty Indians, two at a time. They would come up and shoot at us, just two in a bunch, and we would detail two men who would go out and kill them and ride back. We got pretty hungry, and we came to an Indian hut. Nobody was home, and we went inside. There was a stack of meat, in large slices, which looked like venison. We took some out and cooked it and our wives began to eat it. I smelt it and said to one of the boys that it didn't smell exactly like venison to me. We went back to the cabin and looked for a fresh deer hide. There was none hanging outside, and we went into a little back room. There we found the hide of a big dog, freshly killed."

All "the boys" laughed at this, and then came reminiscences of narrow escapes in the war. Sim Whitsett told of his narrowest escape, Ben Morrow told of his, and Frank James related his. Then Hi George, who is the very man that enlisted Frank James and took him to fight under Quantrill, told his. Hi George is a humorist. It is marvelous that a man who could do serious work like that required in the Lawrence raid and the Centralia fight can be such a jolly old soul.

"The narrowest escape I ever had during the war," said Hi, "was when I was kicked by a government mule and my nose was broken. They thought I was dead, and they didn't send for a doctor for two hours."

Dr. Powell, Frank James' physician, came in and advised his patient not to venture out.

"I'm going, though," said the sick man. "I've got my winter clothes, a thick pair of overshoes and an overcoat, and I feel sure it won't hurt me to go."

Mrs. Samuel sent up advice for her son to stay in bed, but she was told that he intended going to the burial.

"He'll go, then," was the mother's comment. "When Frank James says he'll do a thing, he does it."

Dinner was served in the hotel dining room at 11.30 o'clock, and a few minutes after 12 the little procession started for the farm, the rain having subsided to a mere drizzle. Along winding country roads, deep in mud but fringed with green hedges, wildroses in full blossom, clover and cornfields, the hearse and the carriages wound.

"There is where little Jesse's sister lives," remarked my driver, pointing to a neat white farmhouse upon a hill, half-way out to the Samuel farm. Here in Kearney the son of Jesse James is called "little Jesse," though he weighs 190 pounds, 23 more than his father did, and is big enough to conduct a Kansas City pawnshop. His sister is Mrs. Mary Barr, wife of a prominent farmer. A little farther along, the driver pointed out the home of Mrs. Joseph Hall, one of the half-sisters of Frank and Jesse James. Mrs. William Nicholson, the other half-sister, also lives in the neighborhood. All these were present at the burial today.

Crossing swollen and muddy creeks, one of which is

called Muddy Fork, which fits its condition, and another of which is called Clear Creek, which is a misfit, our procession presently came in sight of the farmhouse where the new coffin awaited us.

It may be noted in passing that Jesse James was baptized in Muddy Fork, in 1868, when he joined the Kearney Baptist Church. I talked today with Mr. Major of Kearney, who witnessed the immersion.

As the procession reached the farmhouse, the rain ceased entirely. The clouds broke into splotches and the sunlight shone out for a moment, just as the six veterans bore the coffin from the house to the hearse.

Mrs. Samuel and Mrs. Frank James, with Mrs. Hi George, sat for a few minutes on the front porch before the remains were brought out. Frank James, during this time, pointed out to his friends the side window through which Pinkerton detectives in 1875 threw the bomb that killed eight-year-old Archie P. Samuel and tore off the right forearm of Mrs. Samuel. John Samuel, who as a boy was in the house at the time, told how the calamity occurred; and Frank James, who was far away that winter night, remarked with some sarcasm that a revolver was found in a field near the house next morning bearing initials which showed that it belonged to a Pinkerton.

"The state," said Frank James, "took the revolver as evidence, but I guess it never got any farther than that."

At the side of the yard Frank James pointed out a whitewashed log cabin.

"Jesse was born there," he said. "I was born three miles from here."

Frank James did not point out the portholes in the log house, nor the bullet holes in the fence and the stable. Some of "the boys" examined these.

After the body was placed in the hearse Mrs. Samuel, supported by young Jesse James and one of the women, walked back to the old grave under the coffee-bean tree. The wrecked coffin had been reburied there. She stood for a moment looking at the grave and then walked slowly to her carriage.

Nature was kind on the trip back to town. It did not rain upon the cortège. A different route was taken on the way back—a road over which Jesse James had ridden on horseback many and many a time, as boy and man.

Hundreds of townspeople were gathered at the grave, where Zach Laffoon and Zip Pollock again performed the duties of sextons. Strangers read the inscription on the only tombstone in the family lot:

"Archie P., son of R. and Z. Samuel, killed Jan. 26, 1875, aged 8 years and 6 months. Our hearts in his grave are lying."

The pretty little poem by Thomas Hood is carved upon the stone, the sex pronouns being altered to suit:

> Our very hopes belied our fears;
>   Our fears our hopes belied.
> We thought him dying when he slept,
>   And sleeping when he died.
> For when the sun came dim and sad
>   And chill with early showers,
> His quiet eyelids closed—he had
>   Another morn than ours.

The widow of Jesse James was buried there a year ago this month, her remains having reposed in a vault at Kansas City for a year after her death. The father of Frank and Jesse James is buried in California, where he died.

Mrs. Samuel, who is a woman of remarkable energy for her years, says she is going back to the farm next March, as soon as the lease expires.

"I can't be contented anywhere else," she said to me. "I have lived on that place fifty-eight years. All my children were born there except Frank. There I have seen one of my sons murdered and another one brought home to be buried, who was murdered at St. Joseph. There my right arm was shot off. Much trouble has come to me there, but I love the old place and want to live there till I die.

"I do not believe that any woman in the world has had as much trouble as I have, or has had so much wrong done to her. I have had trouble enough to have lived 150 years. Do you know Mr. Frank?"

Mrs. Samuel usually refers to her son, in the presence of strangers, as "Mr. Frank."

"I am very proud of him. He is good to me, and he has promised to move out to the farm and stay with me till I die. He is going away next winter to go on the stage, and I don't see how I can stand it. Since he came to Kearney, two months ago, he has been with me more than at any time since he went to the war; and when he made a trip to St. Louis last week, from Friday to Sunday, I could hardly stand it.

"I am so proud that Mr. Frank has won the respect

and good will of the people. He has regained his reputation, and he deserves to be well thought of."

Mr. Major, who told me of Jesse James' immersion in Muddy Fork, told also of his conversion and his joining the Baptist church in Kearney. It is interesting to note that the Baptist church of that day was located upon the spot, since turned into a cemetery, where Jesse James was buried today.

"He joined the church and was baptized in 1868," said Mr. Major. "I notice by the church records that he was 'excluded' the next year, 1869. I was a little fellow then, but I remember hearing my mother tell about Jesse James leading in prayer one night at prayer-meeting. The only thing she recollected about his prayer was that he prayed for the salvation of his brother Frank.

"I remember very distinctly the first funeral of Jesse James in April, 1882. It was preached by the Rev. Mr. Martin, the Baptist minister, and there was a great crowd present. The body was brought here and placed first in a hotel which stood where the Commercial Hotel now is. The coffin was opened and we looked at the face through the glass. The corpse wore a full beard and moustache. Everybody who had known him recognized him."

Mr. and Mrs. Frank James and Mrs. Samuel accompanied the Quantrill veterans to the train this evening and bade them goodby. Before boarding the train "the boys" began talking about horses.

"I can't ride a horse much," said Frank James. "I have a good saddle-horse here, but when I get on him I'm afraid he'll fall down with me."

"I can ride," said Hi George. "You ought to come out to my farm and see me gallop around, attending to my work."

"Precious little work you do these days, I reckon, Hi," remarked Sim Whitsett; "you're too old."

"I'm about sixty-six," replied Captain Hi, "but I get around pretty lively yet. . . . Look out, there, Sim—the Feds are comin'," continued the humorist, and Lawyer Frank Gregg's mind harked back to the fight at Centralia, in which he took part with Frank and Jesse James.

"That was the only affair I was in with Jesse," he said, "but Frank James and I enlisted together."

As the men boarded the train Ben Morrow called out:

"Better call the roll, Frank. Sim Whitsett is missing."

Frank James boarded the coach and looked for Sim, who was sitting in another part of the car.

"Well, goodby, boys, and good luck," called Frank James as the train pulled out.

CHAPTER XXXV

THE DRAMATIC SURRENDER OF FRANK JAMES

THE night clerk at the McCarty House in Jefferson City was drowsy. It was past one o'clock in the morning, October 5, 1882, when two well-dressed men entered the lobby and advanced to the counter. The clerk turned the register around and pulled a pen out of a potato. Some things still were a bit oldtimey and simple in the Missouri state capital. Yawning, the clerk poked the penholder at one of the newcomers, who wrote "Jno. Edwards, Sedalia," on the register. Edwards handed the pen to his companion, who wrote "B. F. Winfrey, Marshall, Mo.," and stuck the pen back into the potato. The clerk languidly read the names and yawned some more.

Messrs. Edwards and Winfrey were assigned to a room upstairs. They went to bed, sleeping double. They had come in from the west on the Missouri Pacific night train, and they were weary. They slept late, not leaving their room until about nine o'clock, when they came down to breakfast and then went out for a stroll.

Mr. Edwards, being none other than our familiar

friend Maj. John N. Edwards, was well known in Jefferson City. He was greeted by many citizens, to whom he introduced Mr. Winfrey, a total stranger. Mr. Winfrey was a tall man, rather thin, with sandy side-whiskers and gray-blue eyes. The sideburns were negligible, but the eyes were interesting; they were active eyes, taking note of everything; keen eyes, always on the alert; restless eyes, never gazing steadily in one direction but shifting from this to that and the other object and back again.

For some hours the noted editor and his friend strolled about town, or sat in the hotel lobby, talking politics with acquaintances of Major Edwards. Both Winfrey and Edwards were staunch Democrats, both knew Missouri politics from A to Z. Mr. Winfrey, it developed, knew also a lot about farming and was a lover of fine horseflesh.

Shortly after the noon dinner the two men went up to their room. Mr. Winfrey lay down and slept for a couple of hours. Major Edwards sat by the window reading the day's newspapers from St. Louis and Kansas City. At five o'clock they walked to the office of Governor Crittenden and were admitted by Finis Farr, the governor's secretary.

Half a dozen men—state officials and plain politicians—were sitting about in the executive chamber. They had been invited thither, they knew not why. But presently they found out. After Major Edwards had shaken hands with the governor he laid a hand upon the arm of Mr. Winfrey, who stood silent, his eyes taking in the assembled company without missing a man.

"Governor," said the major, "allow me to introduce my old friend Frank James."

"I am glad to meet you, Mr. James," said the governor, extending his hand.

"And I am glad to meet you, Governor," said Mr. James.

One of the politicians, sitting back against the wall about twenty feet away, gasped:

"Good God! I can't believe it!"

Nevertheless, it was so. Frank James, cool, calm, collected, master of such emotions as he felt, opened his coat, revealing a thick leather belt crammed with cartridges and showing at the middle a big bronze buckle marked "U. S." He unbuckled the belt and removed it. Attached to it was a holster from which protruded the gleamy handle of a big sixshooter, Remington 44. Holding the belt in his left hand, with his right hand he plucked the pistol from the holster and, deftly moving his fingers down to the polished barrel, extended it handle foremost toward the governor of his native state.

"Governor Crittenden," said the elder and abler brother of the late Jesse James, "I want to hand over to you that which no living man except myself has been permitted to touch since 1861, and to say that I am your prisoner. I have taken all the cartridges out of the weapon," he added, after a brief pause, "and you can handle it with safety."

The gasping politician gasped again, but nobody paid the slightest attention to him. A most dramatic event in the history of human civilization was happening before the astonished eyes of the governor's guests.

Governor Crittenden accepted the belt and the six-shooter, handling the latter somewhat gingerly. He seemed surprised at the weight of the weapon.

"Not since 1861!"—the governor's voice intoned surprise.

"That remark applies to the revolver," explained Frank James. "The cartridge belt has been mine only eighteen years. I got it at Centralia, in September, 1864."

That explained the "U. S." on the buckle. During all the sixteen years of his outlawry and the two years preceding, Frank James had worn a United States army cartridge belt taken from the body of one of the Federal recruits slain in the Centralia massacre. The firearm, notwithstanding its frequent activities through twenty-one years of fighting, was in prime condition.

And thus it was that Alexander Franklin James came in and surrendered, ending at last the Civil War in Missouri.

Although the governor had been expecting his distinguished guest, he was not wholly prepared as to proceedings immediately subsequent. Mrs. Frank James had visited the executive in his office and made plea for her husband. For years, she insisted, he had been living quietly and working hard to support his family. Yet he still was hunted, hounded, always in fear for his life, so that, as Mrs. James told the governor, he was not able to stoop down to split a stick of stovewood without expecting somebody to shoot him in the back. He was eager to "come in" if protection could be assured. He wished to settle down and live like other men.

Correspondence had passed between the governor and the outlaw, the latter's letter being dated at and mailed from St. Louis. Whether it was written in St. Louis is quite another thing. Frank R. O'Neil, a reporter for the Missouri *Republican* (later the St. Louis *Republic*), had visited James somewhere in Missouri hundreds of miles from St. Louis, through arrangement between the outlaw and a trusted friend. James had told O'Neil, in a long interview the account of which was withheld from publication until James surrendered, that he was eager for the sake of his family to be restored to society. The governor had assured his correspondent—the communication being sent to Mrs. James and forwarded to her husband—that the state would guarantee him a fair trial in every respect.

"HE CAME IN"—thus headlined the Missouri *Republican* the day after the event. He had been sojourning in his Nowhere for more than sixteen years, and he came in out of that mysterious Nowhere from the farm home of Sim Whitsett, near Lee's Summit, Missouri, and took train for Jefferson City, Major Edwards joining him at Sedalia. Sim Whitsett, an old Quantrill guerrilla comrade, saw Frank aboard the train at Cole Younger's home town and wished him well. Undoubtedly there were others at the railroad depot there who knew the outlaw, but being his friends they did not "let on." Whitsett alone knew whither Frank was bound; and although he was nigh to bursting with the big news, Sim managed to keep his mouth shut.

So now at last Governor Crittenden had the last of the notorious Missouri outlaw chiefs in custody, including his cartridge belt and his veteran revolver—and didn't know just what to do with him. It was a situation unique. There was a formal discussion. In the end the decision was to send the prisoner to Independence, capital of Jackson County, where it was understood that Prosecutor Will Wallace could disinter a four-years-old indictment charging James with the murder of Pinkerton Detective John W. Witcher, which had taken place in that county in 1874. Frank had hoped to be tried merely for some alleged robbery, but when told of the murder indictment he did not seem to be worried. He said it was absurd, and he expressed confidence in his acquittal on that charge.

On the train with him bound for Independence were Major Edwards, Secretary Farr (custodian of the prisoner), and Frank O'Neil, the only reporter that ever interviewed the uncaught lion of outlawry in his lair. News that Frank James had "come in" had been flashed wide and far. People aboard train crowded into the coach to get a glimpse of him. Nobody knew how he looked. For a man as prominent along certain lines as he, it was most remarkable how slightly he was known in his native state. Major Edwards indicated Finis Farr as the prisoner, and for a time the governor's secretary endured curious gazes. Then the major whispered to somebody that Frank O'Neil was Frank James. Ladies looked admiringly at the newspaper reporter, a handsome and modest man of about thirty-two, who blushed.

"Why, isn't he a fine-looking fellow!" one of the ladies confided to another. "I had no idea such a terrible outlaw could look so nice."

At Sedalia, home of Edwards, the reporter was lionized until the train resumed its way. Frank James, who seldom smiled, enjoyed this immunity from being inspected as a formidable freak.

At the station in Independence a great crowd awaited him. His mother rushed forward and embraced him, thanking God with fervent voice that her son was restored to her at last. She greeted him as "Buck," her oldtime nickname for him. His wife and their four-year-old son Robert welcomed him with fond affection. Mr. and Mrs. Samuel Ralston, his parents-in-law, were on hand. Mr. Ralston served as a sort of master of ceremonies at the hotel, introducing his son-in-law to old friends. Long ago the Ralstons had become reconciled to their daughter's husband. Little Robbie, a beautiful child, had helped, without knowing it.

Cornelius Murphy of Kansas City, county marshal, also was awaiting the prisoner. When Jesse James lived at Kansas City in 1881 he occupied a house on the same block with the home of Con Murphy's father. The marshal was wont to gather his deputies there every now and then, of an evening, and set forth in search of Jesse James and his gang. Jesse got the habit of strolling over to Father Murphy's on these occasions and asking Con how he was progressing in his search. Tradition has it that one night Con invited Jesse to go along and help catch Jesse James.

"No, thanks," replied Jesse. "I'm kind o' timid about such things, Mr. Murphy. But I'll sit on my front porch, and if Jesse passes along maybe I'll recognize him. How does he look?"

"If I only knew," said the marshal, "I might catch him. But that's just the trouble—nobody who wants him knows how the fellow looks."

Whereupon Jesse James smiled.

This, you may be sure, was not bravado on Jesse's part. It was his way of disarming suspicion, and it worked well.

Prosecutor Wallace also was at the station. He turned Frank James over to Marshal Murphy, who put him in the county jail at Independence after family greetings were over. Mr. Wallace found that he had no evidence tending to connect James with the murder of the Pinkerton operative whose body had been found in a road near Independence eight years earlier, at which time the future prosecutor wrote up the incident as a newspaper reporter. After due consideration the state elected to try the prisoner under an indictment found in Daviess County charging him with the murder of Frank McMillan, the railroad workman who was killed when five men held up the Rock Island train near Winston, July 5, 1881.

The trial opened at Gallatin, capital of Daviess County, August 21, 1883, the defendant having remained in jail at Independence until a short time before that date. Circuit Judge H. C. S. Goodman presided. Prosecuting Attorney W. P. Hamilton was assisted by William H. Wallace of Kansas City as principal aid and by four other able lawyers. Col. John F. Philips of Kansas City, a Federal officer in the Civil War and a Federal judge later, represented the defendant as chief counsel. Associated with him were former Lieut.-Gov. Charles P. Johnson of St.

Louis, the most noted criminal lawyer in the state; the Hon. John M. Glover of St. Louis, who served in Congress; Col. C. T. Garner of Richmond; William H. Rush of Gallatin, and Joshua W. Alexander of Gallatin, who served many years in Congress and for a time as secretary of commerce in the cabinet of President Wilson. Frank James was fortunate in the personnel of his battery of defenders.

The trial, which lasted eight days, took place in the Gallatin Opera House instead of the county courthouse. This was not for theatrical effect but because the courtroom was too small to accommodate onefifth of the people who were eager to witness the proceedings. The sheriff issued tickets of admission not to exceed seating capacity of the opera house. Thus no S. R. O. sign was displayed. So far as dramatic interest goes, no theatrical performance in Gallatin or anywhere else ever has surpassed the serious serial that ran there in those hot latter days of August. Frank James was fond of the drama, but he preferred Shakespeare and Marlowe to the Revised Statutes of Missouri.

Mr. Wallace, who made the opening statement, said that evidence would be adduced to show that Frank James, Jesse James, Wood Hite, Clarence Hite and Dick Liddil committed the train robbery in the course of which Frank McMillan was shot to death. Both Liddil and Clarence Hite, he said, each without knowing the other was confessing, had told him these five were the robbers. They had stated that Frank and Jesse James and Wood Hite were the three men who entered the coaches and that Clarence Hite and Liddil were the pair that stood guard over the engine crew.

The defense admitted the presence of Jesse James, the two Hites and Liddil, but contended that the other man was Jim Cummins. Jim had been missing for some years. Jesse James and the Hites were dead, Liddil had given himself up and turned state's evidence under agreement of immunity from prosecution for any crime alleged or admitted.

The case revolved around the identity of the fifth bandit.

Liddil testified that this man was Frank James. Many Daviess County witnesses identified the defendant as one of several horsebacked strangers seen in the vicinity just prior to the crime. A flock of Fords from Ray County, including Mrs. Martha Bolton, sister of the assassins of Jesse James, her two children and her father, "Old Man" Ford, testified that the defendant had been at her house a mile and a half from Richmond near the time of the crime. The defense, in addresses to the jury, denounced all the Fords as utterly undesirable and unreliable.

One of the most interesting witnesses was the Rev. Benjamin Matchett, a rural clergyman of the Christian denomination. He testified that on the day preceding the holdup two men on horseback had stopped at his house near Winston for dinner. One said his name was Scott and that he came from Plattsburg, Clinton County, Missouri, "and the other, the defendant, said his name was Willard," and that he had been in Clinton County for about eight years. Other evidence showed that the man calling himself Scott was Clarence Hite, a youthful first cousin of the defendant.

The preacher said "Willard" asked him what he thought of Bob Ingersoll. There was a discussion, the two disagreed, the minister went into his library and brought out a volume containing Colonel Ingersoll's lectures, Willard read them until he fell asleep. After he woke up, Willard introduced Shakespeare as a topic of discussion more fitting for a preacher. He remarked that "no other man like Shakespeare ever lived," and the clergyman acquiesced. "Then Willard declaimed a piece and remarked, 'That's grand!' which observation I indorsed. I recognize the defendant. I am so confident the defendant is the man who stopped at my house that if he hadn't paid for the dinner I should say, 'Mr. Willard, I would be pleased to have the amount of that board bill.'"

This evoked laughter in court, wherein the defendant failed to join. Frank James, as we know, seldom laughed; and surely that, for him, was no laughing matter, anyhow.

Mr. and Mrs. Allen H. Parmer of Clay County, Texas, testified that the defendant, a brother of Mrs. Parmer, spent several weeks at their home in the summer of 1881, staying upstairs reading most of the time, and that he was there about the time of the Winston affair.

The redoubtable Gen. Jo Shelby took the stand in defense of Frank James, declaring he had not seen the defendant since 1872. Jesse James, Liddil, Cummins and other members of the alleged outlaw band, the general stated, had been at his home frequently in recent years. They were there in the fall of 1881. He had asked Jesse where Frank was and had been told that Frank had been living in the South several years, for his health, which was very poor.

About midway in the trial the defense suddenly abandoned the contention that Jim Cummins (who was no Shakespearean scholar) was one of the Winston robbers. The theory that only four men were in the party—Jesse James, Dick Liddil and the two Hites—was built up. Evidence was introduced to show that Wood Hite and Frank James, who were first cousins, bore a striking physical resemblance. The state controverted this with testimony to the effect that Hite was an unlettered, ungainly, awkward, slouchy, ill-groomed fellow with a stoop, whereas Frank James was erect, tidy, urbane, well-read, highly intelligent. Wood Hite's nickname was "Old Grimes."

In his long and able address to the jury Prosecutor Wallace made a strong point of the testimony of the Rev. Mr. Matchett. Alluding to the conversation on religion and poetry, Mr. Wallace remarked:

"Finally the defendant, he said, got to Shakespeare, and after passing encomiums on this great genius arose and recited extracts from his plays—the slouchy Sphinx, alias Wood Hite, alias 'Old Grimes,' no doubt! A man, gentlemen, may change the exterior of his person, but he cannot change the complexion of the mind within. This is a most remarkable mental characteristic for a Western bandit. To say that it is nothing uncommon for a train robber to go through the land spouting Shakespeare is preposterous. There is no getting away from the identification furnished by Mr. Matchett.

"Dr. William E. Black, one of your best citizens, testifies that since Frank James has been in jail he had a long conversation with him, in which he talked much of Shakespeare and of his plays, naming, I think, Macbeth, Richard III, Hamlet, and others, and passing his opinion on Lawrence Barrett and others whom he said he had had the pleasure of seeing. The nail was driven through by the other witnesses, but the testimony of Matchett and Black, taken together, rivets forever the identity of this defendant. This completes the evidence for the state—abundant, conclusive, irresistible."

After being absent three and a half hours the jury returned a verdict finding Frank James not guilty. But not yet was Frank James free. Prosecutor Wallace had him taken back to Independence, intending to put him on trial for alleged complicity in the Blue Cut train robbery. As at Gallatin, Dick Liddil was to be stellar witness for the state. But whilst James was in jail at Independence awaiting trial on this charge, the supreme court of Missouri rendered a decision in another case to the effect that a person who had been convicted of crime was not competent to testify in a court. Liddil had been sent to the penitentiary for horse-stealing several years before he became a member of the James band; he had been released on three-fourths time, for good behavior. Mr. Wallace requested Governor Crittenden to issue a pardon for this old offence. The governor refused.

"There was nothing left for me to do except dismiss the case, which I did," says Mr. Wallace. "Thus ended the career of the Missouri outlaws. Probably no band in history ever came to a more ignominious ending. Only Frank James escaped."

The year following his acquittal at Gallatin, Frank James was taken to Huntsville, Ala., where he stood trial on an indictment charging him with complicity in the robbery of a Government paymaster who had been held up, in March, 1881, on his way from Florence to Muscle Shoals, to pay off the Government force employed there. The jury found James not guilty. From that time forth the law had nothing against him.

Old indictments against James in Missouri and in other states appear to have been forgotten—at any rate they were ignored utterly—by the respective powers, save in the instances stated. The assumption is that the authorities took one of two views: (a) "We couldn't convict him, anyhow, for lack of evidence, so what's the use to try him?" (b) "Oh, well, the whole gang's cleaned out now, mostly dead and done for, and it will be interesting to watch Frank James make good—if he has it in him."

He had it in him, and he made good. That is in every respect the most boldly outstanding and the most humanly comforting fact in the whole history of the Missouri outlaws. From the moment when he stepped out of the jail at Independence, a free man virtually for the first time since the beginning of the Civil War, and went home to see his mother, to the day nearly thirty-three years later when he died in his bed at the old homestead, Frank James was a thoroughly good citizen. For many of those years I knew him personally, in his home and elsewhere, and I know scores of worthy citizens who knew him still more intimately; and as to the Frank James I knew and they knew I never heard the merest whisper of dispraise.   The chorus in recognition of his commendable qualities of head and heart has been unanimous and enthusiastic.

CHAPTER XXXVI

THE TWENTY YEARS' FIGHT FOR THE YOUNGERS' FREEDOM

EARLY in 1902 I entertained at my home in St. Louis one of the most remarkable men I have known. The late Capt. Warren Carter Bronaugh was remarkable, as I recall him, for two things. He was a Missouri ex-Confederate who had attained the age of sixty years without having learned the rudiments of draw poker, "Missouri's national game"; and for twenty years he had devoted his energies chiefly toward efforts to get the Younger brothers out of the Minnesota penitentiary.

It happened that I was able in a most modest way to assist Captain Bronaugh in this latter capacity toward the close of his long campaign. He was on his way to Minnesota, on one of the latest of his many journeys thither. It happened also, on the occasion mentioned, that I was able to give him elementary instruction in poker-playing, although I knew but little about the game then and, incidentally, have learned virtually nothing since. A few of us had a penny-ante evening at the poker board. My recollection is that I lost to my pupil. You will observe that I take no pride in my poker.

Captain Bronaugh grew up in Henry County, Missouri, where in 1861 he enlisted in the regular Confederate service. At the battle of Lone Jack, in Jackson County, Missouri, Aug. 6, 1862, he fought under Col. Vard Cockrell, whose brother, Gen. Francis Marion Cockrell, served for thirty years as a United States senator from Missouri.

The morning after that exceedingly gory engagement young Bronaugh and a comrade rode a few miles out of camp to forage for breakfast. Returning, they found the camp deserted. Galloping forward to overtake their command, they encountered a group of Confederate pickets, one of whom, learning that they belonged to Cockrell's force, said:

"Colonel Cockrell is on the east side of town, on the Chapel Hill road, in full retreat, and General Blunt is in Lone Jack with 1500 Jayhawkers and Redlegs from Kansas."

Bronaugh and his comrade had been headed directly for Lone Jack and were less than a mile from that place. For nearly an hour they talked with the picket who had warned them. "He was an exceedingly handsome young fellow," said Bronaugh, "stalwart, alert and intelligent, and every inch a soldier. Around his waist, suspended from a glossy black belt, was a brace of fine revolvers. This youthful Confederate picket, by his splendid military bearing, made a peculiar and powerful impression upon me, and also won the gratitude of both my comrade and myself, for undoubtedly, had he not given us timely warning, we should have ridden into Blunt's troops and been captured or killed. From the hour I met him I never forgot his face."

Captain Bronaugh served through the war without making personal acquaintance of either of the Youngers; but after Coleman, James and Robert had been sent to the Minnesota penitentiary at Stillwater under life sentences for their part in the Northfield bank raid in 1876, he conceived a deep and mysterious sympathy for them. He felt an irresistible urge to do something toward getting "the boys" out. In 1882 he was married, and he proposed to his bride a most strange wedding journey. She acquiesced in the plan to visit Minnesota so that her husband might meet the Missourians who had been imprisoned for six years. Bronaugh left his bride at the Merchants Hotel in St. Paul and proceeded to Stillwater, about twenty-three miles distant. Prison Warden J. A. Reed, learning that he was from Missouri, remarked, "We look on all Missourians here with a good deal of suspicion."

"Well, I'm from Missouri and I'm proud of it," said Bridegroom Bronaugh.

"This gentleman," said the warden to his deputy, "wants to see the Youngers, and he's from Missouri. You have him bare his arm to the elbow, and you listen closely to all he says when in the presence of the prisoners."

"Here's a man from Missouri who wishes to see you," said the deputy as the pair paused in front of Cole Younger's cell. Bronaugh poked his bared right arm through the bars and introduced himself to Cole, who gave him a hearty grip; the exile was glad to see anybody from dear old Missouri.

"At my very first glance," said Bronaugh, "I recognized him as the very person who, under such strange circumstances, had hailed me on a public road near Lone Jack on that hot Sunday morning in 1862 and kindly kept me from running into the ranks of the Kansas Redlegs. The Confederate picket, then but a youth, and the man who stood now behind the bars, with his face furrowed with care and his body full of wounds, were one and the same—the redoubtable Cole Younger."

Fate seemed to have directed the footsteps of the happy bridegroom. He began vaguely to comprehend that peculiar feeling of sympathy he had felt for the Youngers since he read about their downfall. This big one-time bandit had saved his life: he would repay by devoting that life in behalf of the picket and his brothers. He told Cole of the Lone Jack incident, which the prisoner recalled but dimly. He pledged his untiring support in efforts toward ultimate pardon. He kept the pledge through two decades of disinterested devotion which I dare to assert has no parallel in the history of mankind.

Warren Bronaugh had no time to learn how to play poker. From 1882 to 1902 he played the nobler game of save-your-saver. He wrote reams of letters, traveled many thousands of miles, spent much of his own money and raised and expended other funds in behalf of the Youngers. He enlisted the moral support of many distinguished Missourians. He played Missouri against Minnesota, and in the end he opened the jackpot and the prison doors. He was a courtly gentleman of the old Southern school, and I pay him here high tribute of respect as a true sporting proposition that never got cold feet.

Many of the high officials in Minnesota, as the years piled up, looked upon Bronaugh as a public nuisance. He was after them hot and heavy all the time. Governors, pardon boards, wardens—he camped upon their trails and gave them no rest. "No missionary in a foreign land ever worked harder than I," he said. His theory was that the Youngers were by no means bad men at heart; that they would make desirable citizens of Missouri if permitted to return home. Minnesotans, with but few exceptions at the outset and for many years, felt that the prisoners fully deserved their fate and should serve out their time.

Former Gov. William R. Marshall was one of the few who enlisted heartily in the cause and gave much aid and comfort to Bronaugh and the Youngers. He visited Missouri and was entertained at Captain Bronaugh's handsome farm home near Clinton. When he got back to Minnesota "he was most outrageously assailed from nearly every quarter of his commonwealth. Partisans fought him without mercy; politicians traduced him; and the press, metropolitan and provincial, joined in criticizing him. Even the pulpit did not spare him." Thus wrote Captain Bronaugh in his book, *The Youngers' Fight for Freedom*, published in 1906.

Ex-Governor Marshall defended his course in a 3000-word communication which was published July 26, 1886, in the St. Paul *Pioneer Press*.

"These men are not as black as much falsehood, much prejudice, much misinformation and the dime biographers have painted them," he wrote. . . . "I am assured by those who knew Cole Younger in the regular Confederate army, in General Shelby's brigade of Price's army—part of the time in the division of General Marmaduke, the present governor of Missouri—that he never was guilty of a cruel or unsoldierly act, but that he was an officer of unusual ability. He was a captain when nineteen years of age. It is not true that either of the Youngers was personally concerned in the killing of Cashier Heywood. That was the act of another of the band, inspired, as a large portion of murderers are, by the bottle. These men have committed crimes enough, without falsely multiplying or exaggerating their offenses. No one claims that they are innocent, or undeserving of punishment. They themselves do not."

At his own expense Bronaugh had 25,000 copies of this letter printed in pamphlet form and distributed throughout Missouri, Kentucky, Tennessee and Arkansas—territory more or less Youngery, so to speak. In a letter to ex-Governor Marshall, Aug. 1, 1886, Cole Younger wrote, in brief part:

"As for the war, I have said that I was engaged in the bloody warfare on the border of Missouri and Kansas. As you truthfully said in your letter to the *Pioneer Press*, it was little better on both sides than murder. That is the original cause of my being in prison today."

In this letter Cole took occasion to pay his respects to the unknown author of the 15-to-1 massacre tale:

"As to the story going the rounds that during the war I captured 15 men, tied them together and tried to shoot through them all, it is false from beginning to end. The whole thing was so absurd that I never supposed any sensible man would believe it. I have always supposed the story was gotten up by some reporter as a burlesque on sensational newspapers."

And yet, strange to record, many Minnesotans are said to have cited this silly story by way of proof that Cole Younger was a devouring demon. A small boy may be forgiven for crediting such trash, but what shall we say of an adult person (physically) who peddles such fools' truck?

Our old friend the untiring and unterrified Major Edwards leaped into the fray and fought valiantly for the Youngers. In 1888, the year before his untimely death, he drew up a celebrated petition to Gov. William R. Merriam of Minnesota, setting forth "ten separate and distinct reasons why the Youngers should be pardoned." They met the fate of President Wilson's fourteen points. This petition was signed by many members of the Missouri legislature and was drafted as emanating from the members of that body.

One of the few Minnesotans other than ex-Governor Marshall who aided Captain Bronaugh in his crusade was Ignatius Donnelly of Bacon-wrote-Shakespeare fame. Donnelly fought for the Youngers with a zeal as fiery as that evinced in his contention for the Baconian cryptogram theory.

Capt. W. W. Murphy, leader of the celebrated seven who charged the Youngers and Sam Wells in the thicket near Madelia and effected the capture of the three brothers and the killing of Wells, also made plea for the pardoning of the prisoners. One or two other members of the seven again fell into line, charging this time upon the board of pardons, which withstood the assault.

Of eminent Missourians who wrote letters in behalf of the prisoners these outstanding figures should be mentioned: Gen. Jo Shelby (of course!); Senator George G. Vest, author of the illustrious defense of the dog; William J. Stone, governor and senator; Thomas T. Crittenden, who had been a Federal officer in the war and in whose administration as governor of Missouri Jesse James was killed and Frank James surrendered; Lon V. Stephens, governor; William Warner, senator; Edwin W. Stephens of Columbia, newspaper editor, publisher of law books, once moderator of the Baptist church in America; Champ Clark, congressman and speaker; William S. Cowherd of Kansas City, mayor and congressman; Shepard Barclay, justice of the Missouri supreme court; Col. John F. Philips, late of the Federal army, congressman, United States district judge; M. E. Benton, congressman, nephew of the great Senator Thomas Hart Benton; and the Hon. William H. Wallace, who as prosecuting attorney of Jackson County had disintegrated the James Boys' Band to the accompaniment of violent staccato music.

Another noted native of Missouri, Senator Stephen B. Elkins of West Virginia, gladly and gratefully aided the cause with cash and a communication to the Minnesota powers. He had even a more intimate reason than had Captain Bronaugh for being friendly to Cole Younger. In October, 1862, near Big Creek, in Cass County, Missouri, Quantrill the Bloodthirsty held captive as a spy young Steve Elkins, who as a school-teacher in that county had had as pupil the big and bright boy Cole Younger, "Bud" to his schoolfellows. Quantrill's camp being in his saddle, he took along no prisoners: horses were too scarce. Bud Younger, a Quantrill trooper, learned of the capture of his friend Elkins and managed to have himself detailed to take the spy out and shoot him. He took Steve some distance away from the Quantrillian presence.

"Well, Bud, I reckon it's all up with me," said Steve. "I know the rules."

"I reckon it is, Steve," said Bud, "unless you light out and run like hell now; and for God's sake keep your mouth shut about this, for you know if Quantrill ever learns I didn't kill you he'll kill me."

The future United States senator and coal baron obeyed instructions, Cole Younger firing his pistol in the air to cause Quantrill to believe he had shot the spy.

Miss Retta Younger, sister of the prisoners, and other family connections worked with Captain Bronaugh. From time to time Bronaugh went to Minnesota carrying pardon petitions in a grip made almost as heavy as that in which Jesse James was wont to tote his surplus supply of cartridges when he went out upon a business venture.

Robert Younger, with a perfect prison record for the thirteen years he had served, died in the penitentiary hospital Sept. 16, 1889, slightly under the age of thirty-four years. Retta was at his bedside. "Please don't weep for me" were his last words. He was buried next to his mother in the family lot at Lee's Summit, Missouri.

Bronaugh was in St. Paul when, on the 10th of July, 1901, the board of pardons signed paroles releasing Cole and Jim after nearly twenty-five years' imprisonment. Permission to leave the state was denied them. Said the *Pioneer Press:*

"The parole of the Youngers is one of those acts of mercy which is twice blessed. It blesseth him that gives and him that takes. It will be approved by public sentiment throughout the state. . . . There has been for several years a distinct change in the attitude of public sentiment. Not that time has softened the general indignation at the crime or crimes of which they were guilty. But the men themselves have changed. They are not the Younger boys who nearly twenty-five years ago belonged to the gang of highwaymen and desperadoes who invaded Northfield, undertook to rob the bank there, and shot the cashier in cold blood. They are called by the same name, but they are not the same persons. They are widely different from the Younger boys of 1876 in character, in all that constitutes moral personality. . . . It has become evident that these men were not radically vicious or depraved, that in their normal elements of character they were brave and kind and just and generous and loyal-hearted. They were led astray by their associations, by the fierce passions aroused by the partisan warfare in which they became involved in the conflict of parties during the Civil War in Missouri. . . . The uniform testimony of all the prison wardens is not merely to their good behavior—their record in this respect being without a blemish during twenty-five years—but to the good character which prompted their good behavior.

"There need be no fear that these men will break their parole or do anything to disappoint the confidence of their friends. There is nothing of the sneak or hypocrite about them. They are ten times better men than are most of those whose unrelenting vindictiveness would have denied to their declining years the poor solace of being prisoners on parole."

Files of the Kansas City *Star* of July 11, 1901, record the scene when Captain Bronaugh visited the prison an hour after the paroles were granted:

"'I said I'd be the first Missourian to shake hands with you, Cole,' said Captain Bronaugh, who was having some difficulty in restraining his emotions.

"'You sure are,' said Cole; and they shook hands again. . . .

"'Well, I reckon (Cole Younger habitually says 'I reckon') you'll keep your promise to walk down the prison steps between us?'

"'You bet I will, and I would have waited twenty-five years more to do it.'

"'Reckon they know it in Jackson?'

"'Yes, you bet!'

"Cole chuckled, his grin broadening until it almost reached his ears.

"'Bronaugh, did you send any telegrams to Missouri?'

"'Lots of 'em, and not a one to anybody that is not your friend.'

"'I sent one myself,' said Cole.

"'Who to?'

"'Lizzie Daniels, down at Harrisonville. You know I knew her when she was a little child—so high. She's a noble girl, too,' and then he added with another chuckle, 'good Methodist, too.'"

Bronaugh was a good Methodist, as Cole knew. Jim Younger came in, and there was handshaking all around. At ten o'clock next morning, Sunday, the Youngers were released.

"Immediately after chapel services," runs the *Star's* account, "while Cole Younger, head nurse, was at his accustomed post in the prison hospital, and Jim, librarian and postman, was in the library, each was informed that he was wanted 'down in front.' They supposed that they were to see a visitor in the reception room. But the brothers met a deputy warden, who handed each of them a suit of civilian clothes and a telescope grip.

"'Put these clothes on,' said the warden; and he added, 'you won't have to go back.'

"The brothers put the clothes on without delay. Then they walked down in town, in company with local newspaper men. Few people recognized Cole and Jim. After dinner at the prison office, the brothers, Warden Wolfer and others enjoyed a naphtha launch excursion on Lake St. Croix.

"'I'm afraid we broke our paroles,' said Cole, 'by getting across the middle of the lake into Wisconsin. I tell you, it was the finest outing I ever had in my life. Wasn't it, Jim?'"

CHAPTER XXXVII

HOW FRANK JAMES AND COLE YOUNGER MADE GOOD

ONLY one of the three Younger brothers who went to Minnesota in 1876, instead of going to the Centennial Exposition at Philadelphia and having a good time, ever got back home alive. That was Thomas Coleman; and this outlaw historian was selected by certain invisible powers as the man to escort Cole into his native state after an enforced absence of nearly twenty-seven years. Now it may be told that the late Captain Bronaugh was chief of these invisibles. Possibly the captain was grateful to me for having taught him nothing serious about playing poker.

A legitimate journalistic plot was involved in the affair. The idea was to have the last of the Youngers re-enter Missouri by way of St. Louis and proceed across state to his old home at Lee's Summit in Jackson County. I was on the staff of the St. Louis *Post-Dispatch*, being dubbed "the outlaw editor" by certain facetious fellows because I had covered many assignments having to do with bold bad men. Through correspondence with Captain Bronaugh and Cole Younger it was arranged that I should meet the latter in Chicago and accompany him to St. Louis, without preliminary publicity, thus giving my paper first chance at the interesting story of his homecoming.

Best-laid plans frequently fail. Cole, at the last moment, balked at the publicity which such a return would have given him. He had the courtesy to send me a wire from Chicago to the effect that he had changed his plans and would enter Missouri from the north, without reportorial company from his old home state. That was about the middle of February, 1903, the Minnesota board of pardons having granted him a full pardon, enabling him to leave that state at will, after watching his course as a hardworking man on parole for more than a year and a half.

When Cole and Jim were released on parole they became commercial travelers, or drummers, for the N. P. Peterson Granite Company of St. Paul and Stillwater. Oddly enough—considering the character of their first activities in Minnesota—the Youngers took orders for tombstones. Each of them received $60 a month and expenses. On one of his rural trips, "making" the graveyard towns by horse and buggy, Jim Younger suffered an accident which laid him up for weeks. He then took up the writing of insurance policies. Before he made much headway at this he was informed that because he was an unpardoned convict any policy he wrote would be held invalid.

Captain Bronaugh continued his efforts to get full pardons for the Youngers. He made another trip to Minnesota in the summer of 1902 and saw Jim Younger in St. Paul. Jim was feeling discouraged. He was in love! Without a pardon he could not marry the young woman to whom he was engaged. She was a newspaper writer in St. Paul and had met Younger when he was in prison. Refined, highly educated, it was said that she circulated in the best society of the Twin Cities. When the lovers learned that they were not to be permitted to wed so long as Younger was merely on parole, the girl went west and left Jim disconsolate.

"I reckon a fellow might as well cut his throat and be done with it," he remarked to Captain Bronaugh, who sought to cheer him up with hope of a pardon not far ahead.

On a Sunday afternoon a few days later the body of Jim Younger was found in his room at the Reardon Hotel in St. Paul. His right hand was clutching a revolver. He had fired a bullet into his head, just above the right ear. Thus the man who had survived terrible wounds and a quarter-century of prison service, always hoping that he might be permitted to return home before he died, succumbed to an affair of the heart almost on the eve of a pardon.

I went to Lee's Summit to witness the burial of James Younger, but arrived one day late because of the peregrinating propensities of Mr. James Robert Cummins, to be treated more fully in the next and final chapter of this chronicle. Jim was buried beside Bob. I found his mound heaped high with flowers still fairly fresh and fragrant. There had been a big funeral, with Sim Whitsett, Bill Gregg and other old guerrilla comrades as pallbearers. Remarked an old citizen standing by:

"'Pears like the Younger boys are all coming home dead. I surely would like mighty well to see Bud get back here alive. I knowed Bud Younger when he was a boy—no finer one in all Jackson County. Bud was bright and ambitious. Folks figured he'd turn out to be a preacher, he was so int'rested in church matters. The war surely done Bud dirt."

"Bud," otherwise Thomas Coleman Younger, returned home from "the war" more than forty years after he left Lee's Summit to join Quantrill. He did not announce his coming. Miss Nora Hall, his niece, told me about it not long ago at her home in Lee's Summit:

"My sister Nettie's husband, Mr. Donahue, was running the hotel here. He never had seen Uncle Cole. The night of Feb. 16, 1903, about midnight, a big man stepped off a train from Kansas City, carrying a grip. He walked to the hotel, near the station. He stood by the stove in the hotel office, smoking his pipe.

"Several persons were there, but nobody paid any special attention to the big man. Another man, a drummer, had got off the same train and gone to the hotel. After a time the big man remarked to Mr. Donahue that he reckoned he'd take a room and turn in. The drummer was eyeing him curiously. So was the landlord. Those two exchanged glances. Finally Mr. Donahue asked the big drummer if he wasn't Cole Younger; and Uncle Cole admitted it.

"He had a good laugh at the drummer's expense. It seems that on the train the drummer had sat near Uncle Cole. He had heard somehow that Uncle Cole had reached Kansas City and was bound for Lee's Summit that night. He mistook another large man on the train for my uncle. He remarked to Uncle Cole, 'Isn't that man over there Cole Younger?' 'I don't think so,' Uncle Cole replied, trying hard to keep a straight face. Well, after they found out who he was, Nettie came downstairs and there was a joyous reunion."

The returned native lived at the hotel for some months but found the life rather too public for a man of his retiring disposition. He told Miss Hall he was going to her house to live, and he did so. After he had earned money at lecturing, chiefly in Texas and other parts of the Southwest, he bought a big two-story house which he presented to Miss Hall, his favorite niece. In that residence he dwelt until his death.

There was a romance in Cole Younger's life, but it happened—that is, started—much earlier than Jim's. The first visit he made away from Lee's Summit after his return was to the home of a prosperous and distinguished citizen whose wife, as a beautiful young girl, had been Bud Younger's sweetheart before the war. Younger was eighteen then, he was fifty-nine now, but he had not forgotten. Nor had the girl. Through all the years of his outlawry and of his imprisonment he had cherished the memory of her; and she had borne him in recollection as a handsome and desirable youth whom the misfortunes of war had overwhelmed. I could tell you—but I won't!—the tale of Cole Younger's lifelong love affair in considerable detail. It would be a love story thoroughly sweet and noble. Half a century from now, perhaps, somebody may write it without violating confidences of the living or of the dead. I violate no confidence in giving this tip to posterity.

Frank James, as we know, was more fortunate in his affair of the heart than was his long-time friend Cole Younger. He married the girl, asking nobody's consent but hers. Despite all untoward circumstances it turned out to be a happy marriage. I fancy that there was no happier woman living than Mrs. Frank James when her husband stepped forth from the Independence jail a free man and a full-blown citizen of Missouri and of the United States. To be a bandit means to be under the ban of society. In the case of Frank James the ban was lifted when the state accepted the verdict at Gallatin and the decision of Prosecutor Wallace that the accused could not be convicted in Jackson County because of lack of competent witnesses. Restored to society, he became a voter under his own name. In Tennessee he had voted regularly under the name of Woodson. He always took a deep interest in public affairs.

At the old Laclede Hotel in St. Louis, for many years the unofficial Democratic state headquarters, the former bandit frequently foregathered in the lobby with politicians and statesmen more or less eminent and talked politics. He had set opinions, and he was not chary in expressing them. You always knew exactly where Frank James stood upon any problem or policy, in politics or in ethics—yes, and in religion and morals. There was nothing equivocative about the man. His words shot home, as had his bullets in earlier days. He had been an intelligent reader and an alert observer from early manhood, and he had achieved rather violent likes and dislikes in the American social scheme. He hated the so-called protective tariff as a huge monster of political trickery devised by ghouls for the devouring of the poor. He never forgave "the damned Yankees" for subjugating the South. To him they were "Black Republicans," "Black Radicals," and the ebon hue never rubbed off.

Nevertheless, Frank James switched over to the Republican party and supported Theodore Roosevelt! Touching upon this point Mr. George S. Johns, for many years editor of the editorial page of the St. Louis *Post-Dispatch*, tells a remarkable story. One day in 1904 James visited the sanctum of Mr. Johns and startled the editor by announcing:

"I'm going to vote for Roosevelt for President, and I'm trying to get all my friends to support him. I like Roosevelt. He says what he means and means what he says. He is a man of my own type."

James remarked that he was sick and tired of the mossback Missouri Democracy. That Democracy, incidentally, had declined to select him as sergeant-at-arms to the lower branch of the state legislature. He had coveted the post because he felt that his elevation thereto would go far toward vindicating the James family. His defeat disappointed him bitterly, and he expressed his disappointment in bitter language. Throughout his long career as a free citizen he devoted himself to the self-set task of trying to convince the people of Missouri, not to speak of Outlanders, that the James boys and the James people in general were a great deal better people than the public had been led to believe.

President Roosevelt visited St. Louis and the Louisiana Purchase Exposition in his campaign year of 1904. A grand banquet was given in his honor. Mr. Johns chatted with the President.

"By the way, Mr. President," he remarked, "our most distinguished Missouri Democrat has declared himself for you in this campaign."

"Indeed! and who is he, may I ask?"

"Frank James."

"What!—the bandit?"

"The former bandit, Mr. President. He is a good citizen now and has been for many years. I would trust him as far as I'd trust any man I know. Frank James is a thoroughly reliable man, a desirable citizen."

"How interesting, now, Johns, how interesting! Tell me about him."

Mr. Johns had been about to turn away, but the President clutched his coattails and drew him back. He told the Strenuous many things about the post-outlaw life of Frank James, how he had made good and was respected by everybody who knew him. The President listened like a schoolboy hearing some thrillful tale to which he could not give full credence on the instant.

"Well! well!" cried Roosevelt. "What a remarkable life-story! A remarkable man, a most remarkable character!"

"He told me the other day, Mr. President," said the editor, "that you and he are men of the same type—you both mean what you say and you say what you mean, he said."

The President's interest deepened. "I want to meet this man," he said with emphasis. "Johns, I want you to come to the White House and take luncheon with me—you know that—standing invitation; but when you do come, I wish you might bring Mr. James along with you. This, you understand, is not in the nature of a command from the President—merely a request."

Mr. Johns explained that Mr. James happened to be in Montana—Frank still was a great traveler—but he would communicate with him, which he did. James, having returned to St. Louis, wrote a letter to President Roosevelt thanking him for the invitation to the White House. He took the missive to the *Post-Dispatch* office with the request that Mr. Johns edit it. The latter read it and said it required no editing, it was an excellent piece of writing. James had assured the President "You are a man after my own heart, a man of my type." He mailed the letter, and no doubt it is in the Roosevelt family archives.

Frank O'Neil, the reporter who had interviewed Frank James shortly before the outlaw surrendered, had become business manager of the *Post-Dispatch*. He advised against taking James to the White House. The elder Joseph Pulitzer, owner of the newspaper, had instituted a somewhat violent campaign against the President's policies. O'Neil fancied that his chief might object to the proposed visit of his editor with the ex-outlaw in tow. So James, who was rather timid about the idea anyhow, never visited the President. Some time later Mr. Pulitzer heard about the incident and expressed explosive indignation because Frank

James had not been escorted to eat with Theodore Roosevelt in the executive mansion of the republic.

"It would have made a great Sunday feature story!" he shouted, with prefatory expletives expressive of his disapproval of Frank O'Neil's well-intended interference.

Sitting in the Laclede Hotel lobby one day, Frank James said to Mr. James C. Espey, a local Democratic politician, that he was going to quit Missouri and never return unless he was brought back on a stretcher. He had not forgiven his native state for failing to give the James family "vindication" in the matter of the job at Jefferson City. Shortly afterward he removed to Oklahoma, where he engaged in farming for a few years. His health failed. He had inherited the old homestead from his mother, recently deceased. Love of his early home still was strong within him. Like his wounded brother, Jesse the young guerrilla, he wished to die at home. He was brought back on a stretcher; but, again like Jesse, he improved in health on the old farm near Kearney.

"If Frank James says he'll do a thing he'll do it," his mother once remarked, in my hearing. Incidentally, I had discovered that. He was a man of his word. He kept faith with those who kept faith with him. He was thoroughly dependable. He deliberated his decisions and stood by them. Frank James was absolutely honest. I used to say, and I meant it, that if I had a million dollars I should as lief trust it to him as to any man I knew—but I never had the million for the test. James despised cowards and hypocrites and cheap-skate crooks.

When Frank James and Cole Younger, some time after the latter returned home, went out together in a Wild West show, James discovered that a group of deadbeats was following the outfit. The management winked at the confidence men who were cheating the people in every town where the performance took place. James began writing letters to mayors and police officials in towns ahead on the itinerary, warning them against the crooks. For this reason those gentry took a strong dislike to James. At a town in northern Missouri several of them cornered him in a store and became openly menacing. He kept his face toward them, a practice acquired in earlier years, and edged out to the sidewalk. He was armed—he carried a concealed weapon by permit—for possible use in self-defense. He feared he might have to make use of his weapon on this occasion, and he was strongly averse to such action.

Cole Younger happened to be riding along the street —on a Missouri mule, according to my informant! He saw the gang of crooks threatening his old comrade, who stood with back to wall. Younger took in the situation at once.

"Hold them off, Frank, till I come!" he shouted, urging his mount forward.

The "con men," arrant cowards anyhow, decided forthwith not to try to beat up old Frank James. That Younger person was a mighty big man and looked much more formidable than did the lean, lank Frank. They drew off, hurling back foul oaths.

If those two oldtimers had been drawn into a mix-up with the crooks, what a newspaper story must have resulted! And many thoughtless persons would have leaped at the conclusion that James and Younger had gone back to their old tricks. James and Younger, being wise, knew this. They had their good post-outlaw reputations to preserve and foster; and they quit the Wild West show in that town, quit it cold.

The first job Frank James got after his release from custody was in a shoe store at Nevada, Missouri, where he clerked for several years. He worked also in a shoe store at Dallas, Texas, for some time. Then he settled down in St. Louis, where he became door-keeper at the Standard Theater, "home of variety," owned by Col. Ed Butler, a Democratic city-politics boss. For years he worked there, supporting his wife and child on a salary which for a long time was only $70 a month. Standing offers at $500 a week, or more if necessary, to appear in a blood-and-thunder melo-drama depicting Missouri outlawry, did not tempt him.

"I have spent my own money, and I certainly haven't had much of it to spend," Frank James told me, "fighting these James-boys-in-Missouri plays that have been on the road. I have had injunctions brought against them in the courts, for two reasons. Such performances traduce the James family; and they cause foolish boys to imagine there's something heroic in being outlaws."

From time to time Frank James served as assistant starter at the Fair Grounds racetrack in St. Louis, the renowned Col. Jack Chinn of Kentucky being chief starter. Now and then James went to other cities as race starter. He earned enough to live modestly and comfortably. As a race-track attaché he became known as one who insisted upon a square deal, and he fought the crooks in that sport as he had fought the con men following the Wild West show. The sneaky cheaters following the races hated Frank James. His contempt for them he expressed in language calculated to curl up a sheet of flatiron.

Frank James never boasted of his outlawry. Yet I have read lying tales to that effect from the pens of several fake writers. He deplored most deeply his period of outlawry, which he never discussed save most guardedly, and then only with men he knew he could trust to keep their mouths closed like gentlemen. When he lay dying at the old homestead in Clay County, Missouri, I read in several newspapers a syndicated feature purporting to come from Spokane, Wash. The story ran that old Frank James, the notorious Missouri bandit, was living in a tough settlement in the state of Washington, and he was quoted in detail as telling thrilling tales of his prowess as an outlaw—boasting of past misdeeds. It was a crime to write and circulate such a tale, a meaner crime than any Frank James ever committed. I enjoyed the privilege of saying so in the press.

The only remark I ever heard him make, or ever heard of his making, which could be construed as in slightest degree boastful—and I did not so construe it —was this, when he had permitted me to borrow for newspaper use a tintype picture of himself and Arch Clements taken in Kentucky after the final disaster to Quantrill:

"This is the first time this picture has been out of

my personal possession in the thirty-seven years since it was made. During my outlawry the detectives would have been glad to get it; but," with a smile such as one seldom saw on the face of Frank James, "they would have had to take me to get the picture."

And but once did I know him to use his past reputation—one might say the sinister magic of his old name —to gain any advantage; and that was but an innocent use of it. The James family occupied a flat in St. Louis, at Laclede and Boyle avenues, next door to the home of some relatives of mine. Neighborhood boys were jamming the electric doorbell push-buttons with matches and other obstructions. The James doorbell suffered. Mr. James said, "I'll fix 'em," wrote on a card "This Is Frank James' Doorbell," pinned the card just above the bell-button—and the boys never played tricks there again.

Frank James died Feb. 18, 1915, on the Samuel farm, known now as "James Farm," where he grew up. Following his expressed wish, his remains were cremated in St. Louis, at the Missouri Crematory. From a signed article, "The Frank James I Knew," which I wrote for the St. Louis *Republic* and which was published a few days after his death, I quote these remarks:

"Following his surrender, trial and acquittal, for a full generation he lived the normal life of the average man in good standing in his community. Leaving aside his outlawry as a matter of history, not to be considered here, I desire to take this opportunity to say a thing which I have believed for many years. I have believed, and still believe, that there never was a vestige of what is called the criminal instinct in Frank James. He never was a criminal at heart. Under happier conditions he would have become, in my opinion, a man of high prominence in the state. His intelligence was of a high order, very far above the average. . . .

"I am painfully aware that there are those who will read with scorn—of a super-superior sort—this estimate of Frank James' real character. They are those who never knew Frank James and who are uninformed as to the antecedents of his outlawry. . . . I hold no brief for the masked bands of desperadoes who have robbed and still rob banks and trains in this and many other states. They are criminals by choice, or perhaps by instinct, by character.

"Nor do I hold a brief in support of the outlaw deeds of the Jameses and the Youngers and their score of followers in the years following the Civil War. They did desperate deeds. Frank James, however, lived down that old, unhappy life. He made good. He fulfilled to the letter the promises he made to the governor of his native state.

"I see men walking the streets every now and then whom I regard as worse criminals, getting right down to the bone and sinew of character, than Frank James ever was. They are social outlaws, business bandits, commercial cutthroats.

"Frank James reformed and repented and rebuilt his shattered temple of life. He is dead. Let us have charity. Whilst charity covereth a multitude of sins, also does it reveal virtues."

Cole Younger, last of the three outstanding figures in border banditry, died at his home in Lee's Summit, March 21, 1916, after a year's illness from dyspepsia and heart disease. He took to his grave, imbedded in his body, seventeen bullets. He had been wounded twenty-six times, but some of the missiles that did not go clean through were removed. My notion is that he was just about the most shot-up man that ever lived to be seventy-two years of age and die in bed with boots off. His vitality was a matter of marvel. An old friend once joked with Cole anent his encysted bullets:

"I reckon," he suggested, "one might drill almost anywhere in you and strike lead."

"I reckon that's so," Cole admitted.

From the Lee's Summit *Journal* of date two days after his death this excerpt is quoted:

"Virtually every one in this community was the former bandit's friend. Many children knew him as 'Uncle Cole,' and he was never too busy or too sick to greet them pleasantly. Younger was a member of the Christian church here, having been converted during a revival meeting held in the summer of 1913. He was a regular attendant up to the time he was confined to his home. He became a good citizen and an active church worker.

"Cole Younger's life since returning to Lee's Summit has been that of a good man, whose only desire was to live peaceably with those loved ones whom he had been denied. Every one here who knew him was his friend, and all gave him that conscious help to make his days and life peaceful."

Younger's pastor, the Rev. J. T. Webb, conducted the funeral services at the Christian church. At the head of his grave, where he lies buried beside his brother James, is a handsome monument bearing this inscription:

COLE YOUNGER

1844–1916

Rest in Peace

Our Dear Beloved

Next to James lies Robert, next to Robert "Mother"—the sole inscription on the tiny headstone of the gentlewoman who suffered so greatly for the sins of the fathers who stole naked negroes from their haunts in the African wilds and shipped them to the American colonies in the filthy holds of slaveships.

CHAPTER XXXVIII

THE COMIC ODYSSEY OF THE REAL JIM CUMMINS

SOMEWHAT suggestive of a vulgarized Odyssey were the wanderings of Jim Cummins, uncaught Ulysses of the bandit brotherhood and sole survivor of the band of men who rode with Jesse James. To be sure, Jim's was a landbound Odyssey, a journeying between two of the seven seas; and the Ulyssean qualities of the wanderer, not to say his antecedents as well, may be subject to cavil of almost Olympian compass. He had been no king of Ithaca nor had his personality exercised any princely sway over even his native county of Clay. Yet it is not to be denied that he had experienced his siege of Troy (as one of the besieged, though always outside the walls); and it is equally undeniable that always his yearnings, like those of the Homeric hero, turned toward home and kindred, the old familiar places and faces.

Like all the others of this outlawed band, Jim Cummins loved his native heath with a devotion that was deathless. His patriotism was increasingly centripetal. Large and wide and wonderful was the world outside, as he made sufficient discovery; but the plebeian old homestead in Clay, between the little old town of Kearney and the newer watering-place of

Excelsior Springs, was to him the veritable seat and center of the universe. Missouri at large he loved chiefly because it contained within its spreading domain the old weatherboarded farmhouse, with the worn stepping-stones leading to each of its two front doors.

"I was raised there," said Jim, long after he had returned from his wanderings and become an honored guest of his native state in the Confederate Home of Missouri. "I was born on that little old farm, and I reckon a man that don't love the place where he was born and brought up ain't much of a man."

The real Jim Cummins is far different from the "Jim Cummings" of blood and thunder. In the summer of 1882 Frank James told Frank O'Neil, the St. Louis newspaper man who interviewed him shortly before his surrender, that Jim was "an easy-going fellow."

"Jim is not at all dangerous," said James, "and the state has no occasion to worry about him. I have no doubt that if he reads what I am telling you he will say, with a most comical drawl: 'Ya-as, there's that fool goin' to turn state's evidence. I'll kill the damn scoundrel as soon as I clap eyes on him—by God, I will!' But Jim won't; that's one of his little plays of fancy. He frequently has them, but he never kills anybody. It's too much trouble."

So far as I have been able to learn, Jim never has killed anybody since the Civil War closed. He notched his pistols plenty of times at Centralia and in other fights under Bill Anderson, when killing was compulsory. But he is not in the least bloodthirsty.

The Jim Cummins of today is a soft-speaking old man with a failing memory. He has forgotten even his own age. When I visited him in March, 1925, for a day's reminiscences he told me he was seventy-four in January. "I'm goin' on seventy-five now," said Jim.

"If you are only seventy-four," I argued, "then you must have been only thirteen when you and Jesse James enlisted together in the guerrilla service; and as you told me once that Jesse was eight months younger than you, then he must have been only a twelve-year-old baby when he was doing some of the hardest riding and sharpest shooting in the Bill Anderson outfit."

"It's a fact I was eight months older than Jess, but I'm only seventy-four now, all the same."

The house manager overheard this preliminary talk. He turned to his books. "Mr. Cummins," he reported, glancing up from the record made when the ex-outlaw was admitted to the Confederate Home, "was born near Kearney, Clay County, Missouri, Jan. 31, 1847."

"This being 1925, that settles it—you must be past seventy-eight now."

"Well, I still don't see it. I reckon a man ought to know his own age."

Half a hundred veterans of the Confederacy were lounging about the lobby of the big dormitory. Those near enough to hear the discussion enjoyed hearty laughter at the expense of Mr. Cummins of Clay. The heartiest laugh came from Ben Sparlin, oldest and smallest man present. A comrade introduced him as a veteran of ninety-six years

"Ninety-six and a half," proudly corrected Comrade Sparlin, who is a halfblood Cherokee from southwest Missouri.

"Some of you in this place live pretty long," I remarked.

"Yes; but we didn't do so much rough ridin' as Jim Cummins done," explained Ben Sparlin, who is so proud of his own age that he has written me a letter, received a day or so before the writing of this paragraph, in which he asks to be recorded as having been born Aug. 17, 1828.

"Jim Cummins," says Ben, "is ashamed of his age, but I'm different."

It is not as a riproaring freebooter that James Robert Cummins should go down to imperishable history. So far as the available facts go, Jim is not known definitely to have participated in a single one of the outstanding episodes in outlawry charged against the Missouri bandits. He is "the goat" of the gang. Jim has been accused, by blood-and-thunder fictionists, of having had a hand in many holdups, such as the robbing of the United States paymaster at Muscle Shoals, Alabama, in March, 1881, of $5200; the holding up of two Mammoth Cave stages in Kentucky in one day, a little earlier; the Big Springs train robbery in Nebraska, in which Jim Berry and the six red bandannas figured tragically; the Glendale, Winston and Blue Cut robberies in Missouri, and other events. The Frank James defense, as we have learned, tried to fasten the Winston label upon Jim, without success. Confessions of Dick Liddil and Clarence Hite virtually exonerate Cummins as to alleged complicity in any of the later crimes of the gang.

It is as the champion surrenderer of all time that your historian essays to send Jim Cummins down to an admiring posterity. Jim surrendered several times but never succeeded in giving himself up to stand trial. "Little" Jesse James, so called in differentiation from his late father of the same name, though he weighed 190 pounds then and said he still was growing, told me in the August of 1902 at Independence, Missouri, that Jim Cummins was the only one of the outlawed ex-guerrilla troopers who never was killed or captured and never came in and stood trial.

The occasion was the annual reunion of the survivors of the Quantrill troop. The date was but a few days before Jim Younger killed himself in St. Paul. Twenty-six of the old Quantrillians, including a few Anderson-ians, responded to rollcall that day. One man, a tall, thin, wiry individual with active blue eyes, stood near the center of the line and answered to the name "J. R. Cummins." Immediately the line broke up, grizzly veterans from each end surging toward Cummins to grasp his hand.

"Well, I'm damned if it ain't old Jim Cummings himself!" exclaimed one. "Put 'er thar, Jim, old pard! I thought you was dead, or still hidin' out. When did you come in, Jim?"

"I come in about three years ago," replied Jim, "if you want to know, after tryin' to come in for about twenty mortal years."

After positively identifying this oldtime guerrilla as the terrible "Jim Cummings" of fiction, I left St. Louis to get the story of his wanderings. He still was a-roving, as I discovered, and for that reason I missed the funeral of Jim Younger. I was chasing Jim Cummins through the entire Jesse James country. At last

I found him, Aug. 28, 1902, at the farm of James Blevins in Lafayette County, some miles out of Higginsville. He had hired out to Farmer Blevins as a horse-breaker, in which line he was an adept.

Jim's lifelong specialty has been horses. He broke more than eighty wild colts for a Clay County farmer in less than two weeks, after he reached the age of sixty. He was accounted one of the miracle-men, as a horseback performer, in the guerrilla outfit. Old guerrillas have told me that Jim was the best rider in the troop. He said himself:

"I could ride at a gallop and pick my hat up from the ground; and I didn't need any stirrups, either, in doing that."

It was at the Blevins farm that Jim Cummins first told me the tale of his Ulyssean rovings, his twenty-years' struggle to get back home, ending triumphantly in 1899. That was seventeen years after Frank James came in and quit, which proves Mr. Cummins to have made the longest record of any of the outlaws as a man "on the dodge." However, his dodging was different from that of the leaders. He came in so quietly, at last, that not even the newspaper reporters discovered him.

"How did you manage it?" I inquired.

"Oh, I fixed it up. I went up to Liberty, my county seat, and saw the authorities before I settled down at home. I got it all fixed up. I've got plenty of friends."

That was the fourth and final surrender of Jim Cummins, if it may be called a surrender at all. He simply rode into town one day, where everybody had known him since boyhood, and "got it all fixed up." It's easy enough when you know how, Jim says.

"So it may be said," I queried, "that you lasted about seventeen years longer than Frank James did?"

"Oh, no; I surrendered, all right, before he was tried at Gallatin in connection with the Rock Island train robbery at Winston. I just thought I'd better surrender. I was living then at Buffalo, Wyoming, a new town that has grown wonderfully since. I was running a shoeshop there, and making good money—$25 a week clear. I picked up cobbling so that I could mend shoes, and then I hired another cobbler to help me. I liked that business, but I concluded it was about time to surrender.

"So I went to the house of a man I had known since boyhood. He was from Clay County, Missouri. I went in at his back door and told him who I was. 'Get out!' he said, 'you're drunk.' He wouldn't believe I was Jim Cummins. I finally convinced him, and he advised me to give myself up. I did so, and the governor of Wyoming was notified.

"He notified the governor of Missouri, Tom Crittenden, and they held me to wait for requisition papers so they could bring me back to Missouri. The people who knew me there at Buffalo in business said I was a crank. 'That's no more Jim Cummings'—they all called me Cummings, you know—'than I am,' they'd say. 'He's either a crank who imagines he's Jim Cummings, or he's a sharper who's trying to work the state for a free pass to Missouri. If they take him to Missouri he'll turn out to be somebody else.'

"It was really a mighty hard matter for me to get anybody to believe I was Jim Cummins—or Cummings, as they understood my name. They even said

I didn't know how to spell my own name. Even the officers at first didn't want to take charge of me. 'What's the use?' they'd say; 'this feller's a cheap faker. Jim Cummings is a fierce proposition, for sure, and this feller ain't fierce a-tall. Why, the real Jim Cummings is a fire-eatin' fiend—and lookee here at this mild-mannered blue-eyed Sunday-school sup'intendent! Shucks! you can't fool us and company.' And so it went. I was ready to come back to Missouri with the officers, and had sold my business for $600; I got a $12 pair of boots and a $10 pair of shoes to boot.

"After I spent one night in custody the authorities out there got a telegram from Governor Crittenden saying he didn't want me. What do you think o' that, now? Been offering $5000 for me, and still I wasn't worth a cent to Tom Crittenden! They seemed to have nothing against me in Missouri, and that made me feel sore—actually it did! Yes, sir.

"Well, sir, the officers turned me loose; laughed at me, and made me feel cheaper'n a last year's straw hat or a left-over biscuit. And I want to tell you I was mighty sorry I'd sold out my shoeshop. I went and tried to buy it back, but couldn't. Since then the town lot I owned, and that went with the business for only $600 in all, has sold for $12,000. I sure missed out big on that deal. Really, I believe I felt worse because I'd sold out so low than if I'd been brought back to Missouri for trial."

The Wyoming failure was Jim's second attempt at surrender. The first one was a success, but it had nothing to do with post-war outlawry. As to that, his skirts as an out-and-out unsuccessful surrenderer remain clear to this day. In the early summer of 1865 it happened. Said Jim as we sat on the Blevins porch in 1902:

"Quantrill had been killed, down in Kentucky; Bill Anderson had been killed, up in Ray County; George Todd had been killed, in Jackson. Nearly everybody I knew had been killed, seemed like. General Lee had surrendered in Virginia, and so I thought it was up to Jim Cummins to surrender in Missouri. Everybody that hadn't been killed had surrendered, except Gen. Jo Shelby and John Edwards, his adjutant, and a lot of his cavalry veterans that refused to surrender and marched into Mexico. I had been down in Texas with George Shepherd, Bill Gregg, Jess James and a lot of other guerrillas, and we all concluded we'd better come in while the comin' was good. So we fought our way up through the Indian Nation, and some of us got back to Missouri alive.

"It was from a spot right down there," said Jim, pointing to Caddo creek, a few hundred yards away, "it was right down there in the Caddo bottoms, between this house and the next one that you see yonder, that we put Jess James in a wagon and started to Lexington to surrender. We had had a fight with some Federal troops at the Missouri river, near Lexington, and Jess was wounded—shot in the right breast. We thought he'd die, but we brought him down yonder and hid him in the brush for a day or two.

"I helped put Jess in the wagon and we drove to Lexington, nine miles, and surrendered. But before

we went in we got assurance that the Federal authorities would grant us our liberty, the same as regular
Confederates. If we hadn't got that assurance we
never would have gone in."

Which, of course, goes to show that Jim Cummins
knew when to surrender and when not to surrender.
His other surrender, which completes a quartet, was
like those already described, entirely of his own voli-
tion. There were no particularly compelling circumstances. No ultimatum had been presented. Jim
just concluded that it was a pretty good time to surrender, and so he surrendered. That was away out in
California, along about 1887.

Many Missourians still remember the daring deed
of a lone robber who boarded the express car attached
to a Frisco train at the old Union Depot in St. Louis,
by presenting a forged letter to Messenger Fotheringham. The letter purported to be an order from the
proper official to let the bearer ride through to Kansas
City, as he was learning to be an express messenger.
Fotheringham took him along. A few miles out the
stranger flashed a gun, overpowered or overawed the
messenger, bound him hand and foot, gagged him, and
took nearly $100,000 from the safe of the Adams
Express Company. Just before he jumped off and disappeared in the darkness he said to the messenger:

"If you happen to see Mr. Billy Pinkerton, give him
my compliments, and tell him if he catches Jim Cummings he'll be doing something I don't hardly expect
of him."

Fotheringham was arrested, accused of complicity,
locked in jail. A few days later the police and the

express company's officials began receiving letters from Chicago, signed "Jim Cummings," declaring that the writer was the robber and that Fotheringham was innocent. The letters led to the arrest of one Fred Wittrock, who was convicted and who served nearly twenty years in the Missouri penitentiary. Fotheringham was released and exonerated.

The real Jim Cummins was living placidly in California, under another name. Jim always retained his Christian name. In some places he was Jim Wilson, in others Jim Johnson, elsewhere Jim Jones, but always Jim. Said Jim as we sat on the Blevins porch:

"I read about this fellow trying to masquerade under my name, and it worried me. I didn't propose to be suspected and accused of anything I hadn't done. That had been an old story to me. I'd been suspected and accused of half the train and bank robberies from hell to nowhere, before the James band broke up. I thought those letters signed 'Jim Cummings' might maybe give me trouble; the detectives might find out where I was and arrest me. The Pinkertons were always after me, as they were after Frank and Jess, but they didn't know enough about me to get me. So I decided to come in and beat 'em to it.

"Well, I went into town, out there in California, and told the authorities just who I was. I told 'em I didn't have a thing to do with that express robbery near St. Louis, neither. I was able to prove I hadn't been out of California since before the robbery. They had nothing against me, they said, and so I returned to my business. I was plumb disgusted, too."

Cummins told me that when he was in California the

authorities offered him $1000 to go into the camp of
Chris Evans and John Sontag, notorious train robbers
and murderers who terrorized the western coast country for years. "I knew those men and was ready to
go into their camp and come out and report," he said,
"but when I got to the vicinity the officers wanted
me to kill the men for $1000. I let 'em keep the
cash."

Jim evidently figured that "it was too much trouble"
to kill the Evans-Sontag outfit.

"There had been a time in Missouri," Cummins
continued, "when I had a similar offer. Sheriff Timberlake of Jackson County, who was trying to arrange
for the capture or killing of Jess James, communicated
with me. He wanted me to come in and quit, showing
good faith and agreeing to help break up the gang.
Timberlake offered me $10,000 and a full pardon from
Governor Crittenden if I would help him exterminate
the boys. I wrote back to take his $10,000 and his
pardon to hell with him."

Jim's tale of Odyssean wanderings must be con-
densed very considerably here. Told in full detail,
it would run far beyond twenty-four cantos. He served
as a government scout in the Indian wars, as a deputy
United States marshal, as a township constable. Between these exciting avocations he cobbled quietly, he
helped thresh wheat, he plowed corn, he broke colts.

"Recollect when the Apache Kid was terrorizing
Arizona? Well," said Jim, "I was out there, and General McCook was called on to find a man to go out and
bring in the Kid, alive or dead—most probably dead,

of course. General McCook selected me, probably because I could shoot straight and ride a horse without falling off. I had been a scout years before under General Shafter, down in Texas, chasing Indians. I agreed to go after the Kid if I could have plenty of provisions and the right outfit of men. They gave me a free hand. I was to get $100 a month and all expenses paid. I had gone to Denver to complete preparations, when I took sick. I had to give up the job of getting the Apache Kid, and I was mighty sorry.

"I went down to my sister's, near Eureka Springs, Arkansas, and was sick for a couple of years. When I got my health back I went into business. I bought a ranch in Barry County, Missouri, close to the Arkansas line, near Cassville, the county seat. I was going under the name of Jim Johnson and was constable for the township. After a while I had to sell out my ranch and leave the state. The officers got onto me, and I wasn't ready to surrender again and didn't intend to be captured. I drifted to Arkansas and bought another ranch, near Beaver, in Carroll County. There I lived some years and was a United States deputy marshal."

"Under what name were you known as a deputy marshal?"

"My own name."

"How did it happen that nobody killed you for the reward the state of Missouri was offering?" I asked him, in surprise.

"Well, it was just this way," Jim explained. "The state had a standing reward of $5000 for me; but down there in Arkansas such an amount of money was too big for the local imagination. If the reward had been $500, no doubt somebody would have killed me for it; but $5000 was so big that they had no confidence in its ever being paid. That's where the state of Missouri made a mistake."

Jim Cummins smiled serenely as he said this, gazing out over the Caddo creek bottom at the big tree under which he had camped thirty-seven years earlier, with the wounded guerrilla boy Jesse James hardly able to draw breath.

"Were you with Jesse much, after the war?"

"I knew where he was. He lived in Nashville a long time, and I remember going down there one time when he was living in the city and Frank was hauling logs a few miles out, in the lumber camps. About the first man I saw was old Uncle Daniel Patton, a Cumberland Presbyterian preacher whom we all knew back in Missouri. A detective named Yankee Bligh was supposed to be looking for us, and we didn't know exactly what Mr. Patton was doing down there so far from home. I went and got a church paper, *The Cumberland Presbyterian*, published in Nashville, and found that the presbytery or general assembly of the church was in session there. That relieved the situation. Uncle Daniel was there for religious purposes only."

Jim told a Jesse James story which bears earmarks of indubitable truth, because it sounds just like what Jesse would have done under the circumstances narrated:

"Jess and I, under assumed names, once went to dine with a state senator in the southern part of Missouri. A young man who had been appointed to

West Point was calling on the senator's daughter. He was telling his sweetheart what he expected to learn at the military academy, and we overheard the talk.

"Jess wrote me a note and passed it over by a negro. 'Tell that young man,' wrote Jess, 'that if he will come outside I'll give him a few lessons in horsemanship and marksmanship that will beat anything he'll ever learn at West Point.'"

A few years after I first met Mr. Cummins he got married. When he returned home there was no slaughter of the Wooers, as in the case of the ancient Ulysses, for Jim hadn't found time to get married. But after I gave him some publicity different from the "Jim Cummings" kind he got a letter from an actress living in Boston, the Hub, and originally from Canada. She was a widow, Mrs. Florence Sherwood. She had known of the "Jim Cummings" of myth and miracle but had had no knowledge of the real Jim Cummins. My contributions toward the building up of the man and the tearing down of the myth penetrated to Boston, and thus unwittingly I became a matchmaker. Indirectly, at any rate, I brought together in holy wedlock the stage and the reputed stage robber. As Florence Sherwood and Jim Cummings the bride and bridegroom went on the stage together, after a happy honeymoon at Excelsior Springs.

Mrs. Cummins felt that Mr. Cummins had in him the makings of a great actor, notwithstanding his nearness to sixty summers. Mr. Cummins responded nobly to the spur; but after a brief career as a James-boys-in-Missouri hero he discovered that the saddle, and not the boards, was his one safe bet. He had a saddle, when first I knew him, which he had ridden for thirty years, beginning in 1872; and if that saddle could but write an autobiography, there indeed were a book of best-seller stride!

"Jim Cummings" retired from the stage in favor of Nat Goodwin and other celebrities of the time who had started young. After the death of Mrs. Cummins the lonely widower returned to the Confederate Home, leaving that hospitable institution to break a bunch of broncos every now and then until infirmities of age retired him from that labor of love.

Jim never made up with Frank James, although the two men met once after Jim came in. Their conversation on that occasion was not altogether of the Walt Whitman camaraderie kind. Jim never forgave Frank because the defense at the Gallatin trial sought to substitute Jim for Frank at the Winston holdup, which happened when Cummins was working on a farm in Kansas at $1.50 a day.

"Frank James put on too much, anyhow," Jim once remarked to me. "He used to spout Shakespeare when we were all a-hidin' out, and that didn't go down with me. What'd Shakespeare have to do with sidesteppin' a bunch o' Pinkertons or a posse o' deputies, I want to know? Huh!"

I requested Mr. Cummins to quote some of the passages from the Bard which were spouted by Frank James in the robbers' rendezvous. He looked at me indignantly at first, then softened.

"If I had come in and surrendered when Frank James was on trial," he said, "and they had put me on the witness-stand and told me to spout some Shakespeare as that there preacher testified the defendant had done, that sure would a-cleared the skirts of old Jim Cummins in the Winston train robbery—why, I'd a-sunk clean through that opry house floor!"

"'Thrice armed is he that hath his quarrel just,'" I quoted.

"There—that's it—that's one line that Frank used to spout; and Jess used to smile kind o' sickly-like when Frank spouted that line."

"Which of the two did you like the better?"

"Me? Why, now, I don't like a-tall to speak ill of the dead, but I think Jess was a more honorable man than Frank—even if Jess did threaten to kill me on sight. But I never did like the way Jess killed Ed Miller."

"And what did you think of Bob Ford?"

"The dirty little coward!"

The last letter from Mr. Cummins before this ultimate page of the outlaw epic is written carries a postscript, "Don't forget to protect my confidence."

I have not forgotten.

THE END